Austriaca and Judaica

Austrian Culture

Harry Zohn
General Editor
Vol. 15

PETER LANG
New York • Washington, D.C./Baltimore • San Francisco
Bern • Frankfurt am Main • Berlin • Vienna • Paris

Harry Zohn

Austriaca and Judaica

Essays and Translations

PETER LANG
New York • Washington, D.C./Baltimore • San Francisco
Bern • Frankfurt am Main • Berlin • Vienna • Paris

Library of Congress Cataloging-in-Publication Data

Zohn, Harry.
Austriaca and Judaica: essays and translations/Harry Zohn.
p. cm. — (Austrian culture; vol. 15)
Includes bibliographical references.
1. Jews—Austria—Intellectual life. 2. Austrian literature—Jewish authors—History and criticism. 3. Austria—Civilization—Jewish influences. 4. Austrian literature—Translations into English. I. Title. II. Series.
DS135.A9Z64 943.6′004924—dc20 94-26810
ISBN 0-8204-2567-2
ISSN 1054-058X

Die Deutsche Bibliothek-CIP-Einheitsaufnahme

Zohn, Harry:
Austriaca and Judaica: essays and translations/Harry Zohn. - New York; Washington, D.C./Baltimore; San Francisco; Bern; Frankfurt am Main; Berlin; Vienna; Paris: Lang.
(Austrian culture; Vol. 15)
ISBN 0-8204-2567-2
NE: GT

Cover design by James F. Brisson.

The paper in this book meets the guidelines for permanence and durability of the Committee on Production Guidelines for Book Longevity of the Council on Library Resources.

Printed in the United States of America.

To Judy,

my life's companion

TABLE OF CONTENTS

PART ONE: Essays

PART TWO: Translations

PART ONE

Essays

"LOVE WITH DETACHMENT"

A Personal Foreword

In an article entitled "Schalom 1988" and published in both New York and Vienna, Peter Marboe, known to many as the longtime director of the Austrian Information Service and the Austrian Institute in New York, concerns himself with the great blow dealt to Austrian culture by the "Vertreibung der Vernunft," the expulsion of the intelligentsia and the horrendous cultural exodus in 1938, as well as by Austria's failure to invite those emigrants to return after the "dunkle Zeit," the seven years of darkness in which some of that country's traditions and its very identity were expunged. In a series of speculations of the "What if?" variety Marboe imagines Viennese university students attending an "overcrowded lecture by Herbert Lederer or Harry Zohn." Such a notion may be flattering to my esteemed Connecticut colleague and to me, but I can hardly imagine that any of my lectures, least of all at the University of Vienna, could be overcrowded. Yet I did have a certain homecoming in mind when I suggested, in March 1987, that some of my Viennese-born American colleagues who, like myself, were teaching their native language, literature, and culture be invited to Vienna to report about their feelings and experiences as cultural mediators. Thanks to Wolfgang Kraus and the Österreichische Gesellschaft für Literatur the symposium that I had envisaged did materialize in June 1988, and while those who offered personal perspectives were considerably younger (and less famous) than the participants in an earlier Viennese symposium, such "grand old men" as Bruno Bettelheim, Rudolf Ekstein, and Ernst Křenek, their continued loyalty to their mother tongue and the cultural values embodied in it was no less impressive and moving. One of them was already a university graduate and successful writer at the time of the *Anschluß,* but the education of the ten other "thirty-eighters" was interrupted in secondary school or at an even earlier stage.

In the spring of 1938 I was in the fifth class (out of eight) in the RGII, the so-called Sperlgymnasium, in the Leopoldstadt, the once predominantly Jewish second district of Vienna. In the 1930s no one told us about a famous graduate of that school who had attended it from 1865 to 1873, when it was called Leopoldstädter Communal-, Real- und Obergymnasium and was located in another building just down the street. In fact, in his first years at that school Sigmund Freud lived on Pfeffergasse, a few steps from my birthplace on Castellezgasse. From June 1938 to September 1940 I had no formal schooling whatever, for in England, where I emigrated in February 1939, I was not able to attend any school. However, after my arrival in Boston the following year I was, on the strength of my Viennese transcripts, placed in the senior class of a high school, which testifies to the quality of the education I had received in the fear-driven authoritarian atmosphere of my Viennese school. After graduating from high school it was necessary for me to go to work, and for five years I held a low-level white-collar position while taking evening and summer courses for a bachelor's degree at Suffolk University (which three decades later awarded me the honorary degree Doctor of Letters and elected me to its Board of Trustees). Unwittingly following in Sigmund Freud's footsteps again I enrolled at Clark University, the only American academic institution that Freud had honored with his presence in 1909. The master's degree that I obtained there in 1947 qualified me to become a teacher, but by that time I had begun to take a more scholarly interest in my native language and its literary creations. (Whether German can be regarded as my mother tongue is open to question; at home in Vienna we spoke precisely that mixture of the Viennese dialect and the Polish variety of Yiddish that Karl Kraus, later one of my *dii minores*, abhorred and excoriated). The receipt of a teaching fellowship at Harvard University then pointed the way to my future career. When it was time for me to choose a dissertation subject, my Jewish heritage became a determining factor. I was initially attracted to Franz Kafka, but that writer was becoming fashionable, even a cult figure, in America and the prey of sociologists, theologians, and psychologists who could not even read him in the original. I had always read Stefan Zweig with pleasure, and my thesis director, the renowned German-born professor Karl Viëtor, sensitively encouraged me to write about Zweig as a translator, critic, and mediator in modern European literature. Before his untimely death in 1951 this outstanding scholar was able to read a significant portion of my dissertation. A sort of elective affinity soon developed between my subject and me, and Zweig inspired in me a desire to become a mediator between my native Austria and my adopted country. As a teacher, lecturer, critic, and translator I have ever since been guided by what Zweig, in his introduction to a collection of his essays, described as his aim: "to understand even what is most alien to us, always to evaluate peoples and periods, figures and works only in their positive and creative sense, and to let this desire to understand and share this understanding with others serve humbly and faithfully our indestructible ideal: humane communication among persons, mentalities, cultures, and nations."

In a veritable "Sternstunde" of my life Zweig's first wife, Friderike Maria, welcomed me to her home in Stamford (Connecticut), and for two decades this noble lady, herself a gifted writer and cultural mediator, was my motherly friend. As she introduced me to her circle of friends, such rare creative or recreative spirits as Fritz von Unruh, Johannes Urzidil, George N. Shuster, René Fülöp-Miller, Hugo Jacobi, Emil Lengyel, and Alexander Gode, the humanism of Stefan Zweig and his circle became a vibrant reality to me. Among Friderike Zweig's wide-ranging activities in which I was able to participate was the American-European Friendship Association and its annual Friendship Week in Stamford. On my first visit to postwar Vienna in 1955 I was privileged to meet some of Stefan Zweig's few surviving friends—the "grand old men" of Austrian letters Franz Theodor Csokor, Felix Braun, and Oskar Maurus Fontana as well as the deaf-mute sculptor-poet Gustinus

Ambrosi. These and others became focal points of my reading, research, and writing. In the summer of 1957 I joined two other "Zweigologists," Erich Fitzbauer and Robert Rie, in founding the International Stefan Zweig Society, which in the ensuing ten or fifteen years issued a number of valuable publications. In 1981 centennial symposia were devoted to Zweig in a number of cities, and I participated in those held at the State University of New York at Fredonia (where Professor Rie, Friderike, and I had helped establish a Stefan Zweig Center) and at Ben Gurion University in Beersheva. In addition to publishing numerous articles on Zweig I edited college editions of "Die Augen des ewigen Bruders," "Buchmendel," and "Schachnovelle," wrote the introduction to a durable paperback edition of *The World of Yesterday*, and translated several of his stories and essays.

However, what tied me to Austrian literature and culture was not so much authors, works, themes, ideas, or currents but very special people whom it was my good fortune to befriend. My friendship with Miriam and Naëmah, the daughters of Richard Beer-Hofmann, was of many years' standing, and so was my close professional and personal relationship with Ernst Waldinger, perhaps the most distinguished Austrian-born poet in America and as a professor at Skidmore College also a colleague. (Waldinger's mother lived in Boston for years, and so did his brother Theo, who in his last years was instrumental in publishing a comprehensive collection of Waldinger's writings in Salzburg). Ernst Waldinger was one of the exiled writers who cooperatively founded the Aurora Verlag, whose publications were distributed by Schoenhof's Foreign Books, a Cambridge firm long managed by Viennese-born Paul Mueller. In the 1950s and 1960s, when I was the director of a German Radio Hour over a Boston station and executive director of the Goethe Society of New England, respectively, I was able to provide a forum for such other Austrian-born authors as Mimi Grossberg, Alfred Gong, Hertha Pauli, Friedrich Bergammer, Margarete Kollisch, and Maria Berl-Lee, all of whom I was privileged to know personally. Alfred Farau (in Vienna Fred Hernfeld), an Adlerian psychologist and as a brilliant, evocative lecturer an eloquent spokesman of the "thirty-eighters," was another Viennese-born friend. Farau took his doctorate in postwar

Vienna and was sometimes tempted to return, but he came to regard emigration as a permanent caesura in one's life and the road to exile as a one-way street. Far from being guided by the usual materialistic principle *Ubi bene, ibi patria*, he subscribed to the Goethean "Wo ich nütze, ist mein Vaterland" (My fatherland is where I can be of service/ do some good), a principle in which the Goethe scholar Karl Viëtor confirmed me many years ago.

My mediating activities have been greatly aided by the stability and continuity of my residence and professional position. I have lived in the same city for fifty-five years and taught at the same university for almost forty-five. Brandeis University, founded in 1948, the same year as the State of Israel, is a non-sectarian institution that represents American Jewry's contribution to higher education. On the occasion of his seventieth birthday the Viennese-born dramatist and poet Frank Gerhard Zwillinger established a personal archives there, and the internationally known book *Wittgenstein's Vienna* originated at Brandeis as the doctoral dissertation of its co-author Allan Janik (now at the University of Innsbruck). My university and my department are small, but the list of the Austrian writers, journalists, actors, and academics who have appeared there upon my invitation in recent decades reads like a Who's Who in Contemporary Austrian Culture: Hilde Spiel, György Sebestyén, Christian Wallner, Ernst Jandl, Friederike Mayröcker, Paul Kruntorad, Herbert Lederer (from the one-man Theater am Schwedenplatz), Susi Nicoletti, Norbert Leser, Gerhard Melzer, Lotte Ingrisch, Viktor Handlos, Marianne Gruber, Judith Holzmeister, Herbert Kuhner, Hugo Portisch, Otto Kerry, Richard Eybner, Angelica Schütz, Gitta Deutsch, Florian Kalbeck, Karlheinz Auckenthaler, Peter Stefan Jungk, Ruth Beckermann. Some of these programs were co-sponsored by the Austro-American Association of Boston, probably the oldest association of its kind, of which I became a charter member in 1944. Viennese-born Walter Toman was a professor of Psychology at Brandeis in the 1950s and the composer Ernst Křenek a visiting professor of Music in the 1960s. Katherine Lichliter, the first Brandeis Ph.D. in German literature (and currently associate director of the Salzburg Seminar), produced a critical translation of three plays by Franz Theodor Csokor as her dissertation, and it has been published as the first volume in Peter Lang Publishing's Austrian Culture series, of which I am the general editor. Other titles issued in that series include a Karl Emil Franzos Reader, a volume of Alfred Farau's essays, monographs on Berthold Viertel and Franz Molnar, a book about and by the composer-conductor Max Schönherr (an idol of my childhood and a friend in the last year of his life), a study of the musician and poet Franz Mittler, and a collection of writings by "Peter Fabrizius" (a dual pseudonym of Max Knight and Joseph Fabry).

Among the thirty books that I have translated are a number of Austriaca, such as the complete Zionist writings of Theodor Herzl, Arthur Schnitzler's novella *Sterben*, Fritz Molden's book on the Austrian resistance between 1938 and 1945, the autobiography of Manès Sperber, a collection of Walter Toman's stories, and two collections of satirical writings by Karl Kraus.

My association with the International Arthur Schnitzler Research Association, which I helped found in Kentucky in 1961, and its quarterly *Modern Austrian Literature* as well as with the American Council on the Study of Austrian Literature has long been a major outlet for my professional work. But again, much of my inspiration and gratification has derived from people rather than publications or organizations. I gratefully remember the work and influence of three Austrian-born emigré journalists, Otto Zausmer of the *Boston Globe*, Ernst Pisko of the *Christian Science Monitor*, and Irene Harand, the courageous editor of *Die Gerechtigkeit* and author of *Sein Kampf*, whose ringing slogan "Ich bekämpfe den Antisemitismus, weil er das Christentum schändet" (I fight anti-Semitism because it disgraces Christianity) was, alas, not heard or heeded in pre-Hitler Austria. The world-renowned composer-conductor Robert Stolz, another idol of my childhood and a person of uncommon integrity and sensitivity, was my fatherly friend for three decades, and his widow Einzi continues to be an inspiration, as does Max Schönherr's widow Lotte. My friendship with the multiply gifted Lola Blonder (100 years young in 1994!) has given me particular satisfaction; her autobiography *Sprache ist Heimat* appeared in the series Materialien zur Zeitgeschichte. In a lighter vein, in recent years I encouraged two young

American singers, Karol Bennett and Pamela Wolfe, to explore the relatively unfamiliar genres of the Viennese operetta and the Wienerlied.

In the 1960s I read Csokor's highly evocative essay "Der farbenvolle Untergang," the title of which derives from Stefan George's characterization of the Austrian *fin de siècle*, and immediately resolved to present variations on this theme in a Reader for college use. Of the nineteen writers represented in this collection, which appeared in 1971, fourteen were Jews or of Jewish descent, and this striking fact indicates the great and imperishable Jewish contribution to Austrian literature. I know that there is another Austrian literature, and like many American Germanists I have long communed with Grillparzer, Raimund, Nestroy, and Stifter. I regularly read and review a number of contemporary Austrian authors, but I have no use for the likes of Waggerl, Kolbenheyer, Brehm, Mell, Hohlbaum, Fussenegger, Jelusich, Nabl, or Zerzer. The lack of attention paid to a very personal book on the Jewish heritage in Austrian literature that I published in 1986 came as a disappointment. Its title, which also describes *me*, comes from a poem by Ernst Waldinger: "*Ich bin ein Sohn der deutschen Sprache nur...*" (I am a son of the German language only...) In addition to essays about Schnitzler, Beer-Hofmann, Herzl, Zweig, Kraus, Farau, Kramer, and others it contains "Wiener Juden in der Literatur," a bio-bibliographical compilation of some 500 writers which I hope to revise and expand some day.

An account of some of my activities on one of the most recent of my eighteen visits to postwar Austria may reveal a typical blend of intellectual and emotional elements. In the fall of 1990 I attended, among other activities, the Innsbruck convention of the Theodor Kramer Society, devoted to the life and work of an exiled poet whom I met in England after a long correspondence friendship; did extensive research, mostly in the form of interviews, for a book on the Wienerlied, a unique product of popular culture to which Jewish lyricists and composers have made enduring contributions; attended the festive opening of a Kafka exhibit at the refurbished Jewish Community Center on historic Seitenstettengasse and the presentation of the latest issue of *Das jüdische Echo*, an annual to which I am a regular contributor; and visited the Chajes-Schule on Castellezgasse, the reopening of which I had attended in November 1984 and whose students furnished impressive evidence of a newly burgeoning Jewish culture in Vienna. (In 1992 I was able to attend the festive first Matura, or graduation, of this school, and I was gratified to note that three of the twelve graduates would be studying at Brandeis University.) Yet I could not suppress the thought that in Nazi Vienna both the old Chajesgymnasium and my own Sperlgymnasium had served as staging areas for the deportation of Jews. This stirred thoughts of the peculiarly Jewish (and perhaps unholy) fascination with the German language and the values embodied in it, which makes the much-discussed German-Jewish symbiosis the most tragically unrequited love affair in world history. Long ago I raised the question whether cultural mediatorship may be regarded as an eminently Jewish trait and answered it with a qualified Yes. In his autobiography Stefan Zweig, that great believer in the Diaspora, discusses the mediating zeal of Jews eager to be active among their host nations in order to improve their position by increasing the store of understanding, tolerance, and humanitarianism in the world: "Their longing for a homeland, for peace, for rest, security, and non-alienation impels them to attach themselves passionately to the culture of the world around them." Nowhere in the modern world, Zweig goes on to say, was this attachment more fruitful than the Jews' attachment to Austrian culture, and as a result "nine-tenths of what the world celebrated as Viennese culture in the nineteenth century was a culture promoted, nourished, or even created by Viennese Jewry."

It is to the interpretation and preservation of this culture that I have dedicated myself, and on the eve of my retirement from full-time teaching this collection of my essays and short translations is offered in this spirit. My feeling for present-day Austria may perhaps best be characterized as a "Distanzliebe," a word once coined by Max Brod to describe the "love with detachment" felt by this "son of the German language only" for the peoples and cultures of the German-speaking realm.

Brandeis University
Boston 02254-9110, U.S.A.
Spring 1994

Harry Zohn

THE JEWISH CONTRIBUTION TO FIN-DE-SIÈCLE VIENNA

Old Vienna, Gay Vienna: is the operetta city of wine, women, and song little more than a myth? The vitriolic Viennese satirist Karl Kraus once observed, "I have shattering news for the aesthetes: Old Vienna was new once."[1] Distance, hindsight, and nostalgia tend to transfigure things, to paper over conflicts and clashes, to bathe the misery, the strife, the poverty of a city or a period in the glow of rosy romanticism. After all, in 1889, 200,000 of Vienna's almost two million inhabitants lived at the starvation level, and shortly after the end of World War I Bruno Frei painted a similarly bleak picture in *Jüdisches Elend in Wien* (1920). To a present-day Viennese, Old Vienna, or *Altwien,* usually means the Biedermeier period, between the Congress of Vienna (1815) and the abortive revolution of March 1848, also known as the *Vormärz*, the *Backhendlzeit,* when everything was still *gemütlich* in the city, when a chicken was roasting on every spit and Schubert's melodies filled the air. (How the Viennese, with their proverbial hearts of gold, treated Franz Schubert and his kind is another story). To a non-Viennese, Old Vienna is apt to mean the age of Johann Strauß, which was the second half of the nineteenth century, and particularly the so-called *fin de siècle,* which is perceived as a period of intellectual brilliance, the kind of cultural florescence that only a politically decaying and socially changing age can produce, the poignant twilight years of a six-hundred-year-old empire that the German poet Stefan George has described as "der farbenvolle Untergang"—the colorful sunset or decline.[2]

Vienna at the turn of the century (which we may define as the dying decades of the Habsburg Empire, from the late 1880s to the end of World War I in 1918) has been very much in the consciousness of today's American intellectuals. Near the turn of another century they are searching for the roots of modernism and parallels to our troubled times, for the guidance and wisdom of a period of tremendous political and cultural change through a better understanding of the problems and solutions (or nonsolutions), the insights and ideas that have shaped the modern world—in music, psychoanalysis, art, architecture, and, of course, literature. Names like Arnold Schönberg, Gustav Mahler, Anton Webern, Alban Berg, Sigmund Freud, Alfred Adler, Adolf Loos, Ludwig Wittgenstein, Otto Wagner, Josef Hofmann, Gustav Klimt, Oskar Kokoschka, and Egon Schiele come to mind right away. The literary contributions of Viennese Jewry have long been one of my own fields of special interest. A little bio-bibliographical handbook I published in 1969 has 238 entries of Jewish men of letters who were born in Vienna or lived there for at least two decades; it lists only those who published one or more books, so it excludes most of the numerous Jewish journalists. An expanded edition published as an appendix to a book of essays contains more than 500 names.[3] To highlight the disproportionate outpouring of talent that this represents, let me review a little history and some statistics.

Jews were first documented as living in Vienna around the year 1200; periods of relative toleration and prosperity were punctuated by expulsions in 1421, 1670, and—most horrendously—1938. The eighteenth century brought some easement under the "enlightened despot" Joseph II, who issued his celebrated *Toleranzpatent* (Edict of Toleration) in 1781-82, even though his mother, Queen Maria Theresia, displayed little fondness for the Jews. Around that time there lived the first Jew, albeit a converted one, who was able to become a force in Austrian intellectual life: Joseph von Sonnenfels, a man of tremendous versatility—a courtier and statesman, a prolific writer on many subjects, and one of the sponsors of Austria's national theater. Thanks to such men as Joseph II and Sonnenfels, Austrian Jews were at last able to take the giant step from the ghetto into the world, and it is hardly surprising that all through the nineteenth century talented and ambitious Jews flocked to Vienna from all parts of the Habsburg Empire. At the turn of the century there was a veritable outpouring of Jewish genius in Vienna, and, as usual, it was far out of proportion to the numbers involved.

Vienna in the reign of Emperor Franz Joseph (1848-1916) was the imperial-royal capital city of a multinational empire comprising about fifty million souls, of whom twelve million were German-speaking. The Jewish population of Vienna grew rapidly in the declining decades of Austria-Hungary, the Dual Monarchy created after the *Ausgleich* (compromise) with Hungary in 1867. Between 1880 and 1938 the Jews amounted to no more than 8 to 11 percent of the population of Vienna. In 1880, there were 72,000 Jews in the city; in 1890, 118,000; in 1900, 147,000; and in 1910, 175,000, which means that before the outbreak of World War I, Vienna was second only to Warsaw as far as the Jewish population in Europe was concerned. At any given time, about 90 percent of Jews in the German-speaking part of Austria lived in the capital city. The steady increase in the Jewish population was due to the fact that Vienna promised greater opportunities, more culture, and less virulent antisemitism—at any rate, not the pogrom variety, though it must be noted that *fin-de-siècle* Vienna had an avowedly antisemitic mayor, Dr. Karl Lueger. This man's Jew-baiting, to be sure, was selective and largely an opportunistic political device (Lueger reserved the right to decide who was a Jew in his eyes), and it did not compare with the menace posed by men like Georg Ritter von Schönerer, whose antisemitism was based on German nationalistic and racial principles and thus foreshadowed the Nazis. Fortunately the time was not ripe for an extremist like Schönerer, who despised other groups and institutions as well: "Ohne Juda, Habsburg, Rom / Bauen wir den deutschen Dom" (Without Judah, Habsburg, Rome / We will build the German dome) was his rallying cry.

Vienna was always the *Wasserkopf*, the hydrocephaloid city, the German-speaking tail that wagged the multinational, predominantly

Slavic dog. Though Emperor Franz Joseph was an intellectual and cultural cipher, the personality of this basically decent and unprejudiced man held the often reluctant and restive nationalities together for a few more decades. At the end of World War I, however, the various nationalities that had served in the army went right from the front to their now independent countries of origin—with one exception: the Jews, who really had no place to go but Vienna; *they* were the true patriots—professional Austrians, almost. In Franz Theodor Csokor's play *3. November 1918* (written between 1929 and 1937, for which a good English title would be "The Army That Never Returned"), Colonel Radosin, a true Austrian patriot, commits suicide when he realizes that multinational cooperation and aspirations will now be replaced by an atavistic, crude nationalism and particularism; another such patriot in the play is Grün, the Jewish army doctor. Such Jews were virtually traumatized by the breakup of the empire. One eastern Jew from Brody, Joseph Roth, a gifted novelist, identified with the various features of Old Austria to such an extent that he intoned dirges for a bygone world, affected the stance of an Austrian army officer, called himself "a Catholic with a Jewish brain," and once signed a letter as "Mojsche Christus."[4] After 1918 Roth was rent by conflicting loyalties and sought spiritual refuge in monarchist ideology, but his Catholic leanings coincided with a fresh creative interest in his Jewish heritage. He strove to create a special symbiosis between *imperium* and *shtetl*, and in *Juden auf Wanderschaft* (1927), a series of vignettes about the life and character of European Jewry, he viewed the Zionist movement as the direct result of internal conflicts within the Habsburg realm. Roth, alas, could not achieve a synthesis between his Jewish origins, his allegiance to, and indeed fixation on, the lost empire, and his desire to embrace the predominant religion of that empire, namely Catholicism, and so he drank himself to death in Paris in 1939, at the age of forty-five.

It is hardly surprising that the majority of Viennese Jews opposed the Zionist movement, though political Zionism was the creation of one of their own, Budapest-born Theodor Herzl, who abandoned his literary career after writing thirty plays and numerous prose works and went to an early grave because of overwork, tension, and frustration. Herzl's greatest support came not from Viennese Jewry but from the Jewish masses of Eastern Europe and the East End of London. He found himself in an untenable position as a "wage slave" of the *Neue Freie Presse,* Vienna's foremost newspaper and probably the greatest liberal journal of Europe at the time. Its proprietors were Jews but, like the great majority of their coreligionists, professional Austrians, as it were. Looking forward to ever more complete assimilation, Moriz Benedikt and Eduard Bacher saw to it that not one word about Zionism and the wide-ranging political activities of their cultural editor, Theodor Herzl, ever appeared in the pages of the *Neue Freie Presse.* While Herzl found little encouragement or understanding among his literary contemporaries, his activities did cause a certain self-awareness and Jewish culture to blossom, inspiring Jewish study associations, athletic organizations, and the like. But how many Jews in *fin-de-siècle* Vienna considered emigrating to a prospective Jewish homeland? These mostly assimilated and sometimes even converted Jews felt they were living in "dos gebenshte Estreich," as the Yiddish writer Avraham Goldfaden once called it. Hebrew writers like Perez Smolenskin, Abraham Broides, Reuben Brainin, and Hayyim Nahman Bialik lived and flourished in Vienna, and so did noted rabbis like Adolf Jellinek, Moritz Güdemann, Zevi Perez Chajes, Max Grunwald, and Israel Taglicht. The old story of assimilation and Jewish attenuation *l'dor vador* is exemplified by the cloth and silk merchant Isak Löw Hofmann, born in 1759, who became Edler von Hofmannsthal in 1835, and thus ennobled cofounded the *Kultusgemeinde* (Jewish community council) of Vienna. His son was already baptized, and his great-grandson, Hugo von Hofmannsthal, one of the giants of modern Austrian literature, born in 1874, was a Catholic (though hardly parochial) writer. One has to look hard for vestiges of a Jewish sensibility in this poet's writings. In "Terzinen über Vergänglichkeit" Hofmannsthal writes: "I existed a hundred years ago, and my ancestors in their shrouds are as related to me as my own hair." In another poem, "Manche freilich...," he repeats: "I cannot shed from my eyelids the weariness of completely forgotten peoples." Presumably these are references to his Jewish ancestry, but why should the Jewish people have been "completely forgotten," except perhaps in the poet's own consciousness? At any rate, in 1905 Hofmannsthal expressed the *Lebensgefühl*, the sense of life, of *fin-de-siècle* Vienna when he wrote: "We must take leave of a world before it collapses. Many know it already, and an indefinable feeling makes poets out of many."[5]

It was a rich literary scene. At one end of the spectrum there are self-hating Jews like Arthur Trebitsch and Otto Weininger; the latter shot himself in 1903, in the house in which Ludwig van Beethoven had died, a newly minted doctor of philosophy at age twenty-three and the author of a very original and sensational book called *Sex and Character* (1903), in which he managed to attack both Jews and women. At the other end of the spectrum there is the only *homo judaicus* of the circle often referred to as Jung-Wien (Young Vienna), the markedly Jewish patriarchal figure of Richard Beer-Hofmann. His orientation may be regarded as a protest against the assimilated, feckless Jewry of his time, and to this end he invoked the heroic biblical period of the Jewish people in a grandly conceived, fragmentary cycle of poetic plays about King David. Beer-Hofmann achieved early fame in 1897 with his "Schlaflied für Mirjam," a philosophical lullaby for his firstborn. While this beautiful poem does express the *fin-de-siècle* feeling that life is impenetrable, disconnected, and evanescent, that we cannot communicate our deepest experiences even to those nearest and dearest to us, and that each generation is doomed to recapitulate the past with its errors and sorrows, it also reminds us that we may derive solace from our community and a definite continuity of existence, with ancestral values and voices shaping us and guiding us to a more meaningful, purposeful life. Even though Mirjam herself and Beer-Hofmann's biographer Esther Elstun stressed the universality rather than the Jewish significance of this poem,[6] I feel that the "Schlaflied," which betokened Jewish dignity even to a man like Rainer Maria Rilke, who was no particular friend of the Jews, is one of the most beautiful *Jewish* poems in the German language. There are several translations of the "Schlaflied" into English. What follows is the one by the poet's younger daughter, Naëmah Beer-Hofmann, whose one flaw is that it is inconsistent about the use of "you," "thee," and "thine."

Lullaby for Mirjam

Sleep, my child, it's late, go to rest.
Look how the sun sets in the west,
Over the mountains its last dying breath.
You—you know nothing of sun and of death,
Turning your eyes to light and to shine.
Sleep, so many more suns are thine.
Sleep, my child, my child, go to sleep.

Sleep, my child, the evening wind blows.
Nobody know whence it comes, where it goes.
Dark and hidden the ways are here
For you, and for me—and for all of us, dear!
Blindly we wander and wander alone,
No companion for you—or for me here below.
Sleep, my child, my child, go to sleep.

Sleep, my child, and don't listen to me,
Meaning for me is but sounds for thee,
Sounds like the wind, like the falling of rain,
Words—but maybe a lifetime's gain.
All that I've reaped will be buried with me.
None can to none an heir here be.
Sleep, my child, my child, go to sleep.

Mirjam—my child, are you asleep?
We are but shores, and blood in us deep
Flows from those past to those yet to be,
Blood of our Fathers, restless and proud.
All are within us, who feels alone?
You are their life—their life is your own.
Mirjam, my life, my child, go to sleep.[7]

Clearly, Beer-Hofmann's vibrant Judaism helped him overcome his own dandyism and decadence, his passivity and pessimism. In his novel *Der Tod Georgs* (1901), the protagonist's reveries and stream-of-consciousness reflections on his aesthetic existence lead him to an affirmation of life and of his Jewish heritage.

In *fin-de-siècle* Vienna, artistic personalities like Beer-Hofmann and Hofmannsthal, and particularly the great Burgtheater, were a formative influence on Martin Buber when he returned from Poland to his native city in 1896 as an eighteen-year-old student. As Maurice Friedman has pointed out, Buber discovered in Vienna "the spokenness of speech...the life of dialogue...This reality of speech-as-event was particularly connected for Buber with Vienna."[8]

Most of the members of the Young Vienna circle were Jews, or at least of Jewish birth or descent. These included—in addition to Beer-Hofmann, Herzl, and Hofmannsthal—Stefan Zweig, Felix Salten (born in Budapest as Sigmund Salzmann), Arthur Schnitzler, Leopold von Andrian-Werburg, Felix Dörmann (originally Biedermann), Siegfried Trebitsch, Raoul Auernheimer, and Peter Altenberg. The characteristic constellation of many of these men of letters was a patriarchally run Jewish family from which the gifted son broke away at the earliest opportunity, spurning the business opportunities provided by the self-made father in favor of a literary career. Cases in point are Stefan Zweig, Siegfried Trebitsch, Felix Salten, and Karl Kraus in Vienna and Franz Kafka and Franz Werfel in Prague. We have Kafka's poignant letter to his father, one of many evidences that he strove to recapture his Jewish heritage and Jewish values. But what Jewish values shall we distill from the life and work of Peter Altenberg, born in 1859 as Richard Engländer, a gentle, lovable ancestor of the beatniks and flower children, a man who tramped around Vienna's streets in sandals and spent his days and nights in cafés, the confidant of cabbies and prostitutes as well as the friend of literary figures, a man who wrote enchanting vignettes about Vienna's little people as well as more exotic visitors from Africa, especially about lovers of all kinds, a bohemian whose nervous breakdowns symbolized the dichotomy between his preachments as a health fanatic and his use of alcohol and drugs, a figure who poignantly reminds us of the transitoriness of a bygone age with its forced gaiety, its surface smiles, its amorous dalliance, and its unheroic passivity? What Jewish values, indeed, except perhaps the fact that Peter Altenberg was both a notable receiver and dispenser of *tzedakah?* And what about the Jewishness of Karl Kraus, the foremost German-language satirist of the past century, a man whose savage satire and mordant wit for decades filled his own periodical *Die Fackel* (The Torch), whose uncompromising blasts aimed at crushing iniquity, deflating pomposity, exposing lies and shams in life, language, and literature, the man who wrote *The Last Days of Mankind* (1919), a mammoth drama widely regarded as the most telling indictment of war ever written, a ringing denunciation of the martial spirit and the corrupt and moribund empire and society that precipitated the carnage? Kraus, like Weininger, is often labeled a self-hating Jew, and in some of his intemperate attacks he was indeed unsparing of his fellow Jews. But Kraus also had a Jew's burning sense of justice, a Jew's reverence for language and its uses, a Jew's quest for truth in human relationships as well as literature.

From an altogether different social class was the Moravian-born writer Jakob Julius David, all but forgotten today, who spent most of his short life in Vienna. Hard hit by poverty and infirmity, David wrote melancholy stories and novels that are marked by a pronounced social consciousness. They include *Das Blut* (1891), about the problems of Jews living in rural areas; *Die am Wege sterben* (1900), about the misery of students in Vienna; and *Der Übergang* (1903), about the decline of a respected Viennese family.

What Jews meant in the culture of *fin-de-siècle* Vienna has been expressed most effectively by Stefan Zweig in his remarkable autobiography *The World of Yesterday.* After making the point that the Jews replaced the somewhat jaded Austrian aristocracy as the carriers of culture and the patrons of the arts, Zweig writes: "Nine-tenths of what the world celebrated as Viennese culture in the nineteenth century was promoted, nourished, or even created by Viennese Jewry." Zweig's rosy picture of the nostalgically remembered Vienna of his youth must, of course, be viewed in the context of his despair at the time he wrote his book near the tragic end of his life, though he was insightful enough to admit that "the world of security was naught but a castle of dreams."[9] A contemporary of his viewed the same scene and sounded an alarm. Jakob Wassermann, a native of Franconia, came to Austria in 1898 and spent the rest of his life there. He found the banks, the press, the theater, the literature, and the social organizations of Vienna in Jewish hands. In his autobiography, *My Life as German and Jew,* first published as *Mein Weg als Deutscher und Jude* in 1921, Wassermann severely criticized the Jews of *fin-de-siècle* Vienna for their servility, lack of dignity and restraint, and their self-seeking opportunism—qualities that Theodor Herzl had also identified as being part of a ghetto mentality. Wassermann's animadversions foreshadow what a German Jew named Moritz Goldstein wrote in 1912, pointing out that the Jews were acting as the self-appointed literary and cultural guardians of a heritage to which their right was highly dubious.[10] It was an alarm that for the non-Jews, particularly the antisemites, only confirmed what they had long felt and what the Jews disregarded at their peril. Among the Jews of Vienna there does not seem to have been a Gershom Scholem to point out forcefully that the German-Jewish symbiosis there had no future. Theodor Herzl tried to respond to the perceived danger, but he merely looked forward to transplanting his own, German-language culture to the Jewish homeland, whereas Scholem saw salvation only in a Hebrew-based Jewish culture.

At that time, however, salvation was sought in greater assimilation and adaptation, even conversion. The two greatest Jewish-born musicians of *fin-de-siècle* Vienna, Gustav Mahler and Arnold Schönberg, both converted to Catholicism. Mahler's act (1897) may be regarded as largely opportunistic, leading to his appointment as musical director of the Imperial Opera House, though it is also true that he found Catholicism intellectually satisfying and more in line with his philosophical and mystical leanings. Schönberg returned to the Jewish fold during the Hitler period. Vienna's chief musicologists and music critics—Eduard Hanslick, Julius Korngold, Max Graf, Egon Wellesz, Richard Specht, Paul Stefan (b. Grünfeld), and Guido Adler—were also of Jewish birth, and so were the foremost contributors to the Silver Age of the Viennese operetta: Charles Weinberger, Emmerich Kálmán, Leo Fall, Oscar Straus, Bruno Granichstädten, Edmund Eysler, and Leo Ascher. Jews even made an imperishable contribution to the quintessentially Viennese genre of the *Wienerlied,* the winegarden songs in which the Viennese, with more than their share of *amour propre,* have long celebrated themselves, their way of life and their beautiful city; suffice it to mention

Gustav Pick (the author of the *Fiakerlied*), Adolf Hirsch (known as Adolfi), and Alexander Krakauer, who in his short life equated his beloved Vienna with paradise.

Jews made no great contribution to the art and architecture of the time; there was no Jewish Gustav Klimt, Egon Schiele, Oskar Kokoschka, or Adolf Loos. The architect Oskar Marmorek deserves to be remembered—if only because he supported Herzl's Zionism and was active in the Vienna Jewish community. Tina Blau (1845–1916) was an impressionist and an associate of Emil Jakob Schindler, the father of Alma Mahler. Richard Gerstl, born in Vienna in 1883, was a promising early expressionist artist whose haunting, manic, bitter paintings were in the mainstream, but his contact was with musicians rather than other artists, and his suicide at age twenty-five was caused by his unrequited love for Mathilde Schönberg. The painter Victor Tischler, born in Vienna in 1890, also deserves mention in this context. Another painter of partly Jewish descent was Max Kurzweil, who took his own life in 1916; he is remembered for his portrait of the young Herzl. Among Jewish artists from other parts of the empire who lived and worked in Vienna for a time may be mentioned Emil Orlik, Mauricy Gottlieb, Isidor Kaufmann, Jehuda Epstein, Eugen Jettel, and Leopold Horowitz. The builder of Austria's Social Democratic party, Victor Adler, was of Jewish parentage, but he embraced Protestantism and in his political pursuits was not above making antisemitic remarks. In the field of education, philanthropy, and social welfare, Eugenie Schwarzwald, a native of Czernowitz and the founder of a legendary girls' school that boasted faculty members like Loos and Kokoschka, deserves to be mentioned.

The story of Moravian-born Sigmund Freud, who spent almost his entire life in Vienna, a city with which he had a love-hate relationship, is too well known to bear repeating here. Suffice it to say that Freud remained conscious of his Jewishness, which by turns was a burden and an inspiration to him, and was a longtime member of B'nai B'rith. In this context a Freudian psychoanalytic apostle turned apostate should not be forgotten. Unlike Freud, Alfred Adler, the originator of Individual Psychology, was a native of Vienna who related with pleasure that he had

had a real Viennese street-urchin childhood, zestfully spoke the city's dialect, and sang its songs.

A writer whom Freud both admired and shunned as his "double" and who in his writings anticipated many of Freud's clinical findings and insights was the dramatist and storyteller Arthur Schnitzler, who was himself trained as a physician. Today Schnitzler is regarded as the perfect literary representative of a declining age, a great diagnostician of earthly evanescence, the psychologically penetrating chronicler and critic of interpersonal relationships and social and cultural decay, in particular the moral relativism of an aristocracy aware that it was fighting a rearguard action against the encroachments of dimly understood economic, social, and political forces. Arthur Schnitzler repeatedly wrote on Jewish themes. Between 1899 and 1912 he worked on his play *Professor Bernhardi* in which he highlighted the burning social issue of antisemitism as well as the problem of euthanasia and its religious considerations. A simple act of mercy on the part of a Jewish doctor is trumped up by prejudice-ridden clerical Vienna and inflated into a *cause célèbre.* In this thesis play the dramatist gives a cheerless picture of Viennese society and weaves into it the many social, religious, political, and ideological crosscurrents that were leading to its disintegration. The *Diskussionsroman* (novel of discussion) *Der Weg ins Freie* (translated as *The Road to the Open* in 1923), which Schnitzler wrote between 1902 and 1907, betrays the influence of Herzl and his largely unsuccessful attempts to win Schnitzler's support for the Zionist cause. It presents a whole typology of Austrian Jewry floundering between the Scylla of anti-semitism and what to Schnitzler appeared to be the Charybdis of Zionist endeavors. The author did not believe that roads to freedom—from prejudice, erotic entanglements, artistic frustrations, and other aspects of an unfulfilled life in a constricting atmosphere—could be traveled jointly. Dr. Schnitzler's only prescription seems to have been that everyone search his soul and find that inner road for himself. He considered it proper that Jews should be a kind of ferment in the brewing of humanity (a position close to that of Stefan Zweig, that great believer in the Diaspora) and that what Herzl called *Judennot* (Jewish distress) should be borne by them proudly, with dignity, and without yielding to the blandishments of any party or movement that promised a panacea. In an undated letter found in 1942, more than ten years after his death, Schnitzler wrote:

> Neither Jewish-Zionist resentment nor the stupidity and impudence of German nationalists will make me doubt in the least that I am a German writer...I would not want Zionism eliminated from the world's political scene of today or from the soul-economy of contemporary Jewry. As a spiritual element to elevate one's self-reliance, as an opportunity to react against all sorts of dark hatreds, and especially as a philanthropic action of the highest rank, Zionism will always retain its importance even if it should some day prove to have been merely a historic episode. I find it proper that authors whose language is Hebrew should call themselves Hebrew writers or Jewish writers. Neither could I object if poets of Jewish background who have hitherto written in another language became outraged at the stupidity and vulgarity of antisemitism, which would deny them membership in a nation on whose territory they were born, in whose speech they were reared and which they even helped to shape; and if, as a result, these poets abjured the beloved language hitherto employed by them and turned to Hebrew as the medium for their creative work. Such poets would thereby have obtained the right to designate themselves as Jewish poets. But as long as they continue to write in German, they must call themselves German poets...They are German poets as surely as Heine, Börne, Gundolf, and a hundred others of Jewish origin are German; as surely as Brandes is a Danish writer and Proust a French writer. Just ask any genuine living German poet, ask Heinrich Mann, Thomas Mann, Gerhart Hauptmann, Hesse, Unruh, whom they feel to be more German: Wolzogen, Dinter, and that crowd, or Wassermann, Werfel, Beer-Hofmann, and a dozen others of Jewish origin that I could name.[11]

By way of summing up, it may be stated that the quantitatively and qualitatively outstanding Jewish community of *fin-de-siècle* Vienna participated wholeheartedly in what one of its descendants, Frederick Morton (b. Mandelbaum), has described as the "nervous splendor" of the time,[12] which betokens a certain isolation, dislocation, political paralysis, cultural pessimism, and other evidences of a spiritual malaise. Most of these Jews were unaware, or tried to deny, that the demise of the liberal tradition which they were experiencing also sounded the death knell of assimilationism. It is undeniable that the Jews of Vienna made many contributions to the culture of the time that are part of the enduring legacy of what has come to be known as modernism. To what extent these contributions may be regarded as Jewish—that is, springing from Jewish self-awareness and embodying Jewish values—is, however, open to argument.

Notes

1. Karl Kraus, *Half-Truths and One-and-a-Half Truths; Selected Aphorisms,* ed. Harry Zohn (Montreal, 1976), p. 60.
2. Stefan George, "Den Brüdern," dedicated to Leopold von Andrian-Werburg and included in his *Der Teppich des Lebens* (Berlin, 1900). See Harry Zohn, ed., *Der farbenvolle Untergang: Österreichisches Lesebuch* (Englewood Cliffs, N.J., 1971), p. 8.
3. Harry Zohn, *Österreichische Juden in der Literatur* (Tel Aviv, 1969); *"...Ich bin ein Sohn der deutschen Sprache nur": Jüdisches Erbe in der österreichischen Literatur* (Wien-München, 1986).
4. Joseph Roth to Benno Reifenberg, February 16, 1926, in *Joseph Roth, Briefe, 1911-1939,* ed. Hermann Kesten (Köln-Berlin, 1970), p. 81.
5. Cited in Jakob Laubach, "Hugo von Hofmannsthals Turmdichtungen" (Ph.D. diss., University of Fribourg, 1959), p. 88.
6. See Esther Elstun, *Richard Beer-Hofmann: His Life and Work* (University Park, Pa., 1983), p. 13.
7. Naëmah Beer-Hofmann's translation of Richard Beer-Hofmann's "Schlaflied für Mirjam" is printed in Klaus W. Jonas, "Richard Beer-Hofmann and Rainer Maria Rilke," *Modern Austrian Literature* 8, nos. 3/4 (1975); 63. See also Rainer Maria Rilke to Ilse Blumenthal-Weiss, April 25, 1922, in Rilke, *Briefe aus Muzot: 1921 bis 1926,* ed. Ruth Sieber-Rilke and Carl Sieber (Leipzig, 1937), p. 145.
8. Maurice Friedman, *Martin Buber and the Theater* (New York, 1969), p. 4.
9. Stefan Zweig, *The World of Yesterday* (New York, 1943), pp. 22, 5.
10. Moritz Goldstein, "Deutsch-jüdischer Parnassus," *Der Kunstwart* 25, no. 11 (March 1912), p. 281-94. See also Goldstein, "German Jewry's

Dilemma: The Story of a Provocative Essay," *Leo Baeck Institute Year Book* 2 (1957); 236-54.

11. Quoted in Harry Zohn, "The Jewish World of Arthur Schnitzler," *Jewish Quarterly* 10 (1963): 29. The original may be found in *Aufbau* (N.Y.) 8, No. 19, May 8, 1942, p. 17.
12. Frederic Morton, *A Nervous Splendor: Vienna 1888/1889* (Boston, 1979).

THE BURNING SECRET OF STEPHEN BRANCH

or

A Cautionary Tale About a Physician Who Could Not Heal Himself

In 1919, shortly after the end of World War I, the publishing house of Scott & Seltzer (New York) issued in book form a fascinating story by a Viennese author still in his thirties who was then only on the verge of achieving the kind of international renown that was evidenced by translations of his works into thirty different languages. The book was called *The Burning Secret,* and the author's name was given as Stephen Branch. This was, of course, Stefan Zweig, and he promptly launched a protest against this unauthorized and quite dubious use of an English version of his name. It must be remembered, though, that in 1919 passions against people and things from the German-speaking world still ran so high that the publishers must have felt their unusual move would produce greater sales of Zweig's story. After all, during World War I sauerkraut became "liberty cabbage," the lowly hamburger was upgraded to "Salisbury steak," the German conductor of the Boston Symphony

Orchestra, Karl Muck, was virtually pushed off the podium and hounded out of the country, and Hugo Münsterberg, a leading light of Harvard's Department of Philosophy and Psychology in its golden age, a man who smarted under the dual burden of being a German and a Jew, died an untimely death of that age-old German disease, a broken heart. But the title of this article derives not merely from my punning proclivities; it is intended to indicate two things: The bit of commercial xenophobia (or xenophobic commercialism) that prompted the *Verfremdung* of an honest and honored name foreshadowed the coming crisis of a man who was then about to embark on the most fruitful decade of his life. And, as a related phenomenon, the title of Zweig's story itself may serve as a reference to a character trait that may help to explain the inexplicable, his final tragedy. Here I should like to adduce as dissimilar but equally authoritative and convincing witnesses two of Zweig's longtime *compagnons de route:* the woman who shared his life for a quarter of a century and a close friend from the years before World War I. The latter is Gustinus Ambrosi, a sculptor and poet who made the only bust of Stefan Zweig that was sculpted from life. That was in 1913, when the artist was only twenty years old but had already achieved such prominence that Emperor Franz Joseph bestowed upon him a *Staatsatelier* for life. At the age of seven Ambrosi contracted a brain fever that made him completely deaf. The boy never attended school and was self-taught to an astonishing degree, ultimately producing more than 2400 works of sculpture, many in the style of Rodin, as well as a large body of poetry, mostly sonnets. Overcoming his handicap with prodigious strength, Ambrosi represented a life-affirming, buoyant, Promethean, Renaissance type of artistry, and his vision of Zweig must be viewed in the light of Ambrosi's basic tenet "All suffering is grace." Two long letters which Ambrosi wrote me in 1954, one year before our only personal encounter in Vienna, are devoted largely to his recollections of Stefan Zweig. He stresses his impression that there was an essentially *feminine* gracefulness about the writer—his figure, his bearing, his hands. Ambrosi describes Zweig as an eternal pilgrim through the human psyche who lived in the past rather than in the present—"dieser in seiner Angst Ansässige, denn Angst war sein wesentlichstes Element, Angst! Angst!" *Angst* has entered the English language as a psychoanalytical term, but what does Ambrosi mean by a life dominated by anxiety? He goes on to elucidate this by saying that Zweig was afraid of force and power. "Stefan Zweig's großer Fehler war, daß er das Mächtige zu erdrückend empfand. Er liebte das Zarte und das dem Starken aus dem Wege Gehende." In this regard Zweig may have been more Austrian than he realized; *Flucht vor der Größe* (Flight from Greatness) is Hans Weigel's title of his collection of essays about great Austrians. Ambrosi claims that while his friend's suicide is incomprehensible to him, it is entirely in keeping with Zweig's evasion of strength: "Zur Stärke gehört vor allem die Geduld und das Wartenkönnen...Und vor allem eine große Logik über das, was 'lebensfähig' und nicht 'lebensfähig' ist." Patience was a virtue that Ambrosi consciously based his life upon, and he missed it in Zweig, whose judgment as to viability and nonviability Ambrosi deemed deficient. According to him, Zweig late in life deliberately shunned those who represented strength, rationality, endurance, viability: "Er hätte bei Friderike bleiben sollen; sie war die Starke, das mächtige, alles verstehende Herz, dem er dann doch aus dem Wege gegangen ist, wie er zuletzt auch Felix Braun und mir aus dem Wege gegangen ist." Ambrosi's religion was his art, and he strove to reach God through it; Friderike Zweig and Felix Braun were born into Jewish families but converted and were throughout their lives rooted in a vibrant Catholic faith. Ambrosi expresses astonishment at the fact that Zweig, who had such a remarkable collection of manuscripts and tried to distill the creative process and the personality from the handwriting of great persons, who was fond of communing with great minds via the graphic manifestations of their genius, should have failed to respond to certain signs indicating the impermanence of evil; he calls him a "zaghafter Traumwandler," a timorous somnambulist who let himself be bedazzled into thinking that a Hannibal, a Napoleon, or a Hitler were eternal features of the world. When Ambrosi, on the other hand, first saw Hitler's handwriting, he recognized him as an epileptic upstart who was bound for eventual self-destruction. All torment, according to Ambrosi, is there to be overcome and to serve for the shaping of works of art; this is how Shakespeare, Michelangelo, and Beethoven have understood it, and even Nietzsche endured madness and was not prepared to end his life. "Wie oft sagte ich es Zweig ins Gesicht: Leid ist Gnade, und man muß sich im Staube wälzen können, um den Himmel zu sehen! Hiebei aber blieb er tauber als die Tauben und ging feminin an aller Schwere vorbei und entschwebte in seinen Gedankenkreis, wo keine schweren Gewichte des Lebens und Schicksals anders als zur Schilderung zugelassen waren." In Ambrosi's view, then, Zweig evaded all grave/heavy/difficult things (the word *Schwere* denotes all of these) and escaped to a realm of thought where the great burdens of life were admitted only for the sake of poetic presentation.

If one accepts Ambrosi's view of Zweig—and I find much of it convincing—it may be argued that Zweig himself was aware of the patrimony of unheroic, effete evasiveness and tried to rid himself of it when the Viennese began to take his first steps on the road to Europe, as it were, and avidly reached for an experience that would enable him to shed the last vestiges of the dalliance, dandyism, and decadence that were the norm in the aesthetically oriented "Young Vienna" circle of writers at the turn of the century. At the age of seventeen he came across a small volume entitled *Les Flamandes,* and in 1902 he met its author, Émile Verhaeren, the Flemish poet who wrote in French and whom Zweig came to idolize not only as a poet but also as a human being. Zweig's initial lack of self-sufficiency despite a sheltered upbringing and early literary successes may have made him respond all the more strongly to certain antithetical traits which he found in the Belgian: the hymnal spirit of Verhaeren's poetry, his prodigious strength and affirmation of all aspects of life, his universal love, his enthusiasm and feeling of exaltation. Verhaeren's watchword "Toute la vie est dans l'essor" became Zweig's own, and the denizen of the intellectual hothouse atmosphere of *fin-de-siècle* Vienna responded enthusiastically to such lines as "Je suis un fils de cette race tenace." To Zweig, Verhaeren appeared as the fulfillment of the social purpose of artistic creativity, and he was to him not so much a literary model (after all, most of Zweig's own poetry was written in his early years and does not loom large in his work) but somehow worthy of emulation because he reflected all facets of contemporary life. What others had regarded as a barren field of poetry—the new machines, the big cities, the burgeoning industrial scene, the earthy rural population and the urban masses, the entire ferment of modern civilization, what today we call urbanism—Verhaeren found eminently fertile for poetic expression. Zweig saw in Verhaeren's work a lyrical encyclopaedia of our time; to him he was the Walt Whitman of Europe who imbued the younger man with the vibrant enthusiasm, the virtuosic use of luxuriant language, and the boundless compassion that shaped Zweig's life and informed his writings as he strove to understand, to interpret, to refine, to preserve, and to transmit a great heritage. During several prewar years Zweig served a unique kind of literary apprenticeship, publishing translations of a number of volumes of Verhaeren's poetry, prose, and plays in addition to producing a monograph about him. It was a great blow to Zweig that after the outbreak of the war in 1914 the unexpected but perhaps all-too-human happened: Even Verhaeren, the proclaimer of the gospel of humanity, endurance, patience, and compassion, fell prey to the hysteria of hatred that bedeviled so many European intellectuals at the same time and in works like *Les Ailes Rouges de la Guerre* and *La Belgique Sanglante* intoned hymns of hate against Germany. By another irony of fate, Verhaeren was struck down and fatally injured in 1916 by a locomotive, one of the machines he had celebrated in his poetry. His hymns and his teachings were soon enough outdistanced and outmoded by the great carnage as well as the economic collapse, the political instability, and the social strife of the postwar years. This was a great setback for Zweig, and Verhaeren's example and influence were only partially compensated for by his second great friend and guiding star, the French writer and humanist Romain Rolland, who in wartime provided Zweig with a focus for his vibrant pacifism. Together the two friends zealously but unsuccessfully tried to rally Europe's intellectuals around the cause of peace and sanity. When Rolland exiled himself from France and went to work for the Red Cross in Switzerland, striving to restore the bonds that the cataclysm had cut and to counteract the poisoning of the arms of which so many intellectuals on both sides were guilty, Zweig in a stirring essay hailed Rolland's modest quarters in the Red Cross building in Geneva as "the heart of Europe." But while Zweig greatly admired

Rolland for his idealistic courage, his friend encouraged him to remain "au-dessus de la mêlée," above the fray. Later the paths of the friends diverged as Rolland adopted a political stance that Zweig could not approve of. Rolland, who was Zweig's senior by fifteen years but ten years younger than Verhaeren, could not replace the strong father figure that the Belgian represented.

At an early age Zweig became aware of the crisis facing his age, and for many years he was bedeviled by the growing antinomy between a bourgeois humanism that had become undermined by the failure of its adherents to commit themselves to positive action and the new, ever-rising current of political and social activism which was compelling individuals to embrace one program or another. While Zweig's knowledge of history, the typology of human motivations and personalities that he presented in his writings, and his skillful psychological probing for the wellsprings of human action could not have left him blind to the need for change, Zweig deliberately adopted an eminently apolitical stance. As late as 1935 he wrote to Hermann Hesse: "I have learned to hate politics...as the counterpole of justice." It was his agonizing dilemma that he knew the world to be irrational and violent yet was rendered incapable of working for change by his aversion to ideological entanglements. His position was that of a secular millennialist characterized by a sort of tolerant detachment. Again and again he was disappointed by the purely practical, by political ventures that foundered on the shoals of incompetence or selfishness, or that were scuttled by dimly comprehended historical forces. Even as he paid tribute to the ill-starred Walter Rathenau, Germany's sometime foreign minister, for extending his horizon from the purely literary to the contemporary scene, Zweig was content merely to hope for the ultimate triumph of reason. His Eurocentric world-view did not allow him to come to terms with contemporary developments that determined the disastrous ascendancy of Fascism and Nazism. One of the great themes running through his work is the dignity and spiritual superiority of the downtrodden and the vanquished. (It is interesting to note that a similar theme has been stated as the poignant essence of Yiddish literature: "The virtue of powerlessness, the company of the dispossessed, the sanctity of the insulted and the injured.") Zweig repeatedly portrayed apolitical individuals (such as that "bibliosaurus," the transplanted Eastern European Jew Jakob Mendel, known as "Book Mendel") caught up in and crushed by the impersonal, unfeeling, cruel machinery of world politics and war. With his collection *Master Builders of the World,* consisting of several biographical triptychs, Zweig wanted to present a typology of the spirit. He was not concerned with the titans of action who moved empires but with the unheroic moral leaders of mankind who have furnished us with enduring examples, though they may themselves have been broken on the wheel of life or history. Zweig's biographical study of Napoleon's minister of police, Joseph Fouché (1928), is a great moral condemnation of *homo politicus;* teaching an object lesson of unprincipled behavior, the author warned the peoples of Europe against falling for politicians of that stripe. In his essay "Ist die Geschichte gerecht?" (Is There Justice in History?), written as early as 1922, Zweig tried to provide a humanistic alternative and antidote to the cult of power and success as he warned the masses against glorifying their oppressors and worshiping their own chains. He pointed out that all too often history has been rewritten in favor of those who have prevailed by virtue of brute strength and that there is a tendency to create myths about the strong and the heroic, while the infinitely worthier and frequently self-effacing heroes of everyday life remain unsung. Might and morality must be clearly sundered; it behooves us not to be bedazzled by the seductive glamor of success and to re-examine history from a humanistic point of view. Military and political hegemony is invariably based on violence and exacts a high price, whereas only a man of mind who gains power honestly and wields it responsibly can enhance humanistic values instead of destroying them. We should never compromise with evil and should resist the blandishments and morally confusing encroachments of material and political forces beyond our control.

In his remarkable autobiography *The World of Yesterday,* which is really the biography of an age rather than a person, Zweig said about himself that as an Austrian, a Jew, a writer, a humanist, and a pacifist he had always stood at the exact point where the global clashes and cataclysms of our century were at their most violent. His response to these blows of fate was an excessive objectivity and feckless neutrality, a reluctance to get involved in the kind of political action that Zweig deemed deleterious, an unwillingness to accept the limitations and vagaries of political activity, and an increasing contempt for merely political adjustments. Zweig's frequently naive stance is reminiscent of the disillusionment, the inaction and near-paralysis of Viennese intellectuals at the turn of the century. Zweig came to regard Europe as his "sacred homeland," and his Europeanism ultimately led him to view the tragedy of the Jews as only part of the larger and presumably more important tragedy of Europe. In the fecund 1920s Zweig's impressive mountain home in Salzburg, the crossroads of Europe, was a shrine to his *idée maîtresse,* the intellectual unification of Europe. But after 1933 the city seemed like an outpost dangerously close to the German border and a hotbed of intolerance, espionage, intrigue, and violence from which he escaped to England four years before the *Anschluß,* though this eventually meant the breakup of his marriage and the loss of his beautiful home with all the cultural treasures it contained. A world increasingly inured to brutality; technical progress coupled with moral regression; the burning of his books in Germany and the loss of most of his German-language readership—all this was anathema to Zweig's sensitive soul and produced an almost hypochondriacal, paranoid uneasiness in him. He felt that he was a member of a generation fated to experience at first hand an uncannily prophetic dictum of the nineteenth-century Austrian dramatist Franz Grillparzer: "The road of modern culture leads from humanity via nationality to bestiality."

Zweig's correspondence with Martin Buber during World War I indicates that he prized the Diaspora and interpreted his Judaism rather wilfully as offering him an opportunity to be a citizen of the world. On May 8, 1916, he wrote: "I would not want to choose Judaism as an emotional prison with conceptual bars separating me from the world outside. I have an antipathy to everything in Judaism that tends to create antitheses." And on May 25, 1917, he wrote to Buber: "This supranational feeling of being free from the madness of a fanatical world has been my inner salvation these past years, and I gratefully acknowledge that what has made this supranational freedom possible for me is my Jewishness. Perhaps it is the purpose of Judaism to show over the centuries that community is possible without country, only through blood and intellect, only through the word and faith." In February 1918 Zweig wrote to Buber: "The more the dream threatens to become actuality, the dangerous dream of a Jewish state with cannons, flags, and decorations, the more I am determined to love the painful idea of the Diaspora, to love Jewish destiny more than Jewish prosperity." Zweig's foremost dramatic work, the pacifist play *Jeremiah,* premiered in Zurich in 1917, must be viewed in the same light. In a letter to Buber dated May 1916 Zweig characterized it as "the tragedy and hymn of the Jewish people as the chosen people—not in the sense of prosperity but in that of eternal suffering, eternal falling and eternal rising—and of the strength deriving from such a fate." Whether cultural mediatorship in the countries of the Diaspora may be regarded as an eminently Jewish quality is open to debate, but surely the career of Stefan Zweig was first and foremost that of a mediator. All his life he strove to translate in a wider and higher sense, to inform, to educate, to inspire, and to arouse appreciation and enthusiasm across personal, literary, cultural, and national boundaries. The key to his life and work is contained in his introduction to a collection of his essays published in 1937 under the title *Begegnungen mit Menschen, Büchern, Städten* (Encounters with People, Books, Cities). There he says about himself that he has made a determined and sustained effort "to understand even what is most alien to us, always to evaluate people and periods, figures and works only in their positive and creative sense, and to let this desire to understand and share this understanding with others serve humbly and faithfully our indestructible ideal: humane communication among persons, mentalities, cultures and nations."

The biographical study of Erasmus of Rotterdam which Zweig published in 1934 is rightly regarded as one of his most personal works, for in troubled times he clearly identified with that *homo pro se* of another century of great strife. Like Erasmus, Zweig found himself buffeted about by wild outbursts of popular passion, and he hoped to derive certitude and courage from his portrayal of the Dutch humanist as a fighter for a "juster, more harmonious structure of our spiritual world...who truly hated only one thing on earth: fanaticism, the enemy of reason." Zweig viewed both his subject and himself as champions of spiritual freedom and opponents of zealotry and all forces bent on abridging or destroying the "divine manifoldness" of *homo sapiens* and God's world. "The man who lives on the spiritual plane may not take sides," he wrote; "his sphere is justice, which is above the battle." Further, it is mankind's highest duty to seek to become "humaner, more spiritual, and increasingly capable of sympathetic, spiritual understanding." In the view of many, Zweig exercised excessive restraint and carried his antifanatical Erasmian attitude *ad absurdum*. The man who never hesitated to associate himself with worthwhile cultural causes and freely shared his considerable material resources with those in need was loath to commit himself to any cause he suspected of being political, including those clearly connected with the desperate fight against Hitlerism. In turning a deaf ear to what seemed to him like appeals to emotion rather than reason, Zweig may have feared that action for the sake of a temporary advantage might compromise his vision of a future age dedicated to a higher human ideal. He may have been motivated by a desire to keep his spiritual resources intact. To the last he clung to his conviction that the world is built on reason and that the individual transcends considerations of religion, ideology, nationality, and politics.

But now it is time to let our second witness speak in supplementation of Gustinus Ambrosi's observations on what may be termed the "burning secret" underlying Zweig's work and his public life. In an essay entitled "Antworten" in the original and "The Final Tragedy" in my translation, Friderike Maria Zweig asks how a world traveler like Zweig could ever have felt homeless and uprooted. Did he not continue to enjoy financial security and a largely undiminished international readership even as an emigrant? Friderike points out that Zweig was attached to his original linguistic instrument and felt lost without it, the way a violin virtuoso feels lost without his Stradivarius or Guarnerius. Also, "he had tried to pretend that his house in Bath was similar to the one in Salzburg." (Some years ago I stood before the handsome villa still called "Rosemount" on Lyncombe Hill, overlooking the old Roman city, where Zweig lived in 1939 and 1940 with his new wife, Lotte, and I was able to understand how Zweig could have felt that way). But in 1941 he felt marooned in Brazil, and closed borders prevented him from returning even to his English replica of his Austrian home. "In thoughts," continues Friderike, "he now passed over his blocked intermediate station, and his memories returned to Austria, the homeland which he now deemed lost to him forever." Despite Zweig's stature as a "great European," his nostalgia for Francisco-Josephinian Vienna, the magnificent old cosmopolitan capital of a seemingly secure old empire, must have grown as his sense of rootlessness and homelessness became overpowering. As his spiritual equilibrium was upset by multifarious personal crises and conflicts, the world situation caused an atavistic uneasiness about the material aspects of his existence to arise in him, and it became evident that he had subconsciously taken the security of earlier days too much for granted. Friderike goes on to ask how a high-minded person like Zweig could have kept on an even keel in that witches' sabbath of conflict. She writes: "I find it somewhat surprising that a man of this kind should have impressed many people, in earlier years and to this day, as a harmonious person who had apparently learned early in life to abreact his 'struggle with the demon.' The almost limitless sources of his inner life flooded his dark inner uproar like a cleansing mountain stream. His faith in the richness of existence, his reverence for living creatures made him a religious man. At the beginning of our relationship I never felt impelled to ask this Faustian man about his attitude toward religion. But how often he spoke of his 'black liver,' saying that it was dangerous to be close to him." In Friderike's view, Stefan was gifted, or afflicted, with an uncanny "second sight" that made him see the shape of things to come, and the historian, the psychologist, the philanthropist, the helper, and the none-too-courageous Erasmian man in him were responsible for this. Cheerful people, innocent children at play, his fellow Britishers (Zweig had received the coveted British citizenship during World War II) fiddling with sporting events and other trivia while the world burned could make him shudder. The man who was so adept at giving to others used to flee from the Christmas celebrations at his Salzburg home and later the bacchanalian carnival at Rio de Janeiro. "For a long time," writes Friderike, "he allowed his pessimism to be mitigated by my optimism; in fact, he counted on it. Later, however, when there were ominous rumblings everywhere, he went so far as to seek a joint descent into profoundest oblivion. This happened some time before the outbreak of the catastrophes. Like Heinrich von Kleist, he now sought companionship in death. He had expressed that dismal desire on two previous occasions, but how can anyone who has not bent over the abyss fathom the seriousness of such a request?" Referring to Zweig's uncommonly empathic essay on Kleist, Friderike writes that "it became frightfully clear to me that only someone who shared a longing for death could muster such an affirmative understanding...It should not be assumed that this macabre trait could be sensed or seen during Zweig's entire life—although, as I reflect upon it, it always was there beneath the surface." Friderike reminds us that Schnitzler, Hofmannsthal, and the early Thomas Mann had established an intimate relationship with death; Zweig only *seemed* sunnier and happier. In this connection, I recall Friderike telling me in private conversation that during the summer of 1941, when she and Stefan were, in the interest of his autobiography in progress, reunited at the summer place of their good friends, René and Erika Fülöp-Miller, at Ossining, New York, Stefan displayed what in retrospect was deemed a suspicious interest in Fülöp-Miller's work in progress, a study of death.

There you have the "burning secret" of Stefan Zweig, alias Stephen Branch: Beneath the surface he was a thanatologist who, having failed to keep the demons at bay, in February of 1942 practiced the ultimate evasion of strength and force, choosing the extreme expression of the kind of *Angst* that Gustinus Ambrosi diagnosed in him.

To avoid ending this essay on such a negative note I shall include a brief tribute to the noble lady who carried on in Zweig's spirit until her death three decades after her former husband's. For many years she set aside her own literary career (as a novelist, essayist, journalist, and sometime lyric poet) to be a helpmate to him. Friderike Zweig was the founder and director of the Salzburg group of the International Women's League for Peace and Freedom. After emigrating to this country she founded the Writers Service Center in New York as a continuation of the Zweigs' activities in behalf of colleagues in need of counsel and help. From early 1943 on the Writers Service Center functioned as more than a literary agency. It aimed at furthering the careers of needy exiled writers by promoting their Americanization, teaching them to adapt to changed conditions and practices, and to write for a relatively limited new market. A combination of secretarial facility, information bureau, cultural cooperative, self-help center, and clearinghouse for vacation opportunities, it placed manuscripts with agents and publishers, supplied translators and illustrators, handled applications for fellowships and grants, researched international copyrights, and arranged lectures and readings. After she moved to Stamford, Connecticut, in 1945, Friderike continued the work of the Center on a more informal basis. The American-European Friendship Association, which she founded in 1943, was not one of the numerous *Landsmannschaften* but a supranational organization that supplemented the work of the Writers Service Center on a more comprehensive cultural and human plane. As Friderike said in her autobiography *Spiegelungen des Lebens,* it would take a book to describe the multifarious fruitful connections and beneficial relationships produced by this cosmopolitan people-to-people organization which for years put on lectures, concerts, theatrical performances, discussions, art exhibits, and social gatherings in several cities. From 1953 on Friderike Zweig organized an ambitious annual Friendship Week in Stamford which attracted people of various backgrounds and ages to an intensive, colorful, and yet relaxing summer week featuring distinguished programs with such comprehensive themes as "The Cultural Unity of Mankind," "The Age of Jefferson and Mozart," "The Comic Spirit," and "Man and the Wonderful World of Science." Even after such wide-ranging efforts ceased, Friderike continued as a one-woman Friendship Association on a less structured but equally effective basis, as witness the hospitality the octogenarian extended to old and new friends attending the International PEN Club Congress in 1966. In a circular letter she sent out in 1954 she wrote: "Let us continue to have America and Europe as our parish and the world as our horizon." That Friderike devoted a life-and-works, a picture biography, and an edition of their correspondence to Stefan

Zweig is a matter of bibliographical record, but what is truly important are the activities, causes, and concerns she carried on or championed in Stefan's spirit: Resources Unlimited for handicapped persons, the Alliance Française, the Connecticut Association for the Abolition of the Death Penalty, and the many fruitful friendships in the spirit of that great master of friendship. In her preface to *Greatness Revisited,* a collection of her essays, which unfortunately she did not live to see published, Friderike wrote: "Now that our horizon is being darkened by question marks about the meaning and values of life, would it not be important to put a few great stars between the ominous signs?"

While Stefan Zweig was, alas, a physician who could not heal himself, his undogmatic and unideological humanism is eminently relevant to our age. While his brand of liberalism may be perceived as old-fashioned today, his contribution to pan-European thought must be regarded as an enduring one. Friderike has reminded us that her husband's was the first voice to call for a cosmopolitan community of the youth of Europe and that he proposed the establishment of an international university functioning interchangeably in several capital cities. In a lecture delivered in 1932, "Die moralische Entgiftung Europas" (The Moral Decontamination of Europe), Zweig called for well-organized student exchanges to reduce political tensions and collective animosities. He felt that the history of culture and of the human spirit rather than political or military history should be taught in the schools of the world. Some things that Zweig worked for tirelessly and that seemed utopian during his lifetime, such as Franco-German understanding and European cooperation, are actualities today. Zweig's apotheosis of Brazil, his last refuge, shows that his interest was not limited to Europe and that he was alive to both the problems and the potentialities of what is now called the "Third World."

Beyond any practical or specific applications of Zweig's work and thought, however, it is the spirit permeating his entire multifaceted *oeuvre,* a spirit as exemplary as it is timeless, that is sorely needed today. In an age beset by horrendous nationalism, chauvinism, racism, fanaticism, violence, crime, and terrorism, much may be found in Zweig's writings to counteract the multifarious dehumanizing forces of our time.

Above all, Zweig's insistent reiteration of the independence and inviolability of the human personality can keep us from becoming inured to these horrors. Even though Zweig's Erasmian "dream of a coming and irresistible humanization of mankind" seems to have receded farther into the distance, we must continue to dream that dream. Zweig's boundless faith in mankind can still sustain us, and his pioneering work in behalf of a brotherly world without boundaries is still capable of inspiring us. Surely Zweig's demand for the humane right of self-determination and the untrammeled expression of the human intellect is of undiminished relevance and may serve as a counterpoise to the woefully reduced view of human nature that holds sway in so much of contemporary literature and thought. "Our greatest debt of gratitude," wrote Zweig in his unfinished last work, a study of Montaigne, "is to those who in these inhuman times confirm the human in us, who encourage us not to abandon our unique and imperishable possession: our innermost self." Half a century after this writer's death there is reason to remember and to read and to be grateful to Stefan Zweig in this sense.

THE HERZL DIARIES:

A SELF-PORTRAIT OF THE MAN AND THE LEADER

In July of 1896 Theodor Herzl entered in his Diary his impressions of a mass meeting in the East End of London. "As I sat on the platform...I experienced strange sensations. I saw and heard my legend being born. The people are sentimental; the masses do not see clearly. I believe that even now they no longer have a clear image of me. A light fog is beginning to rise around me, and it may become the cloud in which I shall walk...This is perhaps the most interesting thing I am recording in these notebooks—the way my legend is being born."[1] As happens with so many great figures, over the years the fog around Herzl has only become thicker, the clouds in which he is enshrouded have increased, and, due largely to his personal magnetism and an early, martyr-like death, his legend has assumed gigantic dimensions. One hundred years after Herzl began his quest for a Jewish state it is high time to reclaim the man and the leader from the sentimental stereotypes that have proliferated about him. A thorough acquaintance with his Diaries is indeed an indispensable prerequisite to an understanding of Herzl's complex personality and may serve as a corrective to some popularly held misconceptions, for this document supplies not only invaluable source material for the early history of political Zionism, but also a vivid, unvarnished self-portrait of a kind that is rare in the history of literature.

The American writer Ambrose Bierce once defined a diary as a "daily record of that part of one's life which he can relate to himself without blushing." "Bitter Bierce" wrote this in his *Devil's Dictionary,* and while it may be true of lesser, more trivial diaries, it does not apply to the remarkably frank record of the incorruptible, outspoken Herzl, who detested dissimulation and self-deception and who noted on the very first pages that his diary entries would be valueless if he attempted to play the hypocrite with himself. The Diaries are therefore a voluminous and *unblushing* compendium of Herzl's triumphs and tragedies, not merely in the arena of world politics, but on a personal plane as well, presenting Herzl from within.

Herzl had started keeping a diary as a young lawyer in the 1880s, but that turned out to be little more than a playful literary exercise. When he began keeping a diary devoted entirely to the Jewish cause, in Paris, around Pentecost 1895, a visionary's instinct told him that he was writing for posterity, that his pages would mirror a vital era in social and political history. A diary, to be sure, is by definition something subjective, capricious, full of loose ends, unexpected shifts, and tantalizing obscurities; it reflects changes of emphasis and attitude, explorations of new paths; it makes snap judgments. Herzl's Diaries are no exception. But their basic veracity has never been questioned, and whole biographies have been based on their contents, quoting from them copiously. In his literary testament, written as early as 1897, Herzl called his Diary his chief literary legacy (elsewhere he had referred to it as "an imperishable treasure of all mankind"—p. 94), and stated that he would like to have it published in both German and English after his death.

Herzl the Zionist leader, the dramatist, essayist, and journalist thus also emerges as one of the great "Dichter ihres Lebens," in Stefan Zweig's phrase, as one of the great adepts at self-portraiture, whose unretouched self-portrait, moreover, offers the reader a rare education in integrity. The emphasis is on the word "Dichter," for Herzl in a certain sense poeticized his life, being ever conscious of the intermingling of life and literature. The phrase "the (serial) novel of my life" keeps recurring in the Diaries. What makes this work so attractive as literature is the diarist's becoming sense of the poetic quality of his undertaking. For years he hovered between "Dichtung und Wahrheit," was not sure whether he was initiating an emergency project of great scope and world-historical significance or merely gathering material for a great utopian novel. The political Zionist and the poet were ever inseparable. *Das neue Ghetto* and *Altneuland* were attempts to let off steam, to gain clarity and strength for his activities in the political arena, to depict poetically and potently the reality he envisioned. While working on his Zionist utopia, *Altneuland*, in 1901, Herzl wrote: "My life is no novel now. So the novel is my life" (p. 1071).

It remains an enigma how the ex-lawyer and journalist, the assimilated and only marginally Jewish Viennese writer of elegant feuilletons, witty essays, and charming but light-weight drawing-room comedies, who called himself "a writer of sorts, with little ambition and petty vanities" (p. 5), almost overnight turned into a statesman with a utopian outlook. At the very beginning of his Diaries the bemused Herzl makes an attempt at self-analysis, reflecting on the great transformation within him, the striking contrast between his desire of just a few years previously to lead a mass conversion of Austrian Jewry and the steps which he was now taking on the road to Zion with almost somnambulistic assurance. After a bit of depth-psychologizing Herzl came to the conclusion that the Zionist idea had had a gestation period of about thirteen years in his mind, which means that the experience of the Dreyfus Affair, so often presented as the sole impetus for Herzl's Zionist program, merely triggered a long-harbored unconscious desire.

As a writer, Herzl is often bracketed with the so-called "Young Vienna" group of men of letters which consisted mostly of Jews and included such major literary figures as Arthur Schnitzler, Richard Beer-Hofmann, Hugo von Hofmannsthal, Stefan Zweig, Hermann Bahr, Peter Altenberg, and Felix Salten. The decade of Herzl's life which is reflected in the Diaries furnishes evidence that Herzl pulled himself up by his literary and ethical bootstraps, thinking, acting, and writing in a way that flew in the face of the *Zeitgeist*. The atmosphere of *fin-de-siècle* Vienna was one of gentle decadence, of world-weary cynicism, of inaction, dalliance and dandyism, of surface gaiety, and many of its literary products were informed by a sort of effete estheticism. While Herzl's more routine and ephemeral literary productions, most of them justly forgotten today, did grow on that soil, his more significant creations have lasted because they are the carriers of both timely and timeless insights and reflect Herzl's vision and his stature as a great moral educator.

What Herzl the educator sought to accomplish was an upgrading of the ethical quality of Jewry. Pride and self-confidence as a driving force in Jewish life and aspirations may be regarded as a major innovation. Proceeding from the insight that he who wants to do great things must first conquer himself, Herzl appears in the pages of his Diary as a rather stern, old-fashioned moralist who opposed drinking and gambling, who believed in patriarchal families, in the moral power of labor, who wished to outlaw suicide as something degrading to the human personality, as a man who wanted to stand immaculate before the tribunal of world history. Yet another side of his personality was that of the showman with a strong flair for the dramatic who was attracted by the pageantry, the pomp and circumstance of the proposed Jewish exodus and transplantation. There was almost Spartan simplicity on the one hand, and love of luxury on the other. With great psychological acumen Herzl proposed to turn the Yellow Badge, hitherto a sign of shame and degradation, into a coveted decoration, called "Jewish honor." "The Promised Land is within ourselves" (p. 150). With such words he wanted to supply a *"sursum corda"* to demoralized ghetto types. Herzl's social philosophy is best expressed in words that he called "the chief tenet of my life": "Whoever wishes to change men must change the conditions under which they live" (p. 856). The man who associated with the lords of the earth as their equal, as he had predicted he would, resolved to be so irreproachable in his conduct that "everyone who comes into contact with me shall get the opposite of the proverbial opinion of the Jews" (p. 693-4). In this he may have been aided by his insight that "the difference between myself and Sabbatai Zevi (the way I imagine him)...is that Sabbatai made himself great so as to be the equal of the great of the earth. I, however, find the great small, as small as myself" (p. 958). In a similar vein, Herzl characterized himself in these words: "He who wills something great is in my eyes a great man—not he who achieves it. For in achievement luck plays a part" (p. 950). Herzl's basic faith in his people never really faltered, and he suggested as his epitaph: "He had too good an opinion of the Jews" (p. 942).

Yet the vision and the reality seldom coincided. In that early *tour de force* of "brainstorming" in Paris, a sort of dress rehearsal for the Address to the Rothschild Family Council, which in turn was a forerunner of *The Jewish State,* Herzl realized that he was mixing sense with nonsense, pipedreams with sound ideas, in a heady brew, that many of his notes smacked of megalomaniacal madness. Herzl early on referred to himself as the "Führer," predicted that he would be "the Parnell of the Jews" (p. 248); yet he repeatedly complained that he was only at the head of an army of "boys, beggars, and prigs" (p. 577). He felt that what entitled him to be and remain the leader was his willingness to accept reverses, to remain undaunted in the face of adversity, his ability to keep several irons in the fire at all times. "It takes certain abilities: to keep silent when a single word could fire enthusiasm; to keep people's courage up even when one is inwardly discouraged; always to grin and bear it; to associate with scoundrels; to be haunted by beggars; and to let oneself be rejected by pretentious boors. These beggars would be like the boors if they had money, and vice versa. On top of this, envy, treachery, insidious attacks, and no rewards—for of course I have done it out of vanity!" (p. 616-7). Levysohn's prediction to Herzl that "those whom you want to help will start by nailing you rather painfully to the cross" (p. 482) soon came true, and Herzl, like so many leaders who are not misleaders, and men of probity generally, found that people constantly impugned his motives. He soon learned to be neither unduly depressed by censure nor unduly elated by acclaim, "because behind the masses who are applauding me I already see the ingratitude, the future envy, and the possible vacillation of the next day" (p. 538-9). Still, all the ingratitude and lack of support were not able to destroy Herzl's belief that "Zionism was the Sabbath of my life...I believe my effectiveness as a leader may be attributed to the fact that I, who as a man and a writer have had so many faults, made so many mistakes, and done so many foolish things, have been pure of heart and utterly selfless in the Zionist cause" (p. 1203).

A man with this kind of self-image must be expected to be a rather autocratic leader. Herzl had no great admiration for democracy and democratic procedures. He felt that despite the best of intentions, most of his co-workers had no idea of organizational problems, of diplomatic exigencies and procedures ("diplomacy is the art of dealing with robbers"—p. 1234). At one time or another, Herzl had occasion to complain, sometimes rather querulously and petulantly, about his co-workers, even such stalwarts as Nordau and Wolffsohn. The exacting Herzl, who could be a rather impatient man, drove his associates hard, and it must have been difficult to pass muster before his uncompromising confrontation: "There are ideas which one cannot escape. One commits oneself by saying yes, by saying no, and by saying nothing at all" (p. 1067). Herzl felt that universal consent could rarely if ever be obtained in a large group, and that even such consent would be no gain. "For then there appear all sorts of windbags, know-it-alls, and busybodies who frustrate sensible, purposeful work. You can't get many heads under one hat. If you ask them first, the result is only talk, perhaps a brawl, and the hat is more likely to be torn to pieces than to be put on. That is why the guiding intellects must simply put on the hat and lead the way; then the others will tag along with admiration and devotion. Do they admire the intellect? I cannot esteem the masses that highly. Rather, I believe that they admire the hat and the courage it took to put it on" (p. 1051).

It was part of Herzl's make-up and economic situation that the writer and the Zionist leader had an uneasy, even excruciating, coexistence for years. Herzl's ambivalence about these frequently conflicting activities is mirrored in many of his diary entries. "Sometimes it happens that a man of worth is active in various fields," he wrote in 1902. "Then he is certain to be recognized only in the field that is not at the real center of his personality. Thus, for example, I am in a field where I have accomplished next to nothing intellectually, but have merely displayed average political skill, such as is attainable by any horse-dealer, in a matter which is crystal-clear to anyone but a blockhead—in the Jewish Question I have become world-famous as a propagandist. As a writer, particularly as a playwright, I am held to be nothing, less than nothing. People call me only a writer of great ability, one who simply didn't give his full measure because he became disgusted and discouraged" (p. 1282-3). Earlier he had written: "I must not live on Zionism. I am not to live on literature. A problem!" (p. 901). Or "Zionism is costing me money and must not yield me anything. On the other hand, I have done myself very great harm as a 'German writer', and they don't quite dare to perform me" (p. 886). Still, despite the fact that he once referred to inner satisfaction as the most expensive of all pleasures, Herzl knew perfectly well that only Zionism enabled him to display the kind of integrity that shines forth from every page of the Diaries.

Herzl's personal situation was far from satisfactory. Throughout the years covered by the Diaries he was the feuilleton editor of the influential *Neue Freie Presse,* probably the top literary post in prestige-conscious Vienna. Herzl's relationship to his superiors, Eduard Bacher and Moriz Benedikt, both of them Jews and "professional Austrians," was the bane of his existence. For years he strove to induce them to take cognizance of the Zionist movement, at least to report on the various Congresses, but despite certain promises they continued to suppress Zionism in the same way they had earlier suppressed Socialism. Moriz Benedikt ("Maledikt" in one of Herzl's sardonic puns) in particular appears as a villainous figure in the Herzl Diaries. Yet, considering Benedikt's assimilationist orientation and what he conceived to be his responsibility to his readership, one wonders whether Herzl was entirely fair to Benedikt, who had assured him that he regarded Herzl and himself as the finest flowering of Viennese journalism. At any rate, Herzl steadfastly rejected a number of chances for journalistic fame and fortune, consistently refused to exploit the news he was making, and even turned down opportunities to acquire a newspaper of his own. Moreover, he lived in constant fear that his frequent trips and the attendant neglect of his duties would bring about his dismissal from the staff. The publishers of the paper undoubtedly considered Herzl, the stylist of repute and the man with worldwide connections, an asset to the paper, despite the embarrassment which his Zionist activities was causing them. However, Franz Servaes, Herzl's successor as literary editor of the *Neue*

Freie Presse, states in his memoirs that his admiration for Herzl was somewhat diminished by the inheritance of an incredible clutter of unacknowledged manuscripts and unanswered correspondence which he found in Herzl's office.[2]

Closely bound up with his unhappy situation as a "wage slave" of the *Neue Freie Presse* was Herzl's unhappy home life. A frustrated patriarchal *pater-familias,* he had a perpetually bad conscience because he was constantly jeopardizing the economic future of his beloved children. Ironically, the one time that he did participate in a business venture (Dr. Marmorek's supposed discovery of a tuberculosis serum), the project failed. It must have taken Job-like patience for Herzl, who insisted that he was not a businessman and never wanted to become one, to engage interminably in financial schemes (such as the Jewish Colonial Trust and the consolidation of the Turkish public debt, with the keen mind of the trained lawyer and the felicitous pen of the writer combining in many projects and outlines) and to deal with a variety of agents and courtiers who were as crafty as they were crooked. The failure of Herzl's marriage to Julie Naschauer, who rarely appears in the pages of the Diaries and then only as a fleeting, shadowy, negative figure, was probably both partially caused and compensated for by his unusually close relationship to his parents. Herzl's thoughts on his father's demise are among the most moving passages in the 2000-page manuscript.

A repeated reference in the Diaries is to Herzl's "riding over Lake Constance." This is an allusion to Gustav Schwab's ballad "Der Reiter und der Bodensee," which tells about a man on horseback who loses his way and finally reaches a village. At first he feels safe; but when the people tell him that he has unwittingly ridden across frozen Lake Constance and that he was in danger of breaking through at any moment, his heart gives out and he falls from his horse, dead. This is what his own ventures and adventures, from the Turkish "Wonderland" to the London slums, his manifold disappointments and sacrifices, his living and writing "with the sound of eagles' wings" over his head and behind his shoulder, reminded Herzl of. As early as March, 1896, he had been told by a physician that he had a bad heart. In the succeeding years the strain got worse, but still Herzl who, paraphrasing Paul Heyse, shuddered to think that he might pass on overnight before the work was accomplished, could not afford to relax and take care of himself. On his deathbed he said that he had given his heart's blood for the Jewish people (*nomen est omen:* "Herz" is the German word for "heart"). In Herzl's Diaries, more than in any of his other writings, the beating of a great heart may be heard.

Notes

1. *The Complete Diaries of Theodor Herzl,* edited by Raphael Patai, translated by Harry Zohn. Herzl Press and Thomas Yoseloff Inc., New York and London, 1960, p. 421. All succeeding page references are to that five-volume edition.
2. Franz Servaes, *Grüße an Wien,* Vienna 1948, pp. 108-9.

TRANSLATING THEODOR HERZL, THE FATHER OF POLITICAL ZIONISM AND "YOUNG VIENNA" WRITER

The five-volume edition of Herzl's Diaries (four volumes of text, one volume of notes) which appeared in 1960, his centennial year, was the first unexpurgated and fully annotated edition in any language. When my distinguished Brandeis colleague Ludwig Lewisohn asked me to bring Herzl's *Tagebücher* to the beach at Gloucester, Massachusetts, where he was spending his summer vacation in 1954, I had no idea that several years later I would be asked to translate, within one year, the three hefty volumes that I took out of the library. The following year I learned that the diaries, which total almost 2000 pages, had been put to very good use in Lewisohn's masterful introductory essay for a volume entitled *Theodor Herzl: A Portrait for This Age*. At that time I did not know that a cultural institute in New York bore the name of the father of political Zionism, that a press by that name was attached to it, and that I would ultimately be entrusted with the translation of Herzl's complete Zionist writings—and all of this, it seems, on the wings of a dove—of "The Legend of the Third Dove," a short piece by Stefan Zweig that had been recited in my translation at a program of the Theodor Herzl Institute.

The connection between Zweig and Herzl is indeed a meaningful one and had long been known to me, for it was Herzl, the *Feuilleton-redakteur,* or editor for the arts, of the prestigious Vienna daily *Neue Freie Presse* who accepted a prose piece by Zweig and thus launched the much younger man on an internationally successful literary career. Herzl is best known as the founder of political Zionism, but he considered himself primarily a German writer—a storyteller, novelist, dramatist, essayist, and workaday journalist. In the history of German literature he occupies a minor place as a member of the "Young Vienna" circle of writers at the turn of the century (and as such the associate of greater and more enduring writers like Arthur Schnitzler, Hugo von Hofmannsthal, and Richard Beer-Hofmann).

Herzl was a man who poetized his life at every turn. When the Hungarian-born Viennese Jew began to work, somewhat quixotically, toward a Jewish homeland overseas, he was not sure whether he was initiating an emergency project on a global scale or merely gathering material for a utopian novel. (He did write one, *Altneuland,* toward the end of his life.) Of Herzl's 30 plays, some of which were produced at the celebrated Burgtheater in Vienna, only *Das neue Ghetto* still merits attention, for it focuses on the wellsprings of Herzl's Zionist quest. Herzl was also one of the foremost practitioners of the feuilleton, a varied and stylistically notable prose form that has survived to this day. Herzl's Zionist activities often led him to neglect his everyday duties as a "wage slave" of the *Neue Freie Presse,* which was owned by assimilated Jews who might be described as professional Austrians and who refused to print even one word about the wide-ranging Zionist activities of their distinguished cultural editor.

On the first page of his Zionist diary, begun at Pentecost of 1895, Herzl refers to his "comically trivial journalistic work," yet this minor literary activity was contrapuntal to Herzl's Zionist endeavors and continued to the end of his short life less than a decade later. At the beginning of the Diaries, a bemused Herzl, still shaken by the Dreyfus

Affair (on which he had reported for his newspaper from Paris) as well as other experiences of anti-Semitism, attempts a bit of self-analysis, trying to fathom how the completely assimilated Jew, an ex-lawyer and journalist, by his own admission "a writer of sorts, with little ambition and petty vanities," almost overnight turned into a bold statesman with a utopian *idée fixe* that repeatedly brought him to the brink of megalomania.

As a translator, I was challenged by the task of rendering a writer with two faces, as it were—one being that of a prophet and leader, the other that of a workaday journalist, a man who aimed at, and achieved, considerable stylistic polish in his essays and stories, but strove for other effects in his Zionist writings. When I started work on the Diaries, for which much material omitted from printed editions had been supplied to me in typescript form, a one-volume abridgment and translation by Marvin Lowenthal had been in print for several years. In an effort to save both time and money, the head of the Herzl Institute asked me to "translate around" that version, not duplicating the roughly 30% of the complete work represented by it. I began to resist that notion when I discovered that Lowenthal's approach was diametrically opposed to mine, for he (a Brandeis colleague at the time!) aimed at a stylistic gloss that the original never had. Lowenthal, who had lived in Europe for a number of years, handled the German language competently enough, but he seemed bent on presenting a rather slicked-up and homogenized Herzl. I did not think that "True, and necessarily true" was a proper translation of "Ja, ich muß," or that a Scottish boat that threatened to "hoch tanzen" on stormy waves had to "dance a Highland fling." Lowenthal's very first paragraph turned me off, as the saying goes, with "Ich arbeite an einem Werk" rendered as "I have been pounding away at a work" and "die komisch kleine Journalistenarbeit" Englished as "my funny little journalistic work." What filled me with wonderment, awe, and a great sense of responsibility was the fact that I was privileged to produce the first complete edition of this important work, though the need to render half a million words in just one year left me little time or energy for self-congratulation. I learned only later that several English translations of the Diaries had been produced as labors of love but had failed to achieve publication, and that Hans Herzl, the diarist's hapless son, had once been hired to translate his father's Zionist journal. (That version, it turned out, is completely *verschollen;* it seems that no one has been able to locate it.) The five-volume edition of the *Complete Diaries* was co-published by the Herzl Press and the firm of Thomas Yoseloff; the latter offered it as a selection of one of its subsidiaries, a Jewish book club. As a translator who has seldom been offered, or settled for, a royalty arrangement rather than a straight fee, I have no way of knowing how many sets of the Diaries wound up on American bookshelves as likely but unread bar mitzvah presents.

The translation of a dialect always poses a special problem. When Herzl, as part of his political quest, called on Austrian Prime Minister Ernst von Koerber, a bachelor who lived with his mother, in the spring of 1900, he was so intrigued by the fact that this man used the Viennese dialect that he took the trouble to make a faithful transcription of his speech. This dialect, which was and is spoken with zest by most Viennese from governors to garbage men and professors to proletarians, is really untranslatable. I attempted to achieve a comparably relaxed tone in English, but I had to point out in a footnote that this speech does not necessarily denote a low educational level or carelessness on the part of the speaker. Here are a few examples: "Der Kaiser traut sich net, mit mir so zu reden wie mit'n Badeni oder Thun, weil er si' denkt, ich leg' ihm's Amt nieder...Do schaun S', gestern, wie i z'Haus komm zu Mittag, wird mir telephoniert, i soll zum Erzherzog Franz. Na, i bin net glei' 'gangen. I hab z'erscht a Löffel Suppen und a Stück Fleisch 'gessen... Am Abend, wie i z' Haus komm, liegen scho wieder Akten da. Na, da hab' i bis um eins in der Nacht g'arbeit't. Und i steh' um fimfe in der Fruah auf!"—"The Emperor don't dare to talk to me like he did to Badeni or Thun, 'cause he thinks I'm gonna resign on 'im...Like yesterday, see, I get home for lunch, and they phone me to come 'n' see Archduke Franz. Well, I sure didn't dash right out. First I had a spoonful o' soup an' a hunk o' meat...In the evenin', soon's I get home, I find papers layin' there again, waitin' for me. Well, so I kept on workin' till one in the ayemm. An' I get up at five in the mornin'!"

As a sort of pendant to the Diaries, I translated for volume 4 of the *Herzl Year Book* recently discovered letters and other documents that illuminate Herzl's relationships with William Hechler, a charmingly eccentric British clergyman who was in sympathy with Zionist aims because of his conviction that the Jews' return to Zion had been prophetically foretold, and with the Grand Duke of Baden, a helpful potentate to whom Hechler had introduced Herzl. When in the late 1960s the Herzl Press decided to issue a new translation of Herzl's book *Der Judenstaat*—the concise Zionist Bible, as it were—I was again chosen as the translator. I was astonished to discover that mine was the first completely new English translation of that seminal work since Sylvie d'Avigdor's of 1897. This version of *The Jewish State* had been worked over by generations of scholars and non-scholars whose German was often mostly Yiddish and who added, subtracted, and emended until the book itself became a legend. I looked over several versions that had achieved print over the decades, but I did not feel impelled to crib from any of them, for they had misinterpreted several key Zionist concepts. For example, "öffentlich-rechtlich gesicherte Heimstätte" was rendered as a "publicly recognized, legally secured homeland," whereas Herzl meant simply a homeland recognized under "öffentliches Recht," or public law. "If you will it, it is no dream" has received wide dissemination as a ringing Zionist slogan. What Herzl wrote, however, is "Wenn ihr wollt, ist es kein Märchen," but apparently a dream is more inspiring than a fairy-tale or a legend.

There is, as I found out, such a thing as the politics of translation. While I was embarked on the translation of the Diaries, my attention was drawn to an editorial in the *Bulletin of the American Jewish League for Israel* for October 1959. Permit me to quote it in its entirety: "It seems to be the intention of the authorities responsible for the celebration of Herzl's anniversary to use his Diaries as the basis of a program of propaganda. In Jerusalem they are to publish about twenty volumes in Hebrew. In the United States the Herzl Press is to print five volumes in English. There seems to be plenty of money around for an unlimited program of books based on the Diaries. It is a question of whether it is politically wise to do this. The Diaries call for a thoroughgoing review of the value of what they contain before printing them. That has been the view from the beginning. It is all the more desirable now when it is intended to give publication to a definitive edition. In our view, the larger part of the Diaries should be left to rest in the Jerusalem archives as material for research and not be put forth for general reading purposes." In taking up the cudgels in behalf of an uncensored and complete Herzl, my polemical exchange with the editor of the *Bulletin* was aided by my ignorance of the dynamics or politics of Jewish organizational life. I was able to refute most of the points in the editorial and deal with a printed reply to my first letter that had spoken of "libelous" or "damaging" material in the Diaries that made them unsuitable for the "lay reader." "It may shock some people to learn," I wrote, "that the refined Herzl had a temper and was not above using a word like *Scheißkerle*. The sons and daughters of some men might cringe at Herzl's derogatory remarks about their fathers. But they will be at liberty to present their own evidence to the contrary, if they have it, and the cause of learning and truth will be advanced."

By the time the Herzl Press called upon me to translate Herzl's Zionist essays, addresses, and occasional papers, to be published in two volumes in 1973 and 1975, I had become aware of the sensitivity surrounding some of Herzl's terms in light of the contemporary political situation and the need to avoid what had become "buzzwords." In the Hebrew edition of Herzl's collected writings, which was to include ultimately one or more volumes of his letters, certain decisions were made that affected the American edition as well. For those collections of short prose my very competent editors were Marie Syrkin, a retired Brandeis colleague, and Gertrude Hirschler, a Viennese-born editor-translator. In a letter dated June 1972 it was pointed out to me that the manuscript would be edited "from the point of view of the contemporary reader, who may find the perfectly accurate and literal translation of Herzl misleading" and that "there are often dangerous political implications if Herzl is left starkly in his own 'lingo'." It became clear to me that Herzl's "zionistische Kolonisationsprojekte" had to be rendered as "Zionist settlement projects" and that terms like "colonization," "colonial," or "colonists" wouldn't do. Yet I resisted the notion of prettifying "Kolonisationsbarone" and turning them into "patrons of settlement." And how does one render Herzl's appellation *Mauschel* for an anti-Zionist? (The word is derived from a variant of the name Moses; it has long been a German epithet for a haggling Jewish trader, or for a Jew generally, especially one whose German is largely Yiddish). Surely terms like "sheeny," "kike," or "Yid" could not be used. By leaving *Mauschel* untranslated, we were able to contrast the term with *Jude,* or Jew, a person of culture and dignity, reflecting Herzl's hope that *Judenjungen* would become *junge Juden.* Herzl's essay "The Menorah," written in 1897, is of autobiographical significance. In the form of a poignant parable about a *baal teshuvah,* a man who returns to the Jewish fold, Herzl highlights the symbolic beauty, growth, and acceptance of his Zionist idea as the darkness of suppression and of a ghetto mentality gives way to the splendor of Jewish auto-emancipation and a new Zionist fervor lights the way to a Jewish state. Here is the first sentence of this essay: "Es war ein Mann, der hatte die Not, ein Jude zu sein, tief in seiner Seele empfunden." I interpreted the word *Not* in light of yet another term often used by Herzl, *Judennot,* by which he meant the distress of the Jews. My editor pointed to earlier translations of that essay. Here is one by Maurice Samuel, a competent translator: "Once upon a time there was a man who had discovered deep in his soul the need to be a Jew." The rendition of Bessie London Pouzzner, an incompetent translator, reads: "Deep in his soul he began to feel the need of being a Jew." I felt that all of these were mistranslations. I lost that particular argument as far as the book edition was concerned, but I was able to publish my version elsewhere: "There once was a man who had felt deep in his soul how hard it was to be a Jew." In his biography of Herzl, issued in 1975, Amos Elon agrees with my reading; the man in question "felt in his heart the distress of being a Jew." In the two-volume edition of essays a problem was posed by the editorial decision to print the addresses that Herzl made in English just as he delivered them. In a letter of protest dated February 9, 1975 I expressed my position as follows: "The effect of having Herzl speak, or write, two different kinds of English—his own and mine—is a bit startling. It is like an actress who comes on stage looking like a frump, and a tongue-tied one at that, with the prompter standing behind her and whispering in her ear, and who then reappears all gussied up, wearing an elegant dress and a lot of makeup, and speaking her lines fluently."

Since the writings of Herzl have long been in the public domain, I later took the opportunity of translating, as a labor of love, some of his short non-Zionist prose. Stefan Zweig has characterized these writings as follows: "His essays are still enchanting in their wealth of sharp and ofttimes wise observations, their stylistic animation and their aristocratic charm. Whether light or critical, they never lost their innate nobility; they were the most cultivated in journalism and were the delight of a city that had schooled itself to every subtlety." When I had done a number of these translations, I read them in 1972 at a special program of the Herzl Institute under the title "The Unknown Herzl." "Die linke Glocke" (The Bell on the Left) dates from 1901; it is one of Herzl's "philosophical tales" with a twist. "Die Romantik der Armen" (The Romance of the Poor), written in 1895 and based on a court case involving a rake who preyed on gullible women eager to get married, shows Herzl's sympathetic interest in Vienna's "little people" and his concern with life's little tragicomedies even during his preoccupation with the Zionist cause. "Trudels Träne" (Trudel's Tear) is one of several sensitive prose pieces that Herzl devoted to children, his own as well as those of others. "Juli-Sonntag im Prater" (July Sunday in the Prater), finally, is one of several feuilletons in which Herzl depicts the Viennese and their city in a way that differs markedly from most accounts of "gay Vienna." Translating these pieces presented no particular difficulties, but I would like to share with you one instance in which a play upon words posed a real challenge. In his description of a lower-middle-class family on its tedious trek to the joylessness and ultimate despair of the Prater, Vienna's fabled pleasure ground, the author guesses, on the basis of the man's large workman's hands which seem to consist of all thumbs, that he must be a butcher who has married the boss's only daughter. She seemed charming and lovable to him as she sat at the cash register, and "er schnitt es gern in jeden Schinken ein." This is an unmistakable punning reference to a line from "Ungeduld," the seventh song in the Schubert-Müller song cycle *Die schöne Müllerin:* "Ich schnitt' es gern in alle Rinden ein...(I would fain carve it in every bark...that my heart is yours.) Herzl had a bit of condescending fun with an inarticulate man who probably had only limited opportunities to express his love. A proper English translation would have to present a bit of poetry or a snatch of song as recognizable to most Anglo-American readers as the line from a famous *Lied* was, and is, to readers in German-speaking countries—and it would, furthermore, have to include a reference to a tool or other item available to a butcher. After much thought I came up with this: "To him, love was a many-rendered thing." At a subsequent brain-storming session, however, someone suggested another solution: "Two hearts beat in three-quarter rind." Both versions, involving songs written well after Herzl's time, are anachronistic, but at least the songs are recognizable and the reference to the Robert Stolz tune does preserve the Viennese ambiance.

No one can translate thousands of pages of an author and not feel a certain sympathy for him. In recent years I was sorry to notice that Herzl has been widely ignored, criticized, or maligned—for one thing, because he fought the right battle with the wrong weapons and was incredibly naive as far as the acceptance, or non-acceptance, of the Zionist philosophy and the Jewish settlers by the indigenous population of Palestine, the Arabs, was concerned. But I feel that I have kept faith with an important, albeit somewhat controversial literary and historical figure by serving him as a translator ever mindful and appreciative of both the power and the poignancy of his production.

THE VITRIOLIC VIENNESE

An Introduction to Karl Kraus

The essential untranslatability of the Austrian satirist Karl Kraus has been axiomatic for a long time, and this is why only a small fraction of his voluminous literary output has appeared in translation and Kraus is relatively unknown beyond the confines of the German-speaking world. There is much truth in Kraus's observation that "a linguistic work translated into another language is like someone going across the border without his skin and putting on the local garb on the other side."[1] The vitriolic Viennese, a man who hauled the powerful and the pitiful alike before a tribunal of total satire, was a legend in his lifetime (1874 to 1936), a person adored or vilified by many of his contemporaries. Following a decade of desuetude, his work was rediscovered and republished in Germany and Austria after the Second World War, and a number of books on Kraus in English as well as translations from his writings are in print. Yet the problem of limited access to him remains. As Erich Heller put it, "Karl Kraus did not write 'in a language,' but through him the beauty, profundity, and accumulated moral experience of the German language assumed personal shape and became the crucial witness in the case this inspired prosecutor brought against his time."[2] Kraus's timelessness (and, at long last, his *relative* exportability and translatability) derive at least in part from certain parallels between his age and ours, and from the need of our age for his vibrant pacifism, his defense of the spirit against dehumanizing tendencies, and his "linguistic-moral imperative," which equates purity of language with purity of thought, a return to the sources of spiritual strength, and steadfastness of moral purpose.

Karl Kraus lived a life that oscillated between love and hate. ("Hate must make a person productive," he once wrote; "otherwise one might as well love.")[3] He was born on April 28, 1874, at Jičin, a small Bohemian town northeast of Prague, as the son of a prosperous manufacturer of paper bags. In 1877 the family moved to Vienna, and Kraus spent the rest of his life in that city, with which he—like Sigmund Freud, another Czech-born Jew—had a love-hate relationship. His was a family constellation that was typical at the turn of the century: the sons of Central European Jewish businessmen—often self-made men and heads of patriarchally organized families—rejected the family business in favor of a literary career. Franz Kafka, Stefan Zweig, Franz Werfel, and others joined Kraus in following this path.

Having attended the University of Vienna without taking a degree, Kraus attempted a career on the stage. His failure as an actor irrevocably turned him to journalism and literature, though his talent for mimicry and parody found ample expression in his later public readings. He once said of himself that he was perhaps the first writer to experience his writing as an actor: "When I give a reading, it is not acted literature, but what I write is written acting."[4] In 1892 Kraus began to contribute book reviews, theater criticism, and other kinds of prose to various newspapers and periodicals. In his twenties, however, the satirical impulse became too strong for any sort of accommodation, and Kraus rejected the prospect of becoming a sort of "culture clown" absorbed by a deceptively slack and effete environment. Because work within the Establishment seemed to be hedged in with multifarious taboos and considerations of a personal and commercial nature, Kraus turned down a job offer from Vienna's most prestigious daily, the *Neue Freie Presse,* and founded his own journal. The first issue of *Die Fackel* (The Torch) appeared on April 1, 1899 and turned out to be anything but an April Fool's joke. Kraus at first enlisted the services of other writers, though these never contributed more than about one-third of this aggressive journal's contents. From 1911 to 1936 *Die Fackel* carried Kraus's writings exclusively: "I no longer have any collaborators. I used to be envious of them. They repel those readers whom I want to lose myself.[5] This statement indicates the uncompromising nature of this unique satirical journal in which Kraus effectively clipped his era and put it between quotation marks. Quotation is the hallmark of his satire, and in its use he was guided by the conviction that what was most unspeakable about his age could be spoken only by the age itself.

The thirty-seven volumes of *Die Fackel* represent a gigantic effort to fashion the imperishable profile of an age from such highly perishable materials as newspaper reports. They contain the major part of Kraus's literary output; most of the satirist's publications in book form represent distillations from the pages of *Die Fackel.* The journal is an enormous pillory, a running autobiography, and a world stage on which Kraus dramatized himself and his mission. The small-format, red *Fackel* had a remarkable satiric *genius loci;* material that might have attracted scant attention elsewhere received heightened relevance in its pages, and "little" people became "great" there. Thus Kraus's periodical continued to have numerous "contributors," albeit unwilling and unwitting ones. J.P. Stern has attempted to assess the uniqueness and significance of the *Fackel* in these words: "To delimit the intellectual region in which to place this journal, one would have to think of Péguy minus his Catholicism and patriotism; of F.R. Leavis uninvolved in any education 'establishment,' plus genius; of the satirist in George Bernard Shaw as milk-and-water to Kraus's vitriol; of the early Wittgenstein's equation of 'language' and 'world'; of H.L. Mencken's criticism of the leisure class; of the poet Siegfried Sassoon's 'scarlet major at the base'; of the early Evelyn Waugh's satirical type-casting—and all this would have to be translated into the peculiar medium of Vienna."[6]

Kraus began to write when a century top-heavy with historical and cultural events and innovations was approaching its end. In the specific case of his homeland, which was both the source and the target of his satire, the Habsburg dynasty, worn out after a reign of some six hundred years, was coming to an end, and so was Austria-Hungary, the political constellation of its last half-century. The reign of Emperor Franz Joseph, a prime target of Kraus's satire, spanned almost seven decades and witnessed the slow, inevitable dismantling of an old political, social, and cultural structure. It was a time of overrefinement and overripeness to the point of decay and death, and Kraus's marked apocalyptic stance as a "late" warner and prophet of doom derives from his epoch's *Zeitgeist:* transitoriness, disintegration, and inner insecurity. Ironically, Karl Kraus shared his initials with Imperial-Royal Austria, the *kaiserlich-königlich* empire, designated by K. K.—a country which Robert Musil, in his novel *The Man Without Qualities,* called "Kakania." Kraus came to regard this centrally located empire as a proving ground for world destruction.

Kraus's first major satirical work was a literary satire entitled *Die demolirte Literatur,* a witty diatribe about the razing of a Vienna café frequented by the literati. His pamphlet *Eine Krone für Zion* is a lampoon of political Zionism, the creation of Theodor Herzl, an editor of the *Neue Freie Presse,* written from the standpoint of an assimilated European Jew and sympathizer with Socialism. Kraus has been called everything from a "shining example of Jewish self-hatred" (Theodor Lessing) to "an arch-Jew" (Berthold Viertel).[7] His writings lend support to all of these judgments, but it must be borne in mind that the man who once noted that according to the latest census Vienna had 2,030,834 inhabitants—"that is, 2,030,833 souls and myself"[8]—refused to be part of *any* ethnic, political, or social group. In 1899 he left the Jewish fold, and after remaining *konfessionslos*—religiously unaffiliated—for some years, he secretly converted to Catholicism in 1911. Eleven years later he left the Catholic church again to protest publicly what he regarded as its unwholesome participation in pseudo-artistic and commercial aspects of the Salzburg Festival, the creation of two men he disliked, the poet Hugo von Hofmannsthal and the theatrical director Max Reinhardt. Frank Field's view that Kraus's Jewishness is "of vital importance in understanding the particular extremism and sense of the apocalyptic which pervades his work" and that Kraus "attacked his own people in the same way that the prophets of the Old Testament castigated the unworthiness of the Israelites of the trust which God had placed in them"[9] is supported by Kraus's own statement of 1913: "I believe I can say about myself that I go along with the development of Judaism up to the Exodus, but that I don't participate in the dance around the Golden Calf and, from that point on, share only in those characteristics which were also found in the defenders of God and in the avengers of a people gone astray."[10]

If Kraus's early satiric writings were directed largely against standard aspects of corruption, the second period of his creativity may be dated from the appearance of his essay "Sittlichkeit und Kriminalität" (Morality and Criminal Justice) in 1902, which became the title essay of a book-length collection issued six years later. On the basis of contemporary court cases Kraus concerned himself with the glaring contrast between private and public morality and with the hypocrisy inherent in the administration of justice in Austria. In turning a powerful spotlight on a male-dominated society with its double standards, its shameless encroachments on privacy, and its sensation-mongering press, Kraus expressed many ideas and attitudes that are germane to present-day concerns: women's rights, child abuse, sexual mores, education, "gay liberation." The gloomy, bitter wit of this collection gave way to lighter humor in Kraus's next book, *Die chinesische Mauer* (The Great Wall of China, 1910). Writing about Peary's contested discovery of the North Pole in 1909, Kraus remarked with awful prescience that "progress celebrates Pyrrhic victories over nature, making purses out of human skin."[11]

Kraus's unremitting satirical warfare against the press was motivated by his view of journalism as a vast switchboard that concentrated and activated the forces of corruption and dissolution. Recognizing a disturbing identity between *Zeit* and *Zeitung*, his age and the newspapers it spawned, with *Worte* (words) usurping and destroying *Werte* (values) and news reports *causing* as well as *describing* actions, he had apocalyptic visions of the destruction of the world by the black magic of printer's ink. One of Kraus's aphorisms belongs in this context: "One ought to acknowledge the significance of the fact that gunpowder and printer's ink were invented simultaneously."[12] Kraus was convinced that the moving forces of his time were not entrenched in parliaments but in editorial offices, controlling capital and the government, influencing public opinion as well as the arts and sciences, and destroying thought, taste, receptivity, and imagination. Decades before Hermann Hesse coined the phrase "das feuilletonistische Zeitalter" in his utopian novel *The Glass-Bead Game,* Kraus recognized his age as "the age of the feuilleton" in which newspaper reports took precedence over events, form eclipsed substance, and the style, the atmosphere, the "package" were all-important. The press was seen as the polluter of language and poisoner of the human spirit. In his polemic essay "Heine and the Consequences" (1910) Kraus excoriated the nineteenth-century German-Jewish poet and essayist for introducing the feuilleton in Germany and providing an inheritance on which journalism has drawn ever since: its function as an intermediary between art and life and as a parasite on both, creating a deleterious, linguistically deceitful mixture of intellect and information, reportage and literature. "To write a feuilleton," wrote Kraus, "is to curl locks on a bald pate; but the public likes these curls better than a lion's mane of thought."[13]

"My language is the common prostitute that I turn into a virgin."[14] This aphorism illuminates both Kraus's mission and his method. While many poets have striven to restore pristine purity to language and make it once more a serviceable vehicle for poetic expression, Kraus's obsession with language went considerably beyond such a pursuit. He saw an absolute congruity between word and world, language and life; the unworthiness of his "language-forsaken" age was for him defined by its treatment of language. For him language was the moral criterion and accreditation for a writer or speaker. J.P. Stern, to be sure, suspects that what he has called Kraus's "moral-linguistic imperative" may be an indication that the satirist was "succumbing to the curse of Vienna—the city in which the experiment of replacing morality and politics by the life of the imagination was carried to the point of moral paralysis and political disintegration."[15] To Kraus language was the mother of thought, not its handmaiden, the divining rod capable of finding hidden sources of thought. Despite the fact, however, that Kraus raised language to an almost apocalyptic significance, he never developed a theory or philosophy of language, being essentially un unsystematic and anti-philosophical thinker. Yet the Vienna Circle of logical positivists was greatly interested in Kraus's relationship to language, and there are certain parallels between Kraus's thought and the ideas of Ludwig Wittgenstein, the foremost figure of that circle—for example, their insight into the fundamental connection between, or even identification of, aesthetics and ethics. Wittgenstein learned from Kraus how to think in and through language, yet he thought *against* language—which, for him, was an obstacle to thought that had to be painstakingly surmounted—whereas Kraus fought *for* language, mystically uncovering thought through it. What Kraus and Wittgenstein really had in common was their endeavor to fashion a fortress capable of standing inviolate against the corruption of language and morals they saw all around them.

It is all but impossible to convey in English an idea of Karl Kraus's style. Its allusiveness, its attention to verbal associations, and its artful plays upon words make reading Kraus in the original a rare intellectual delight. Kraus was not only a master of the art of punning, with a deep seriousness underlying his verbal wit, but also a skillful practitioner of various subtle stylistic devices based upon the spirit of German grammar and Kraus's enjoyment of what he termed *Sprachlehre.* Punning often constitutes a *reductio ad absurdum* of language and serves to test the truthfulness or mendaciousness of a statement or a mentality. The aphorism was a literary form which Kraus, an admirer of his forerunners J.C. Lichtenberg and Johann Nestroy, used extensively. Some aphorisms were distilled from a longer text in prose or poetry; in other instances an aphorism was lyrically expanded into an epigram or served as the nucleus of a prose piece.

Kraus began to write poetry comparatively late in life; his first poems were printed in *Die Fackel* in 1912-13, but then nine volumes of poetry appeared between 1916 and 1930 under the collective title *Worte in Versen.* In his poetry Kraus admittedly was an epigone, indebted to Goethe and Shakespeare, rather than an innovator. He was "unoriginal" in that he needed some occasion to trigger his art, the way an oyster needs a grain of sand as an irritant to produce a pearl. His poems are seldom "romantic" in the sense of being products of poetic rapture; rather, they spring from the rapture of language and logic. Some of Kraus's poems are versified satires and polemics or autobiographic excursions. Others are *Gedankenlyrik,* with a cargo of thought in

Schiller's tradition. Still others represent a satirist's holiday in the sense that in the poetic realm Kraus felt free to reveal himself unabashedly in his love of mankind and the human spirit, and in his enjoyment of nature and animals. In one of his best-known poems, "Nocturnal Hour," Kraus alludes not only to his working habits (like Balzac, he read and wrote at night, sifting the world through the sieve of the word and filling one sheet after another with his minuscule, all but undecipherable handwriting), but also to the recalcitrant material with which he had to work and live. What has been described as the claustrophobic intensity of his work may have been one reason why Kraus never married. The man who made himself the measure of his era's moral bankruptcy strove to lead an exemplary, wholly consistent, almost ascetic life. While he did not lack friends, his existence was of necessity a lonely one. He did know several women of uncommon physical and spiritual beauty, foremost among them Sidonie Nádherný, a Czech aristocrat whom Kraus met in 1913 and with whom he had an affectionate relationship, with relatively brief interruptions, until his death, frequently visiting her at her family estate, Janoviče Castle south of Prague. Kraus's thousand letters and postcards to the woman who turned down his proposals of marriage were long presumed lost, but they were rediscovered in 1969 and published in Germany in Kraus's centennial year. Reading them is a shattering experience. Apparently Kraus the man needed this searing, though often frustrating and sometimes even degrading, emotional attachment to keep Kraus the satirist cold as ice and hard as steel.

The outbreak of the war in 1914 marked a turning point in Kraus's life and creativity, and the outraged convictions of the pacifist and moralist inspired him to produce his most powerful and most characteristic work. Following several months of silence at a time when other writers were rushing to the ramparts of rhyme and boarding the bandwagon of banality, Kraus delivered a sardonic public lecture on November 19, "In These Great Times...," which may be regarded as the germ cell of his extensive wartime output. He viewed the war as a tragedy of mankind enacted by figures with all the stature, substance, and truthfulness of characters in an operetta. Without waiting for the detachment which time might have brought him Kraus wrote the 209 scenes of the five acts of *The Last Days of Mankind* as well as the ten-scene Prologue and the Epilogue between July 1915 and July 1917. In Kraus's lifetime, only the Epilogue, "The Last Night," was performed in a special stage version; after World War II both abridged and complete versions of the drama, prepared by Heinrich Fischer, Leopold Lindtberg, and Hans Hollmann, have been presented on the stage and on television in Europe.

The Last Days of Mankind begins with the voice of a newsboy and ends with the voice of God. It is set in the streets of Vienna and Berlin, in offices and army barracks, churches and cafés, places of amusement and military hospitals, railroad stations and army posts. The play's many hundreds of characters include emperors and editors, poets and prostitutes, professors and politicians, teachers and tradesmen, soldiers and sycophants, children and churchmen, journalists and jesters. There are actual persons as well as fictitious ones, and through their authentic speech patterns they reveal and judge themselves in an enormous phonomontage. This dramatic typology of man's inhumanity to man is a striking amalgam of naturalistic and symbolic elements. There is no hero or plot in the conventional Aristotelian sense. The scenes range in length from one-line "black-outs" in the tradition of the cabaret (more often than not, what is blacked out is the human spirit) to lengthy dialogues, dramatized editorials, and phantasmagoric tableaux.

The twenty-three conversations between the Grumbler and the Optimist function as the choruses of the tragedy; they are oases of relative repose and reflection. In his running commentary, the Grumbler, a Kraus figure, constitutes the voice of reason, presenting eschatological views rather than espousing *Realpolitik.* Kraus's wartime waxworks of "Goethe's people" and his fellow Austrians includes such characters as the two fatuous privy councillors who vie with each other in mangling one of the glories of German poetry, Goethe's "Wanderer's Nightsong;" the Bavarian storyteller Ludwig Ganghofer, who yodels his way along the front, writes war reports for the *Neue Freie Presse,* and swaps jokes with an appreciative Kaiser; "patriotic" pastors of the "praise-the-Lord-and-pass-the-ammunition" variety; and Alice Schalek, the first woman accredited to the Austrian army as a correspondent, whose gushy effusions and insensitive search for "human-interest" material amidst degradation, destruction, and death made her a macabre joke and a frequent target of Kraus's satire. As the tragedy rushes toward its cataclysmic end, surrealistic touches are introduced. The rhymed Epilogue is a harrowing poetic satire raised to a supernatural plane in which many motifs of the play are recapitulated in cinematographic or operatic form. After the silence that follows utter destruction, God's voice is heard speaking the words of Kaiser Wilhelm at the beginning of the war: "Ich habe es nicht gewollt" (I did not will this).

The story of Kraus's postwar writings and polemics is basically the history of his disillusionment. The best that Kraus could say about the Austrian Republic was that it had replaced the monarchy and rid Karl Kraus of that troublesome companion, the other K. K. The satirist engaged in extended polemics with the German-Jewish journalist Maximilian Harden (once an admired model), the German-Jewish critic Alfred Kerr, and the Prague-born poet Franz Werfel (formerly an admirer). One of several apostles turned apostates was the psychoanalyst Fritz Wittels, who presented an anti-Kraus paper at a 1910 meeting of the Vienna Psychoanalytic Society. Kraus's running fight with the "psychoanals," as he called that fraternity, produced such celebrated aphorisms as "Psychoanalysis is that mental illness for which it regards itself as therapy."[16] In the middle and late 'twenties Kraus castigated the unholy alliance between a police chief (Johannes Schober) and a corrupt press czar (Imre Békessy). With bureaucratic *Gemütlichkeit* Schober retouched the police record of Békessy, who in turn ordered his editors to print nothing about ninety dead people on the police chief's conscience. (The reference is to the police riot that followed the burning of the Ministry of Justice by an enraged mob in July 1927). Prevailing against a clique and a claque, Kraus almost single-handedly waged a spirited, protracted, and ultimately successful fight to remove Békessy from the Viennese scene. The literary fruit of the Schober-Békessy affair was another documentary drama, *Die Unüberwindlichen* (The Unconquerables), which was premiered in 1929. Other plays written in the 'twenties include *Wolkenkuckucksheim* (Cloudcuckooland), a verse play based on Aristophanes and presenting a sort of Last Days of Birdkind, but with a Shakespearean solo by the Lark at the end promising conciliation and peace.

Kraus's public readings of his own works and those of others may be regarded as an integral part of his creativity and perhaps even as the apogee of his effectiveness. From 1892 to 1936, with a hiatus between 1899 and 1910, Kraus presented seven hundred recitals in a number of European cities, with the proceeds frequently going to charitable causes. After 1925 Kraus used *Theater der Dichtung* (Theater of Poetry, or Literary Theater) as a designation, reading poetry, prose, and entire plays to sizable audiences in spellbinding one–man shows. Kraus may be credited with the modern revival of interest in the nineteenth-century Viennese actor–playwright Johann Nepomuk Nestroy, whose works he adapted and presented to show Nestroy in his full stature as a powerful social satirist and a linguistic genius. Kraus often added *Zeitstrophen,* topical stanzas of his own creation, to the *couplets* in Nestroy's comedies. Shakespeare was a living force in Kraus's life, and over a period of decades Kraus recited his adaptations of thirteen dramas of the Bard; he also issued two collections of plays and the *Sonnets* in his translation. In fashioning his own versions from existing translations, Kraus, who knew little English, was guided by his superior poetic sense and unerring linguistic instinct. The satirist's special relationship with Jacques Offenbach dated back to his boyhood. He adapted and performed, with a piano accompanist, many of Offenbach's operettas, whose *esprit,* enchanting wit, and telling social satire he appreciated in programmatic contrast to the Viennese operetta of his time (Franz Lehár, Emmerich Kalman, etc.), which Kraus regarded as inane, meretricious, false, and unwholesome.

Karl Kraus can perhaps best be described as a basically apolitical man with an *ad hoc* attitude toward politics based on personalities rather than parties or issues. Though he supported the Social Democrats at various times in his life, that party, which held a majority position in postwar Austria, was increasingly at odds with what it regarded as Kraus's carping criticism, his deficient understanding of economics, and his blindness to the achievements and promises of modern technology.

"*Mir fällt zu Hitler nichts ein*"[17] (I cannot think of anything to say about Hitler). This is the striking first sentence of Kraus's work *Die Dritte Walpurgisnacht* (The Third Walpurgis Night—the title refers to both parts of Goethe's *Faust* as well as to the Third Reich), written in the late spring and summer of 1933 but not published in its entirety during Kraus's lifetime. That sentence, the germ cell of the misunderstandings and conflicts that marked and marred Kraus's last years, may be indicative of resignation (though Kraus *could* think of many things to say about Hitler and did indeed say them), but it is primarily a hyperbolic, heuristic device for depicting the witches' sabbath of the time. There had been no *Fackel* for ten months when No. 888 appeared in October 1933. Its four pages contained only Kraus's funeral oration on his friend, the architect Adolf Loos, and what was to be his last poem, with a particularly poignant last line: "Das Wort entschlief, als jene Welt erwachte"[18] (The word expired when that world awoke). Kraus sadly realized the incommensurability of the human spirit with the unspeakably brutal and mindless power structure across the German border. Once again language was in mortal danger (Kraus's remarks on the subject anticipate and confirm the dictionaries of the language of inhumanity and the murderers' lexica that appeared after the end of the "Thousand-Year-Reich"), and the perpetrators of the new horrors obviously were *not* characters from an operetta. As Kraus attempts to deal with the early excesses of the Nazi regime, which made him foresee much of the full fury to come, he seems engaged in a desperate rearguard action; his writing is like the rambling monologue of a worried man who talks incessantly in an effort to keep the demons at bay. In voicing genuine concern over Germany's pressure on his homeland, Kraus for once found himself in Austria's corner. Paradoxically and sadly, this led him to side with what has been widely recognized as the clerico-fascist regime of Chancellor Engelbert Dollfuß, whose assassination in 1934 came as a severe shock and blow to Kraus. Many of the satirist's erstwhile leftist adherents, some of them now Communists and/or emigrants, expected Kraus to join them in their struggle and perhaps to stop Hitlerism with a special issue of *Die Fackel*, but they were disappointed at what they regarded as his equivocation. Kraus, for his part, seemed content to reduce his readership to people who, in those perilous times, did not abandon their interest in Shakespeare, Nestroy, Offenbach, and German style, including Kraus's unique "comma problems." His death of heart failure on June 12, 1936, at the end of a long period of physical and spiritual exhaustion, during which he had pathetically and futilely tried to pit the word against the sword, mercifully saved him from witnessing the Nazi take-over of Austria to the cheers of most of its population, the destruction of his belongings, the death of close friends in concentration camps, and untold other horrors. "In the twelve years that followed the accession of Hitler to power in Germany," writes Frank Field, "things were to happen that surpassed the most pessimistic insights of the satirist: the building of the concentration camp at Buchenwald around Goethe's beech tree, and the processions that took place into the extermination chambers of Auschwitz while elsewhere in the camp the orchestra played selections from Viennese light music—all this only becomes a little more explicable after reading the works of Kraus."[19]

To draw parallels between Kraus's time and *his* language and *our* time and language is a risky undertaking, but apart from the importance of the timeless humanitarian ideals that Kraus espoused, the relevance of his satire to our age is readily apparent. It is not difficult to imagine what Kraus would have said about the "Newspeak" of our day, about the "Doublethink" described in George Orwell's novel *1984,* or about the denatured language of Watergate, a language that conceals, not reveals, human thought and feeling. Certainly our linguistically permissive and heedless age is as "language-forsaken" as Kraus's time was. Surely a parallel may be discerned between Alice Schalek's use of the word *ausputzen* (clean out) in connection with enemy trenches, or the Viennese vulgarism *obidraht* for a similar act, and our present-day military's use of terms like "waste" or "off" as euphemisms for "kill." Hardly a day goes by on which the biased reporting of the press and the shameless invasions of privacy committed by journalists and radio and television reporters fail to confirm the satirist's bleak vision. The fact that there is no Karl Kraus today to do battle with the polluters of language and the defilers of the human spirit is one of the minor tragedies of our time.

Notes

1. Kraus, *Beim Wort genommen* (Munich: Kösel 1955), p. 245. All the aphorisms quoted in this article may be found in English translation in *Half-Truths and One-and-a Half Truths: Selected Aphorisms of Karl Kraus,* ed. and trans. by H. Zohn. Montreal: Engendra, 1976; University of Chicago Press, 1990.
2. E. Heller, "Karl Kraus," in *The Disinherited Mind,* New York: Farrar, Straus & Cudahy, 1957, p. 239.
3. *Beim Wort genommen,* p. 270.
4. *Ibid.,* p. 284
5. *Ibid.*
6. J.P. Stern, "Karl Kraus's Vision of Language," *Modern Language Review* 61 (1966), p. 73.
7. T. Lessing, *Der jüdische Selbsthaß,* Berlin: Jüdischer Verlag, 1930, p. 43; B. Viertel, "Karl Kraus, Ein Charakter und die Zeit," in *Dichtungen und Dokumente,* Munich: Kösel, 1956, p. 259.
8. *Die Fackel,* 315/316, Jan. 26, 1911, p. 13.
9. F. Field, *The Last Days of Mankind: Karl Kraus and His Vienna,* New York: St. Martin's Press, 1967, p. 68.
10. Kraus, "Er ist doch e Jud," in *Untergang der Welt durch schwarze Magie,* Munich: Kösel, 1960, p. 333.
11. Kraus, "Die Entdeckung des Nordpols," in *Die chinesische Mauer,* Munich: Kösel, 1964, p. 272 (in English translation in *In These Great Times: A Karl Kraus Reader,* ed. by H. Zohn, Montreal: Engendra, 1976 or University of Chicago Press, 1990, p. 56).
12. *Beim Wort genommen,* p. 380.
13. *Ibid.,* p. 191.
14. *Ibid.,* p. 293.
15. J.P. Stern, *op. cit.,* p. 83.
16. *Beim Wort genommen,* p. 351.
17. Kraus, *Die Dritte Walpurgisnacht,* Munich: Kösel, 1952, p. 9.
18. Written on September 13, 1933. English translation in *In These Great Times,* p. 259.
19. F. Field, *op. cit.,* p. 212.

TRAKL, KRAUS,
AND THE *BRENNER* CIRCLE

On November 7, 1912 *Die Fackel,* which had contained only Karl Kraus's writings for a year, printed the following aphorism: "Siebenmonatskinder sind die einzigen, deren Blick die Eltern verantwortlich macht, so daß diese wie ertappte Diebe dasitzen neben den Bestohlenen. Sie haben den Blick, der zurückfordert, was ihnen genommen wurde, und wenn ihr Denken aussetzt, so ist es, als suchte es den Rest, and sie starren zurück in die Versäumnis. Andere gibt es, die denkend solchen Blick annehmen, aber den Blick, der dem Chaos erstatten möchte, was sie zu viel bekommen haben. Es sind die Vollkommenen, die fertig wurden, als es zu spät war. Sie sind mit dem Schrei der Scham auf eine Welt gekommen, die ihnen nur das eine, erste, letzte Gefühl beläßt: Zurück in deinen Leib, o Mutter, wo es gut war!"[1] This aphorism, which appears near the end of a section headed "Nachts," seems like an elaboration of the preceding one in which Kraus says, with his vaunted verbal play: "Kindspech ist eben das, womit man auf die Welt kommt."[2]

The "Siebenmonatskinder" aphorism is prefaced with the words "Georg Trakl zum Dank für den Psalm." Kraus's reference is to the second version of one of Trakl's most characteristic poems, entitled "Psalm," bearing the notation "Karl Kraus zugeeignet" and first printed in *Der Brenner* for October 1, 1912.[3] Kraus's aphorism in turn elicited the following telegram sent by Trakl from Innsbruck on November 9: "Ich danke Ihnen einen Augenblick schmerzlichster Helle."[4] This exchange on the highest literary and human plane takes us *in medias res,* as it were, of the relationship between the two men, but it may well constitute its very essence: Kraus's intuitive understanding of Trakl's knowledge and feeling of being appreciated on his own terms. Decades later their mutual friend Ludwig von Ficker remembered Kraus's aphorism when he wrote to Werner Meyknecht on January 28, 1934: "Kraus mußte in Trakl auch geistig den Zukurzgekommenen, das Siebenmonatskind, sehen..."[5] One need not, of course, agree with Ficker's interpretation of this profound aphorism, but perhaps Kraus's view of Trakl and his limited viability is best expressed in a letter to Sidonie Nádherný of November 1914 that refers to the poet's death: "Er ist wohl kein Opfer des Krieges. Es war mir immer unbegreiflich, daß er leben konnte. Sein Irrsinn rang mit göttlichen Dingen."[6]

Perhaps the "Siebenmonatskinder" aphorism sums up an attitude toward the world which Kraus and Trakl shared, though with an important difference. Both desired a return, a flight, to the *Ursprung,* but Trakl's bleak images, which seemed to disarm thought, were essentially alien to Kraus, at least before the advent of "the last days of mankind." That Trakl may have viewed Kraus as a model of wholeness and integrity in contrast to his own *Zerrissenheit* is suggested by a change he made in the version of "Psalm" that is dedicated to Kraus. The first version[7] mournfully depicts an empty, disconsolate, godless world, with this final sigh: "Wie eitel ist alles!" The last line of the second version is "Schweigsam über der Schädelstätte öffnen sich Gottes goldene Augen." This evocation of Golgotha seems to be in contradiction to the rest of the poem, which is about the loss of wholeness, innocence, and dreams, and it offers some hope of redemption and transfiguration.

Among the critics who have discerned some resemblance between the poetry of Trakl and of Kraus are Wilma Iggers, who even calls Kraus a Trakl epigone,[8] and Leopold Liegler, who sees Traklian elements in "Verwandlung," a poem by Kraus that might be regarded as a delayed response to "Psalm."[9] It was written on March 14, 1915 in a painful situation as a wedding present for the faithless Sidonie Nádherný.[10] The theme is renewal and transformation, the overcoming of sorrow through the spirit, and a return from a wintry world to a paradisiac state. There are Traklian words like *Herbst, Grab, blasse Schwester, Mond,* and *fliehende Sterne.* But Kraus's apostrophe to Spring as "zitternder Bote des Glücks" is comparable to Trakl's restoration of the lost island paradise in his "Psalm." It may be a counterpoem to Trakl's world, born of Kraus's general happiness in the Garden of Eden that was Janowitz Castle, though its chatelaine on more than one occasion turned it into a hell for him. Kraus asserts harmony between man and nature, the possibility of an individual paradise as a counterpoise to the chaos of the world.

The personal relationship between Trakl and Kraus dates from the summer of 1910, when Trakl spontaneously addressed a letter to Kraus. This communication has not been preserved, but we do have a letter to Erhard Buschbeck, dated the latter part of July, in which Trakl writes: "Ich habe an Karl Kraus geschrieben, ganz unpersönlich und kalt—werde von ihm wohl nichts zu erwarten haben."[11] Trakl's move into Kraus's orbit coincided with his loss of faith in salvation through artistic productivity, in the possibility of conquering chaos by aesthetic means. Why, then, did Trakl approach Kraus at a time when he seemed to be despairing of the Word? Possibly because he regarded Kraus as a moral model with marked charitable impulses, as the intrepid champion of humane values in an unfeeling age, as a guide and healer. In more practical terms, to be sure, Trakl may have sought publication in the *Fackel* and a chance to alleviate his desperate material situation. Kraus in turn may have sensed in Trakl a congruity between art and artist, life and literature, one of those rare poets whose work expresses an intimate relationship between language and being, a man whose uncompromising truthfulness exacted the price of isolation and loneliness that was also paid over and over again by the satirist. The two men were clearly fated to meet, and from late 1911 on a mutual friend, Karl Hauer, whom Trakl had met in September in the Salzburg society Pan, was at work as a mediator.

Their first meeting, however, did not take place until early August 1912, presumably at the home of Trakl's new friend Ludwig von Ficker at Mühlau near Innsbruck. Earlier that year the circle had widened as Trakl had met other members of the *Brenner* group (Carl Dallago, Karl Borromäus Heinrich, Max von Esterle, Karl Röck). In August of the following year Kraus and Loos made it possible for Trakl to spend his vacation in Venice with Kraus, Adolf and Bessie Loos, Oskar Kokoschka, Peter Altenberg, and Ludwig and Cissi von Ficker. Kraus seems to have tried to help Trakl in other ways as well. In early April of 1913 Erhard Buschbeck wrote to the poet: "Wegen Deines Gedicht-Bandes wird Herr Kraus mit Ficker in München sprechen. Herr Kraus will ihn nämlich zu Rowohlt empfehlen."[12] That Kraus was increasingly regarded as Trakl's mentor and sponsor is demonstrated in rather unedifying fashion by Robert Müller, one of the few enemies of Kraus among the contributors to the *Brenner* and the man who had introduced Trakl to that circle. Müller blamed Kraus for inducing Trakl to withdraw his poems from *Die Pforte,* an anthology of Austrian poems that Müller had edited for the Saturn–Verlag of Heidelberg. On September 4, 1913 Müller wrote to Buschbeck: "Wie kann ein Mensch nur so wenig Rückgrat haben und sich von dem buckligen Juden, dem Kraus, kommandieren lassen?...Das will ich dem Kraus nicht vergessen, so ein Krüppel an Leib und Seele."[13] In somewhat less odious fashion the painter Oskar Vonwiller wrote on May 25, 1914 to his schoolmate Trakl, who had appealed to him for material assistance: "Ich würde Dir empfehlen, Dich an Kraus zu wenden, der mit leichter Mühe eine weitergreifende Aktion für Dich in's Werk setzen kann, die Dir viel mehr Vorteil bieten kann, als ein Palliativmittel wie dieses von Dir gewünschte."[14]

In the *Fackel* of December 15, 1913 Kraus reprinted excerpts from Karl Borromäus Heinrich's *Brenner* essay "Die Erscheinung Georg Trakls" (March 1, 1913),[15] and soon thereafter Trakl thanked him with "Gefühle meiner respektvollsten Verehrung und Liebe."[16] In the *Fackel* for March 28, 1914 Kraus comes to the defense of Trakl and polemicizes against Paul Schlenther, who had written in the *Berliner Tageblatt* that Trakl displayed a frighteningly "krasser Naturalismus" and that "seine Kunst ist noch viel zu unausgeglichen, alle fünf Seiten ein anderer Stil." Kraus's comment was that Schlenther ought to be made to forego his pension as the retired director of the Burgtheater in favor of Trakl.[17] Having attended Kraus's Vienna reading on November 9, 1913, Trakl wrote Kraus on December 13 and enclosed the first version of his poem "Winterabend" (beginning "Wenn der Schnee ans Fenster fällt"), asking him to accept this poem, written "in rasender Betrunkenheit und verbrecherischer Melancholie...als Ausdruck der Verehrung für einen Mann, der wie keiner der Welt ein Beispiel gibt."[18] That Trakl's epistolary style may be indebted to Kraus's example and that some of his letters may have been written, as it were, "mit der Fackel im Ohr" to an even greater extent than was the case with Elias Canetti has been suggested by Peter Horst Neumann,[19] though as yet without the requisite documentation.

In the Salzburg Trakl Symposium of 1978, Gerald Stieg and Eberhard Sauermann disagreed with each other on the significance of such Trakl dedications to Kraus, on whether Trakl's relationship with the satirist may be interpreted as a dialogue with a father symbol and whether both Trakl's admiration for Kraus and his possible criticism of him can be deduced from these poems.[20] Stieg, who answers these questions positively, elsewhere gives an analysis of the poem contributed by Trakl to the "Rundfrage über Karl Kraus" which Ludwig von Ficker arranged for the *Brenner* (Nos. 18, 19, 20) of June and July 1913 and issued in book form four years later.[21] Intended in part as an answer to the vicious anti-Kraus polemic which the satirist's reading of March 29 had elicited in the pages of "Zeit im Bild," the "Rundfrage" carried Trakl's invocatory poem "Karl Kraus":[22]

Weißer Hohepriester der Wahrheit,
Kristallne Stimme, in der Gottes eisiger Odem wohnt,
Zürnender Magier,
Dem unter schwarzem Mantel der blaue Panzer des Kriegers klirrt.

In this poem Kraus is apostrophized as a high priest, a prophet, a magician, and a warrior—all Old Testament, pre–Christian attributes or functions. As Gerald Stieg has pointed out,[23] *weiß* in Trakl denotes death —not the blackness of physical destruction, but a sort of neutral color expressive of the lifelessness and bloodlessness that precede redemption and as such symbolizing the imperfection of earthly existence. It is the color that Otto Weininger has characterized as "dieser falsche Schein der Vollkommenheit."[24] The realm of the unredeemed dead is akin to that of magic, and the magician's animal, the snake, is reminiscent of the loss of paradise. (Compare the "weiße Magier mit seinen Schlangen" in the poem "Psalm").[25] Does the white high priest officiate where God is dead? Is he a usurper of God's function, speaking in a congealed, icy, sterile voice the truth of a ghostly intermediate realm? God's icy breath presumably is Truth, and since to be truthful means to judge, the vulnerable truthseeker needs to wear a warrior's armor. While Trakl appreciates Kraus's *saeva indignatio* and his ardent fighting spirit, he cannot have faith in the satirist's classical, humanistic artistic ideal because it is not founded on Christianity. Thus, so reasons Stieg, this seemingly adulatory poem may well contain hidden criticism, and he concludes that "als einziger Beiträger der 'Rundfrage' hatte Trakl *in nuce* die spätere, religiös bedingte Kritik an Kraus vorweggenommen."[26]

The news of Trakl's death, which Ficker wired Kraus on November 9, 1914, was the first of several blows that Kraus was to sustain in the years to come: the deaths at the front of his friends Franz Grüner and Franz Janowitz as well as the suicide of the dancer Elisabeth Reitler. On December 16, 1914 Kraus included two Trakl poems, "An den Knaben Elis" and "In ein altes Stammbuch," in his Vienna reading in memory of the poet, though he did not attend the *Gedenkfeier* for him. If the *Fackel* had propagated and advertised Trakl's poetry in his lifetime, it now actively raised funds for a tombstone on his new grave near Innsbruck. For example, in April 1923 Kraus announced that 300,000 Kronen from the proceeds of his Nestroy cycle had gone toward the *Brenner* Fund for Trakl's grave, and in June 1928 Kraus noted that a Munich performance of his *Traumstück* had been followed by Eugen Auerbach's settings of five Trakl poems.[27] In June 1919 Kraus sent Ficker a critique by

Alexander Lernet–Holenia in which Trakl was painted as a plagiarist of K.L. Ammer. Instead of basing a *Brenner* item on it, Ficker provided Kraus with evidence that it was Lernet–Holenia who had plagiarized Trakl. Leopold Liegler's recollection, written down in the 1940s, that Trakl was among the contributors to the *Fackel* between 1910 and 1914 and that Trakl's "Anerkennung in so kurzer Zeit ohne den Einfluß und die Patronanz der *Fackel* gar nicht möglich gewesen wäre"[28] surely is faulty, but there is evidence that Kraus missed few opportunities to draw attention to the poet. In April 1927 Kraus mentions Trakl among those Austrian poets (Berthold Viertel, Richard Schaukal, Franz Janowitz) "die durch Zeilen wertvoller sind als die beliebteren durch Bücher."[29] His last word on Trakl the following year indicates that he placed the work of his contemporaries Trakl and Else Lasker-Schüler on the very pinnacles of poetry: "Nur auf den höchsten Gipfeln deutscher Lyrik...in wenigen Strophen von Claudius, Hölderlin oder Mörike, heute in Zeilen Trakls oder der Lasker-Schüler, ist, im erhabenen Einklang von Gesicht und Gehör, so Gestalt geworden, was ein Herz und die Natur einander zu sagen haben."[30]

Some remarks about the relationship between the *Fackel* world of Kraus and the *Brenner* world of Trakl and Ficker may be in order here. Gerald Stieg has chronicled in detail the multifarious connections, collaborations, and conflicts between these two journals, which shared not only aims but also numerous contributors and readers. The prewar *Brenner* was strongly supportive of Kraus, who was seen as a prophet and precursor of Christianity. Thinkers like Ficker, Dallago, K.B. Heinrich, Theodor Haecker, and Ferdinand Ebner appreciated in Kraus his courage in championing moral values and castigating iniquity and unworth, his purity of thought, and his striving for perfection of form. Of these men, Theodor Haecker, who had approached Kraus via Kierkegaard, came most strongly under Kraus's satiric spell ("Ich bin ohne Karl Kraus nicht denkbar").[31] The *Studien über Karl Kraus* which the Brenner Verlag issued in 1913 bring together essays by Dallago, Ficker, and Heinrich. Kraus's *Sprachdenken* appealed to the *Brenner* Circle, as did his "Blick in die Welt—Heraustreten aus gedanklicher Eingesponnenheit" (Ferdinand Ebner).[32] Only the *Brenner* is comparable to the satirist's exemplary stance in wartime. Its non-appearance matched Kraus's own silence after the outbreak of the war, with vol. 5 appearing as the *Brenner-Jahrbuch 1915* in memoriam Georg Trakl, whereupon publication ceased until 1919. The Trakl poems contained in the *Jahrbuch* may be regarded as artistically perfect representations of decline and as such stand in programmatic contrast to Kraus's satire, which was viewed by many as the only proper artistic response to an apocalyptically experienced present.

The end of the war marked the beginning of a process of detachment and dissociation between the *Brenner* and the *Fackel.* Now Trakl loomed especially large as the embodiment of the paradox and mystery of Christianity, representing Christian idealism in contrast to Kraus's ethical idealism. From this point of view Kraus lacked Trakl's religious depth and was wasting his satiric talent on *Schein* rather than *Sein,* on external and relatively insignificant phenomena. Kraus in turn regretted what he perceived as a narrowing of the postwar *Brenner*'s viewpoint. Moreover, the latent anti-Semitic tendencies of some members of the *Brenner* Circle—religiously based rather than the ethical-aesthetic kind practiced by Weininger and by Kraus himself—now came to the fore, and in marked contrast to the prewar journal, Franz Janowitz was the only Jew to appear in its pages. It should not be forgotten that at one time or another the *Brenner* Circle included such strange figures as the self-hating Jew Erich Messing, a major contributor to the fund for Trakl's grave, and Jörg Lanz von Liebenfels, who declared Kraus a sort of honorary Aryan. From Karl Röck's diary we know, however, that Trakl resisted the diarist's attempts to wean him away from Kraus and had no use for Röck's anti-Semitic attitude, though Trakl was not above making an occasional anti-Semitic dirty joke.[33]

The postwar *Brenner* increasingly reflected a rejection of idealism, as the last representative of which Kraus was perceived. When Kraus was discussed, the loving lyric poet was given pride of place and the hating satirist was de-emphasized. By 1934, when vol. 15 of the *Brenner* was dedicated to Kraus on his sixtieth birthday, Ludwig von Ficker had integrated Kraus into his Christian conception of the world as an example of Christian self-sacrifice. This view was promoted by Kraus's championship of the murdered Chancellor Engelbert Dollfuß, whose assassin turned him into a Christian martyr, though Kraus's support of Dollfuß's political position was not conceded any eschatological significance. The aforementioned *Brenner* issue carries an article, "Das Bild des Menschen bei Georg Trakl," by Werner Meyknecht, who was working on a dissertation with the same title, and Meyknecht recalls to memory the poems which Trakl dedicated to Kraus.[34] But it is in the highly revealing letter from Ficker to Meyknecht of January 28, 1934 that Ficker's presumably definitive assessment of the relationship between Trakl and Kraus may be found.[35] "Ich glaube, daß Kraus wohl das Ungewöhnliche der Erscheinung spürte," he writes, "aber im Grunde nichts Rechtes mit ihr anzufangen wußte...Kraus liebt die idealen, die klassisch aufgeräumten Geisteshorizonte, die leicht aufzuhellenden, die durch keine Emotion der Wahrheit, die über ihnen ist und ihre Schatten auf sie wirft, im Pathos ihrer Eigenmächtigkeit zu erschüttern sind. Gerade die Dichtung Trakls aber spiegelt einen solchen, durch Einbruch der übernatürlichen Wahrheit in die Sphäre seiner natürlichen Idealität bis auf den Grund erschütterten Geisteshorizont."[36] According to Ficker, Trakl found that while Kraus's intellect was nourished by the substance of truth, it also seared truth in the medium he had chosen for his creativity, namely satire, so that his effectiveness was confined to the limited opportunities of this form to fashion a truthful response to trying times. Trakl knew that he was a lost soul, but his profound faith made him a courageous visionary and realist who was ahead of his time. "Ihm gegenüber darf...Kraus als der letzte Idealist dieser Zeit gelten—er, der sich mit der furchtbaren Realität herumschlägt...ohne anders mit ihr fertig zu werden, als indem er ihr Tödliches viviseziert, aber zugleich im Laboratorium seines konsequent auf Konservierung bedachtes Geistes revivifiziert der Nachwelt überliefert. Trakl aber hat aus der Hölle seines Lebens durch ihre Wirklichkeit hindurch (nie über sie hinweg!) bis in die Wirklichkeit des ferngerückten Himmels gesehen. Das ist der Unterschied, der himmelweite Unterschied auch im Wesen der Selbstaufopferung der beiden."[37]

From Kraus, then, Trakl elicited the rarely given "Ja des Neinsagers," to use Werner Kraft's phrase.[38] For Trakl the very dissimilar

Kraus may or may not have been a father or an older brother, but at the very least he was an admired guide and helper in the troubled last years of this *poète maudit.* For Ludwig von Ficker and the *Brenner* Circle both men were interwoven as exemplary figures of their time—singly and jointly serving as inspiration, touchstone, and challenge.

Notes

1. *Die Fackel* 360–362, p. 24.
2. *Ibid.*
3. Now in Trakl, *Dichtungen und Briefe,* ed. by Walther Killy and Hans Szklenar, Salzburg: Otto Müller Verlag, 1969, vol. 1, p. 55.
4. *Ibid.,* p. 492
5. Ludwig von Ficker, *Denkzettel und Danksagungen,* München: Kösel-Verlag, 1967, p. 120.
6. Karl Kraus, *Briefe an Sidonie Nádherný von Borutin,* München: Deutscher Taschenbuch Verlag, 1977, vol. 1, p. 83.
7. *Dichtungen und Briefe,* vol. 1, pp. 366-367.
8. Wilma Iggers, *Karl Kraus: A Viennese Critic of the Twentieth Century,* The Hague: Martinus Nijhoff, 1967, p. 13.
9. Gerald Stieg, *Der Brenner und die Fackel,* Salzburg: Otto Müller Verlag, 1976, p. 265, 285.
10. It first appeared in *Die Fackel* 406-412, p. 136.
11. *Dichtungen und Briefe,* vol. 1, p. 479.
12. *Dichtungen und Briefe,* vol. 2, pp. 753-754.
13. *Ibid.,* p. 707. In 1914 Müller, the sometime editor of *Der Ruf,* a journal in which Trakl appeared, published an anti-Kraus pamphlet, *Karl Kraus oder Dalai Lama, der dunkle Priester. Eine Nervenabtötung,* as a special issue of his own journal *Torpedo.* Kraus struck back by lampooning him as Harald Brüller in his "magische Operette" *Literatur oder Man wird doch da sehn* (1921). Müller committed suicide three years later.
14. *Ibid.,* p. 788.
15. *Die Fackel* 389-390, p. 27.
16. *Dichtungen und Briefe,* vol. 1, p. 532.
17. *Die Fackel* 395-397, p. 27.
18. *Dichtungen und Briefe,* vol. 1, p. 530. The second version of "Winterabend" may be found on p. 102.
19. See *Internationales Georg Trakl-Symposium,* ed. by J.P. Strelka, Bern: Peter Lang, 1984, p. 41.
20. Gerald Stieg, "Georg Trakl und Karl Kraus," Eberhard Sauermann, "Die Widmungen Georg Trakls," in *Salzburger Trakl-Symposion,* hrsg.

von Walter Weiss und Hans Weichselbaum. Salzburg: Otto Müller Verlag, 1978.

21. Stieg, *Der Brenner,* pp. 267-268.
22. *Rundfrage über Karl Kraus,* Innsbruck: Brenner-Verlag, n.d. (1917), p. 17. In subsequent printings of this poem the word "schwarzem" was replaced by "flammendem." See *Dichtungen und Briefe,* vol. 1, p. 123.
23. Stieg, *Der Brenner,* pp. 267-268.
24. Otto Weininger, *Über die letzten Dinge,* Wien–Leipzig: Wilhelm Braumüller, 1904, p. 130.
25. *Dichtungen und Briefe,* vol. 1, p. 56.
26. Stieg, *Der Brenner,* p. 270.
27. *Die Fackel* 613-621, p. 58; 781-786, p. 68.
28. Leopold Liegler, "Meine Erinnerungen an Karl Kraus," *Kraus-Hefte* 25, January 1983, p. 9.
29. *Die Fackel* 757-758, p. 28.
30. *Die Fackel* 781-786, p. 97. This accolade is not diminished by the unfortunate context in which it appears, "Aus Redaktion und Irrenhaus," one of the few instances in which Kraus was the victim of a hoax, a misjudgment, or an illusion.
31. Quoted in Stieg, *Der Brenner,* p. 153.
32. Werner Kraft, "Ferdinand Ebner und Karl Kraus," *Mitteilungen aus dem Brenner-Archiv* 1, 1982, p. 15.
33. See, for example, Trakl's postcard to Erhard Buschbeck, Salzburg, November 13, 1911, *Dichtungen und Briefe,* vol. 1, p. 485.
34. Stieg, *Der Brenner,* p. 9.
35. *Denkzettel und Danksagungen,* pp. 116-122.
36. *Ibid.,* pp. 119-120.
37. *Ibid.,* pp. 120-121.
38. W. Kraft, *Das Ja des Neinsagers: Karl Kraus und seine geistige Welt* (München: edition text + kritik, 1974) contains a section on Georg Trakl and Else Lasker-Schüler, pp. 191-198.

THREE AUSTRIAN APHORISTS:

KRAUS, KUH, CANETTI

This essay begins with an aphorism about aphorisms and an epigram about aphorisms. The first one is by Wystan Hugh Auden and Louis Kronenberger: "Aphorisms are essentially an aristocratic genre. The aphorist does not argue or explain: he asserts. It is for the reader to decide whether an aphorism be true or false."[1] The epigram is by Roy C. Bates: "In the literary prism / Nothing more enlightens, nothing hooks / Ampler meaning than the aphorism, / Scoring better than a shelf of books. / Half a truth is ideal, / Three-quarters would be unreal." Note that both the aphorism and the epigram contain the words "true" or "truth." The epigrammatist was willing to settle for half a truth; perhaps he had in mind the derivation of the word "aphorism" from a Greek root denoting a delimitation or a setting of a boundary. Those defining "aphorism" seem to be partial to partiality; thus J.A. Cuddon, in his *Dictionary of Literary Terms,* says that "a successful aphorism exposes and condenses at any rate a part of the truth."[2] It never occurred to me to ask Roy C. Bates (whom I knew in his last years as an erudite Boston attorney, but who had had an earlier identity as a Berlin poet and thinker named Kurt Bauchwitz) whether he was acquainted with the writings of Karl Kraus and in particular with this often-quoted aphorism: "Der Aphorismus deckt sich nie mit der Wahrheit; er ist entweder eine halbe

Wahrheit oder anderthalb" (An aphorism never coincides with truth; it is either a half-truth or one-and-a-half truths).[3] Or with another Kraus aphorism, which continues, or expands upon, the one just quoted: "Ein Aphorismus braucht nicht wahr zu sein, aber er soll die Wahrheit überflügeln. Er muss mit einem Satz über sie hinauskommen." (An aphorism need not be true, but it should overtake truth. It must get beyond it in one sentence / with one leap). Here you already have a taste of Kraus's celebrated amphibolous word-play, his virtuosic groping along the rope of language. When Kraus pronounced the word "Satz," with its dual meaning of "sentence" and "leap," his expressive hands would do a bit of jumping or vaulting. Bates-Bauchwitz may or may not have read Karl Kraus, but W.H. Auden, that *Wahlösterreicher* (Austrian by choice), certainly did, and appreciatively so; the *Viking* (or *Faber) Book of Aphorisms* that he co-edited in 1962 with my then Brandeis colleague Louis Kronenberger contains dozens of Kraus aphorisms in Auden's translation.

Kraus, Kuh, and Canetti had in common more than the alliterative nature of their names and their interest in one particular literary form; behind all their linguistic brilliance and the fireworks of their wit there were a deeply serious moral concern and more than a little of Juvenal's *saeva indignatio,* a quality that has over the ages produced many a concentrated shot of venom. Like many great satirists, they set out to question commonly held assumptions, deflate pride and pomposity, combat stupidity, and subvert practices thought to be in need of changing. In his discussion of such dissimilar Austrian writers as Franz Grillparzer, Ernst von Feuchtersleben, Hugo von Hofmannsthal, Arthur Schnitzler, Richard von Schaukal, and Karl Heinrich Waggerl, the historian William M. Johnston speaks of the "gentle aphorists of Vienna." None of the three under discussion here fits that description. If Marie von Ebner-Eschenbach, the Moravian-born storyteller and aphorist (whose lifespan, 1830-1916, happened to coincide with that of her monarch, Emperor Franz Joseph), was "the great apostle of forgiveness,"[4] Kraus, Canetti, and Kuh are, by and large, exemplars of unforgiveness. An aphorism by Elias Canetti dating from 1943 says that "Die großen Aphoristiker lesen sich so, als ob sie einander gut gekannt hätten" (The great aphorists read as if they had known one another well). The great aphorists do seem to constitute a certain brotherhood, but in writing "*lesen* sich so" Canetti may have meant to indicate the *Zusammenschau,* the synoptic work, that the *reader* must do as he or she tries to glean practical wisdom from all those nuggets of thought and insight that are presented from a great variety of viewpoints and reflect so many different personalities. Aphorisms virtually force the reader to assent or dissent, to come to terms with capsules of commentary.

Kraus (1874–1936), Kuh (1890–1941), and Canetti (*1905) were contemporaries and certainly knew one another, or at least *of* one another. The young Canetti came under Kraus's spell and then had to free himself of his domination by putting himself through a "Schule des Widerstands," a school of resistance, in order to find his own voice. Anton Kuh was in many ways an antipode and adversary of Kraus, whom he once apostrophized, in a brilliant impromptu speech, as "Der Affe Zarathustras."[5] As one of the minions of Imre Békessy, the corrupt Hungarian-born press czar who led postwar Vienna's dance around the Golden Calf and against whom Kraus waged an ultimately successful campaign, Kuh was clearly beneath the satirist's contempt, if not his notice. Those acquainted with the writings of Kuh may well wonder whether as a satiric aphorist he was not the "ape" of Kraus, illustrating, despite himself, the old adage that imitation is the sincerest form of flattery.

Somewhat disarmingly, Canetti asks in an aphorism dating from 1954: "Welche Sätze, die man in einer Aphorismensammlung findet, schreibt man sich auf?" (Which of the sentences that one finds in a collection of aphorisms does one write down?). He goes on to suggest that it may be those that confirm one's own beliefs and justify one's existence, those that amuse one because of an unexpected turn of phrase or their witty concision, or those that embarrass one and put one to shame in salutary fashion by holding up a mirror to oneself or to mankind generally.

As I treated myself, in preparing this article, to the collected aphorisms of Kraus, Kuh, and Canetti (in perilously large and addictive doses) as well as to their own statements about this particular aspect of their work, I found that Karl Kraus was the only one who was quite comfortable with the genre and expressed satisfaction with it, the only one who had no reservations about it, made no apologies for it, and did not try to rename it. The aphorism, then, occupies a correspondingly important position in his oeuvre. His best aphorisms may be found in the prewar *Fackel* between 1906 and 1917, and he issued three collections in book form: *Sprüche und Widersprüche* (Dicta and Contradictions, 1909); *Pro domo et mundo* (1912); and *Nachts* (At Night, 1918). All of these are combined in the posthumous collection *Beim Wort genommen* (1955), the title of which alludes to this Kraus aphorism: "Weil ich den Gedanken beim Wort nehme, kommt er" (Because I take an idea by the word/ at its word, it comes). In the postwar period Kraus favored the form of the epigram, and his verse epigrams are often expanded aphorisms, just as a Kraus aphorism was often distilled from a longer text in prose or poetry, or else served as the nucleus of a subsequent prose piece. In his review of Kraus's collected aphorisms, Heinz Politzer aptly remarks that "they share in the German Latinity of Georg Christoph Lichtenberg, the abysmal Viennese wit of Johann Nestroy, the Christianity of Søren Kierkegaard, the anti-Christian aggressions of Friedrich Nietzsche, and the Jewishness of Franz Kafka."[6] In Kraus's work there is no dearth of thoughtful and lapidary aphorisms about the form itself: "Einen Aphorismus kann man in keine Schreibmaschine diktieren. Es würde zu lange dauern." (One cannot dictate an aphorism to a typist. It would take too long.) This could be taken to mean that even the fastest typist could not handle the flash of inspiration, or that the cerebral process producing an aphorism is endless and that no typist could wait long enough. "Einer, der Aphorismen schreiben kann, sollte sich nicht in Aufsätzen zersplittern." (Someone who can write aphorisms should not fritter away his time writing essays.) Kraus's aphorisms are such an integral and suggestive part of his total satire that those acquainted with his uniquely language-based work will not only find his wisdom disturbingly applicable to present-day situations, but will be tempted to fashion aphorisms in his spirit to give satiric expression to the "brave new world" that he was mercifully spared from seeing. Here is one contemporary insight in this spirit: "They started by processing cheese. Now they are processing *words!*"

Wolfgang Mieder, the foremost American expert on proverbs, their versions and perversions in literature, journalism, politics, and advertising, has traced Kraus's satiric use of proverbs and proverbial phrases by supplying a list of such sayings and their frequently mordant adaptations by Kraus.[7] Kraus delighted in subverting, perverting, undermining, distorting, or "alienating" traditional saws or clichés in order to reflect actual conditions or define current phenomena. By depriving these proverbs of their euphemistic aura and cutting through their poetic, aesthetic, and figurative veneer, Kraus unmasked them, as it were, and by means of punning distortion made them serve as a stark, unvarnished expression of the "great times" in which he lived. A case in point is the trite German saying "Man lebt nur einmal," which has an equivalent in the (equally trite) hedonistic "You only live once." In his aphorism "Man lebt nicht einmal einmal" Kraus utilizes the possibilities of the German language to give verbal play to an idea directly derived from this language. "Einmal," stressed on the first syllable and meaning "one," is preceded by "einmal," stressed on the second syllable and meaning—in conjunction with "nicht"—"not even." To reproduce the syntactical uniqueness of German and still convey Kraus's thought (which is basically life-affirming), one would have to use the analogous (though not fully equivalent) resources of the English language, ending up with a version of Kraus's pithy aphorism that would read something like this: "Your chances of living a happy, productive life are not even even." Here is another seemingly trite Kraus aphorism: "Je größer der Stiefel, desto größer der Absatz." On the face of it, this is a shoemaker's truism: "The bigger the boot, the bigger the heel." Kraus's principled pacifism adds the dimension of militarism and all the associations it evokes. But in colloquial German, "Stiefel" also means "blather" or "nonsense," and another meaning of "Absatz" is "sale." My translation, "The bigger the bull, the bigger the bull market," still does not convey all the levels of meaning and the language-derived ideas in Kraus's aphorism, especially when one considers that yet another meaning of "Absatz" is "paragraph."

(In view of Kraus's interminable paragraphs, the satirist's detractors might well use this aphorism against him.)

Karl Kraus and Anton Kuh were both consummate *Sprechkünstler*—reciters, rhetoricians, raconteurs. Kuh was a *Sprechsteller* rather than a *Schriftsteller* (the latter being the common German word for "writer"—one who fashions writing; Kuh crafted *speech).* "Die Wenigsten wissen," he once wrote, "daß auch das Nichtschreiben die Frucht langer und mühseliger Arbeit ist." (Very few people realize that non-writing, too, is the fruit of long and arduous labor.) This *Stegreifredner,* or impromptu speaker, who was as brilliant as he was brash, viewed his aphorisms as *Sprechergebnisse,* the results of speaking—"nicht so sehr Höhepunkte eines geschriebenen als die Überreste eines geredeten Daseins"[8] (the residue of a spoken life rather than the high points of a written one). Kuh shunned the term *Aphorismus:* "Der Aphorismus ist der größte Schwindler. Er simuliert durch Sparsamkeit Hintergründe, die er gar nicht hat."[9] (The aphorism is the greatest swindler. Through economy it simulates backgrounds that it does not possess.) In one of his collections of aphorisms Kuh says: "Die vorliegenden Aphorismen haben den Vorzug, keine zu sein."[10] (The aphorisms presented here have the merit of being none.) He preferred to call them *Aussprüche* (remarks, or sayings). In 1922 he published a collection under the title *Von Goethe abwärts: Essays in Aussprüchen. Aussprüche* is also the subtitle of a later collection, *Physiognomik* (undated, but probably 1931). Kuh attempts to convince the reader that these *Aussprüche* are different from *Aphorismen,* which he describes as "aus der Selbstbespiegelung der Sprache entstandene Formeln"[11] (formulas produced by the narcissism of language), a phenomenon that Kuh likened to premature ejaculation. Kuh thought of his *Aussprüche* as memory-joggers, crude mnemonic devices that preserved material for feuilletons (such as are contained in his book *Der unsterbliche Österreicher,* 1931), "Endglieder ungeschriebener Gedankenketten, deren Stolz oft die unaphoristische glanzlose Prägung, die blendende Pointenlosigkeit bildet"[12] (final links in unwritten chains of thought that pride themselves on being unaphoristically unglamorous and brilliantly pointless). It is hard to think of a more un-Krausian intention or formulation. Kuh thus makes a virtue of *Ungeschliffenheit* (lack of polish) as he wants his *Geistesblitze* (flashes of inspiration) viewed as beginning, middle, or final sentences of essays that the reader is invited to fashion or finish for himself. One really does not mind doing so, for Kuh offers Nietzschean cultural criticism and Schopenhauerian pessimism in witty, attractive, assimilable, and up-to-date form. In the manner of Kraus, Kuh displays considerable ingenuity in retrieving, augmenting, adapting, rewriting, interpreting, or nullifying famous sayings, accepted wisdom, or cultural norms. A case in point is his punning adaptation of the Latin saying "Post coitum omne animal triste est": "Ante coitum omne animal est Tristan." If, as Kuh says, Arthur Schopenhauer created "Aphorismen zur Lebensweisheit" (aphorisms embodying practical wisdom) and Johann Nepomuk Nestroy wrote "Aphorismen zur Lebensnarrheit" (aphorisms reflecting the absurdities and follies of life), Kuh seems to shuttle back and forth between both camps as a self-styled "Chauvinist der Wirklichkeit,"[13] a zealot of reality who aims at presenting a physiognomy of his time, with many of his contemporaries, particularly literary figures, as recipients of his "Reverenz der Bosheit"[14] (tribute of malice) as he wrests his *aperçus* from their physiognomies, as it were, by way of self-defense. Kuh's aphorisms often read like the witty and somewhat snide effusions of a brainy *Gymnasiast* (secondary-school student) or other *enfant terrible,* and from a Krausian perspective he was an "Einfallspinsel" in the tradition of Heinrich Heine, whom Kraus despised as an overly facile writer with an insufficient reverence for language and all the values inherent in it. (Kraus's pun is based on the words *Einfaltspinsel,* which means "simpleton," and *Einfall,* idea—thus, a simpleton who thinks he is inspired.) Karl Kraus, who carried on a protracted fight against the "psychoanals," might, however, have appreciated at least *some* of Kuh's definitions (daffynitions?)—for instance this one: "Die Psychoanalytiker: Asocia-Zionisten." (The German sonic pun combines "association" with "Zionists.")

Elias Canetti, on the face of it, is another reluctant aphorist, yet he appears to have availed himself copiously of this genre. *Die Provinz des Menschen,* subtitled *Aufzeichnungen 1942 bis 1972,* contains but a small selection of his writings in this form; he has withheld the rest from publication.[15] Canetti's notes or jottings, ranging from one-liners to miniature essays and presented in the form of a diary, are a pendant to his non-fictional magnum opus *Masse und Macht (Crowds and Power)*[16] and represent a sort of counterpoise to, or safety-valve for, the author's prolonged, almost obsessive preoccupation with his monumental work. Canetti made a selection from his aphoristic notes at a much later date, when he presumably had sufficient detachment from the great prose work that had prompted those musings as an offshoot. Ingo Seidler considers these aphorisms, together with *Masse und Macht,* as Canetti's main work, pointing out that they follow a long tradition of unsystematic but incisive and illuminating "minimal writing:" "The French *moralistes,* G.C. Lichtenberg, and (in method, though hardly in message) Nietzsche are his most obvious predecessors."[17] Uwe Dick identifies *Verläßlichkeit* (dependability) as the hallmark of Canetti's aphorisms and regards them as guides for the *Lebens-Partitur* (the score of life), "lebenswerte Leitgedanken" (guiding thoughts, or basic ideas, worth living by) and "ein Ozeanien voller Denkinseln" (an Oceania full of cerebral islands).[18] A third critic, David Turner, finds in the *Aufzeichnungen* "aphoristically expressed hypotheses which question the norms of human life" and feels that any one of them might have been expanded into a play, just as Canetti's three plays are built on "an idea basically so simple that it might have been expressed in the form of an aphorism."[19] Canetti himself displays a becoming sense of what the trouble with his *Aufzeichnungen* is: they tend to be too personal, not fluid or flexible or transformable enough. It is probably in the nature of the form that aphorisms tend to carry a considerable cargo of autobiographical elements. Canetti's notes are universal and quotable enough, but to a greater extent than Kraus's and Kuh's they gain from being read and understood in context, in the context of the author's life and thought. It is in this form that Canetti's rebellion against, or detachment from, Karl Kraus becomes most apparent. Despite the acuity of his critical analysis and frequently judgmental stance, he does not join Kraus in a rejection of the world as it is constituted or in an all-out attack on its inhabitants. "Ich habe es satt, die Menschen zu durchschauen," Canetti writes; "es ist so leicht und es führt zu nichts." (I am tired of seeing through people; it is so easy and does not lead to anything.) Canetti's aphorisms are more varied and less predictable than Kraus's; even where he is passionately involved, he is not primarily concerned with making his points through linguistic wit or brilliant verbal play. Often his relatively plain language and matter-of-fact approach contrast effectively with the boldness of his statements. His love of mankind and belief in the relative educability of people are always in evidence.

In the early 1950s Canetti commented on his drama *Die Befristeten* (variously Englished as *The Deadlined, The Numbered,* and *Life-Terms*) and included material from his travel book *Die Stimmen von Marrakesch (The Voices of Marrakesh).* Some of the *Aufzeichnungen* read like entries for his work *Der Ohrenzeuge (The Earwitness):* "Der Satte" (The Sated One), "Der Belesene" (The Well-Read One), "Der Lobsammler" (The Praise-Collector), "Der Restaurator" (The Restorer). Occasionally Canetti includes *Lesefrüchte* in the manner of a commonplace book. When he writes "Er legt Sätze wie Eier, aber er vergißt, sie zu bebrüten" (He lays sentences like eggs, but he forgets to hatch them) he may have had himself in mind, but surely the statement applies to aphorists generally. Canetti's recurring themes are war, history, myths, power, language, psychology, philosophy, and especially death, with which Canetti has been combatively obsessed to the point of denial and a quest for immortality. The author appears in these notes as an ethical humanist with a radical bent who has no patience with any power, religion, or philosophy that brooks or sanctions dehumanization, strife, carnage, and death, but also as a man with a pronounced sense of the essential ineradicability of prejudice, profiteering, and the martial spirit—many of the manifestations of what Max Brod has termed "unedles Unglück" (ignoble misfortune). Of great literary interest are Canetti's capsule characterizations of, or tributes to, such dissimilar spirits as Mohammed, Hieronymus Bosch, Montaigne, Hobbes, Goethe, Lichtenberg, Francis Bacon, Stendhal, Kafka, and Robert Walser. Some aphorisms are of an attractive childlike naiveté: "Was ein Tiger ist, weiß ich wirklich erst seit dem Gedicht von Blake." (What a tiger is I have really known only since Blake's poem.) Canetti's wartime aphorisms are of the greatest density and effectiveness; they are indicative of his attempt to use language as a weapon and to derive solace from the word.

It should also be noted that Canetti tried hard to come to terms intellectually with the phenomenon of Hitler: "Daß dieses Gesicht es bis zu diesem Krieg gebracht hat, und wir haben es nicht vertilgt! Und wir sind Millionen, und die Erde wimmelt von Waffen, Munition wäre da für dreitausend Jahre, und dieses Gesicht ist noch immer hier, über uns weit ausgespannt, die Fratze der Gorgo, und wir im Morden alle versteinert." (To think that this face has lasted till this war, and we have not destroyed it! And there are millions of us, and the earth teems with weapons, there would be enough ammunition for three thousand years, and this face is still there, stretching wide over us, the gargoyle of the Gorgon, and we have all become petrified in murdering.) Among several suggestive aphorisms on Canetti's own Jewishness is this breathtaking one from 1944: "Die Sprache meines Geistes wird die deutsche bleiben, und zwar weil ich Jude bin. Was von dem auf jede Weise verheerten Land übrig bleibt, will ich als Jude in mir behüten. Auch *ihr* Schicksal ist meines; aber ich bringe noch ein allgemein menschliches Erbteil mit. Ich will ihrer Sprache zurückgeben, was ich ihr schulde. Ich will dazu beitragen, daß man ihnen für etwas Dank hat." (The language of my intellect will remain German—because I am a Jew. Whatever remains of the land that has been laid waste in every way—I want to guard it in me as a Jew. *Their* destiny, too, is mine; but I bring with me a universal human legacy as well. I want to give back to their language what I owe it. I want to contribute to their having something that others will thank them for.) It is hard to think of a more affecting or a more poignant summation of the German-Jewish intellectual symbiosis—and it comes from a man who did not have German as his first language.

If I had to give a final characterization of these three aphorists, I would say that Karl Kraus is the most aphoristic thinker, the pithiest, most powerful, most quotable, the closest to language in his effectiveness, the most determined foe of commonplaces, and the complete satirist *in nuce*, but also a man who limited his range somewhat by deliberately excluding from his experience and attention so much of technology, philosophy, and fiction; that Kuh is the wittiest, the most irreverent, the most abrasive, the most reality-centered, and the most practical; and that Elias Canetti is the most wide-ranging, the most consistently humanistic, and, despite his skeptical, uncompromising attitude, the most conciliatory spirit (as befits the sole survivor among the three), as well as the most dependable guide—if only because he plays the role of *advocatus diaboli* relatively seldom. Whether Kraus, Canetti, and Kuh should be regarded as part of the "Viennese School of Aphorists, 1880–1930" that William M. Johnston discerns is debatable. I feel that Kraus's words, used in another context, "O laßt uns diese Dichterschule schwänzen"[20] (Oh, let's cut this literary school), are applicable here. There is such a thing as a school of fish, but given the frequently satiric and thus exclusive nature of this genre, can there be a school of aphorists in the sense of James Lipton's *Exaltation of Larks*? Perhaps Kraus, Kuh, and Canetti form an Acerbity of Aphorists, or an Affrontiveness of Aphorists.

Notes

1. W.H. Auden and L. Kronenberger, eds., *The Viking Book of Aphorisms,* New York; Viking Press, 1962, V-VI.
2. Garden City: Doubleday, 1977, 49.
3. All translations are my own. A selection of Kraus aphorisms may be found in *Half-Truths and One-and-a-Half Truths,* ed. and trans. by H. Zohn, Montreal: Engendra, 1976; Manchester: Carcanet, 1986; Chicago: University of Chicago Press, 1990.
4. W.M. Johnston, "The Vienna School of Aphorists, 1880-1930: Reflections on a Neglected Genre," in G. Chapple and H.H. Schulte, eds., *The Turn of the Century: German Literature and Art, 1890-1915,* Bonn: Bouvier, 1981, 278.
5. Wien: J. Deibler, n.d. (delivered in Vienna on October 25, 1925). An English translation may be found in Harold B. Segel, *The Vienna Coffeehouse Wits 1890-1938,* W. Lafayette: Purdue University Press, 1993, pp. 310-343.
6. *Books Abroad,* Winter 1959, 66. Politzer discerns a kinship between Kraus's aphorisms and the work and quest of Otto Weininger, Sigmund Freud, Arnold Schönberg and Adolf Loos, "all of whom tore the shallow decor from the crumbling facade of the Franz Joseph empire in their search for a purer form of man and his cultural pursuits." (*Ibid.*)
7. W. Mieder, "Karl Kraus und der sprichwörtliche Aphorismus," in *Deutsche Sprichwörter in Literatur, Politik, Presse und Werbung,* Hamburg: Buske, 1983, 123-131 (originally published in *Muttersprache,* 89, 1979).
8. A. Kuh, *Physiognomik,* München: Piper, n.d., 7.

9. A. Kuh, *Von Goethe abwärts,* Wien: Forum, 1963, 154.
10. *Ibid.,* 155.
11. *Physiognomik,* 8.
12. *Von Goethe abwärts,* 153-154.
13. *Physiognomik,* 7.
14. *Ibid.,* 8.
15. München: Hanser, 1973; *The Human Province,* trans. by Joachim Neugroschel, New York: Seabury, 1978.
16. *Masse und Macht,* Hamburg: Claassen, 1960; *Crowds and Power,* trans. by Carol Stewart, New York: Viking Press, 1962.
17. I. Seidler, "Who Is Elias Canetti?," *Cross Currents,* 1982, 112.
18. U. Dick, "Canetti—Sätze für die Lebenspartitur," *Literatur und Kritik,* 177/78, Sept./Okt. 1983, 383.
19. D. Turner, "Elias Canetti: The Intellectual as King Canute," in *Modern Austrian Writing,* ed. by A. Best and H. Wolfschütz, London: Oswald Wolff, 1980, 88.
20. Kraus, "Dichterschule," *Worte in Versen,* München: Kösel, 1959, 269.

GUSTINUS AMBROSI

The Sculptor, the Poet and the Man

Gustinus Ambrosi was active as a sculptor and a poet for seventy years and his works repose in some fifty places from San Francisco to Yokohama and Amsterdam to Johannesburg, yet he is virtually unknown outside his native Austria. He has been undervalued and neglected both as an artist and a poet, for all too many people have considered the deaf-mute artist, writer, and thinker as an epigone not in the mainstream of either sculpture or poetry and have been unwilling to regard his art, his poetry, and his life as all of a piece, with one illuminating the other. In its totality Ambrosi's creativity represents a tireless search for the meaning of the artist-poet's harsh fate and the significance of art and life in general. There is no denying Ambrosi's relative obscurity, yet he achieved fame at a very early age, receiving the State Prize of Austria-Hungary as the first of numerous honors, and in 1913, when Ambrosi was only twenty, Emperor Franz Joseph took the unusual step of bestowing upon him a "Staatsatelier auf Lebenszeit," a lifetime studio guaranteed by the government. Over the years Ambrosi had a number of studios—*Arbeitsstätten,* as he called them—in various locations, including the Prater in Vienna. His last atelier, on the edge of the Augarten, where he was domiciled from 1958 until his death, has since 1978 been an Ambrosi Museum, part of the Österreichische Galerie, and it includes more than two hundred works donated by the artist himself.[1] Twenty years after his passing Ambrosi has only a relatively small circle of admirers. It is not surprising that a Nuremberg periodical called *Der gute Menschenkenner (Illustrierte Zeitschrift für praktische Natur- und Menschenkenntnis)* should in recent decades have devoted illustrated articles and even a special issue to Ambrosi,[2] for it reflects the thought of a man by whom the artist was influenced: Carl Huter (1861–1912), the discoverer of the Grundkörperbau- und Naturelltypen (body-build and constitutional types) and a pioneer in the study of psychophysiology. Considering Ambrosi's great handicap and his lifelong heroic efforts to overcome it and compensate for it, it is only logical that at least one noted psychoanalyst should have attempted to interpret Ambrosi's prolific and wide-ranging creativity in psychoanalytic terms.

Augustus Arthur Matthias Joseph Ambrosi was born on February 24th, 1893 at Eisenstadt in the Burgenland (then part of Western Hungary and known as Kismarton) as the youngest of five sons of Friedrich Ambrosi, a k.u.k. (imperial and royal) army officer who was also (and primarily) a musician and painter. His equally artistic Hungarian mother, Nathalie de Langh, the daughter of one of Metternich's archivists, had been raised on the Hungarian puszta. Gustinus was a *Tornisterkind* (army brat) who was at the tender age of 18 months taken to St. Pölten and then to Prague. His musical talent manifested itself early on, and at the age of four his parents began to instruct him in both the violin and the piano. In 1899 the boy came down with meningitis and became completely deaf on his seventh birthday. He is said to have smashed his fiddle—which would have been the first of a number of outbursts of rage, though these were mostly of the verbal variety.[3] Later he came to regard his deafness as a blessing, a shield from the multifarious disturbances and distractions of the world, and a spur to inwardness.[4] At any rate, his son's tragedy was a severe blow to the elder Ambrosi, who had hoped to have his frustrated artistic ambitions realized in his son, and after years of severe depression he died in a Prague mental institution in November 1908. After the death of her favorite son in Siberian captivity in 1916, the narrowly religious mother became a bit of a recluse, and she outlived her husband by three decades.[5] For several years Gustinus Ambrosi received instruction at an institution at Smichov in Prague, but he was self-taught to an astonishing degree and by the age of thirteen was reading the Bible, Dante, Plato, Horace, and Nietzsche. Having been apprenticed to Jakob Kozourek, a Prague master of several trades, the vigorous young man became an accomplished carpenter, locksmith, and stone mason as well as a sculptor, and he thought of handicraft as the exalted foundation and indeed the goddess of all art.

Ambrosi characterized death, specifically that of his father, as his spiritual teacher. His sculpture "Der Verstoßene" (The Outcast, 1909), depicting the hunched-up figure of a man, may be regarded as a monument to his father as well as a poignant portrayal of his own isolation and loneliness. However, it was the sculpture "Der Mann mit dem gebrochenen Genick" (The Man With the Broken Neck), reminiscent of Auguste Rodin's "Man With the Broken Nose," that made the sixteen-year-old famous. This depiction, ultimately in marble, of a roofer who had plunged to his death while working on the same Graz building as Ambrosi undoubtedly has autobiographical significance as a haunting likeness of a human being deprived of speech, but this powerful personal statement was soon perceived as a frightening symbol of the collapse of a stable humanistic order and as an adumbration of nameless horrors to come that were to strike millions as dumb as that woeful workman.

When Ambrosi was fourteen, he already produced a terracotta model of the Belgian artist Constantin Meunier, and at age seventeen Elizabeth Foerster-Nietzsche commissioned a bronze bust of Friedrich Nietzsche from him, making her brother's death mask available for that purpose. The following year the artist made a bronze bust from life of August Strindberg, to whom he had written a few years earlier that deafness meant the ability to hear the language of nature ("Taubheit is das Gehör für die Sprache der Natur").

After the completion of his training ("Freisprechung"), early exhibits, and other successes in Graz, Ambrosi and his mother in 1912 moved to Vienna, where the artist was to spend the rest of his life and create as many as 2500 sculptures in plaster, bronze, marble, iron, wood, aluminum, tin, and clay.[6] Hundreds of these were plundered, destroyed, or damaged by the ravages of wartime. These sculptures range from several hundred busts that constitute a veritable Who's Who in European culture and government to such large allegoric, mythological, and symbolic sculptures as "Der opfernde Abel" (Abel Sacrificing, 1917), "Promethidenlos" (Prometheans' Lot, 1917-18), "Die Erschaffung Adams" (The Creation of Adam, 1919), "Der Mensch und das Schicksal" (Man and Fate, 1920), "Kain" (1922), "Ikaros" (1923), "Phaidros" (1954), and "Die Blüte" (The Blossom, 1965-69). Among his monuments may be mentioned one of Franz Schubert in Vienna and one of Engelbert Dollfuß in Graz, but plans for a Joseph Haydn monument in Eisenstadt did not materialize. Among the noted writers portrayed by Ambrosi, some of whom became his friends and wrote about him, were Hugo von Hofmannsthal, Stefan Zweig, Romain Rolland, Gerhart Hauptmann, Rainer Maria Rilke, Peter Altenberg, Richard Dehmel, Franz Theodor Csokor, and Felix Braun. In 1919 Alfons Petzold described "the Viennese sculptor with the Giotto figure and the Florentine head of a young Medici aristocrat" as "the most revolutionary artist of Austria, if revolution can be defined as the violent uprising of long-suppressed forces bent on creating something new and great."[7] The art critic Fritz Karpfen first wrote about Ambrosi in the same year and published a book about him in 1923.

It did not take art and literary critics long to discern in Ambrosi certain Promethean qualities of Renaissance artistry. The ancestry of the man who was the prototype of a titan striving to endure and transmute a harsh fate in creative solitude and Dionysian self-affirmation has been traced back to 15th–century Florence (according to other sources, to Trieste). Ambrosi was keenly aware of this heritage and viewed himself as a latter-day Renaissance artist. "Hätte es Michelangelo nie gegeben, ich hätte ihn erfunden!" (If Michelangelo had never existed, I would have invented him), he once said.[8] Ambrosi managed to find a link between Michelangelo, the ecstatic biblical man *par excellence* (to whom he planned to devote a hymnic biography), and Rodin, to him the synthesis of modern man, whose naturalistic style the Austrian strove to emulate.

Like Michelangelo, Ambrosi early on felt an urge to give literary as well as plastic expression to his feelings and insights. This in turn related him to Rodin, who, as Rilke has told us, was bent on listening to his inner voice and plumbing his own depth. Ambrosi felt that he was making music in words when he wrote poetry and in stone and metal when he sculpted. The artist started writing when barely into his teens and produced, in addition to voluminous diaries, some stories and plays, but it is logical that the strictest and most disciplined of all lyric forms, the sonnet, should have become his favorite and most characteristic form of literary expression. Through these poetic invocations, exhortations, and monologues Ambrosi attempted to breathe life into his stones and to integrate himself into an exalted tradition.[9] The form of the sonnet was intended to help him escape "ewigen Wechsels ewiger Wahn" (the eternal delusion of eternal change).[10] Far from being the production of an aesthete, Ambrosi's poetry was intended to help himself and others cope with life and may be regarded as a running commentary on his very existence and an *apologia pro vita et arte sua,* reflecting his basic motif "Alles Leid ist Gnade" (All suffering is grace). Only a small fraction of his thousands of poems was printed in five volumes; of his series of sonnets addressed to Savonarola, Machiavelli, Michelangelo, Petrarca, Dante, and Shakespeare only a few appeared in *Festschriften,* catalogues, and the like, for he typically worked on these poems for decades and then deemed them too imperfect for publication.

In the forty-nine *Sonette an Gott,* begun at age sixteen and published in 1923 (Zürich-Leipzig-Vienna: Amalthea), the "O Mensch" rapture of the Expressionists is transformed into "O Herr" invocations of a man who has come to regard his tragedy as a blessing because it has enabled him to find *his* God and who, while intoning paeans of praise to the Lord, still vacillates between childlike faith in God, abysmal doubts, and fits of anger. Even as he praises the Christian God of love and employs the language of the church, the world of the Greek deities looms in the background as a counterpoise and challenge. The forty-six *Sonette vom Grabe einer Liebe,* published in 1926 (Vienna-Leipzig-New York: Stein Verlag) are a poetic expression of the failure of his second marriage, the "grave of a love"—to Leopoldine Luise Janik, called Did, for whose sake he had left the Catholic church. His first wife, the Graz teacher Anna Murmayer, bore him a daughter, Ingeborg (1919–1940), and Beate, whom he married in 1928, died in 1991. Ambrosi worked on the sixty-five *Sonette an Beethoven* for more than five decades and finally allowed them to be printed in 1974 (Vienna: Georg Prachner). In these poems of defiance as well as consolation Ambrosi communes with another artist who was vouchsafed the boon of pain and inspired to rage by it ("durch Pein begnadet und zur Wut entfacht," p. 29). The poet assures the musician, whose music he heard and played as a child, that his tones can penetrate Ambrosi's deafness ("Da wird die Taubheit plötzlich zum Gehör, / denn die Musik aus deinem tauben Hören / hallt in die Taubheit, der ich angehör" 20), that a deaf person can reach regions where music resounds as in a dream ("Der Taube kann sich hinbegeben / wo die Musik erklingt wie aus dem Traum," 65), and that deafness was not too high a price to pay for closeness to Beethoven ("Den bittern Kelch der Taubheit trank ich gern, / wußte ich doch: du warst mir niemals fern," 81).

For over two decades Ambrosi had *Neujahrsblätter* printed as a New Year's greeting for friends and admirers. Each of these contained, on two to eight pages, numerous illustrations as well as a poetic *Jahresspruch,* usually in a facsimile of the poet's handwriting. These hortatory or didactic poems, rarely sonnets, constitute *Gebrauchslyrik,* practical wisdom, often an interpretation of the sculptor's art. The *Jahresblatt* for 1955 is a pictorial record of a rescue: the chaos and destruction of 1945 is juxtaposed with the new productivity and creative order of 1954. The richly illustrated *Jahresblatt* for 1960 presents four variations on the theme of the sculptor's busts, but the poems contain little more than the rather trite observation that an artist's endeavor is to capture mankind in imperishable fashion. The New Year's greeting for 1972 depicts "Leid und Freude" (Sorrow and Joy), a dual statue in marble and bronze, along with this characteristic Ambrosian thought: "Gutes wird durch Leiden oft vollbracht" (The good is often accomplished through suffering). To the well–wishers on the occasion of his sixty-fifth birthday in February 1958 Ambrosi responded with a juxtaposition of a recent photograph with the likeness of the ten-year old boy, who seemed cheerful enough despite his affliction.

After my interest in Stefan Zweig had led me to correspond with Ambrosi for a year or two, my only meeting with the writer's longtime friend took place in Vienna in the summer of 1955. In his historic studio in the Prater, which had been utilized for the World's Fair of 1873 and had once been occupied by the painter Anselm Feuerbach and the sculptor Kaspar Zumbusch, we communicated with each other in the manner of Beethoven's *Konversationshefte.*[11] Shortly thereafter I made part of my collection of Ambrosiana available to Dr. Felix Deutsch, a Viennese-born Boston psychoanalyst[12] who was working on the psychology of the sculptor and was pleased to add Ambrosi to his other exemplars, Rodin and Käthe Kollwitz, gaining additional insight by asking a friend, the Viennese actor Paul Barnay, to get in touch with the artist.[13] In December 1955 Deutsch wrote me that Ambrosi had confirmed what he had found in the life history and works of Käthe Kollwitz—namely, that the wellsprings of the artist's creativity lay deep in the experiences and fantasies of early childhood. In a paper on "The Creative Passion of the Artist and Its Synaesthetic Aspects," delivered before the Boston Psychoanalytic Society in June 1957, Deutsch sees Ambrosi's artistic and poetic work as a compulsion to make restitution, as a quest for the recovery of his lost identity by creating a new reality through his art, and as an attempt to bring his father back to life in the busts of the great men with which he surrounded himself. According to Deutsch, "The passionate need for restitution of this image of a brother, of a father, and last not least of himself, who had lost a part of his body, gave his artistic work an almost hypomanic character."[14] The psychoanalyst believes that Ambrosi's super–Whitmanesque feelings might have led to insanity if he had not been able to transmute them into artistic productions. Thus he turned the past into "versteinte Gegenwart" (petrified present—*Die Sonette an Gott,* p. 13). Since his love was petrified and buried in the past, the sculptor himself became a bisexual love object; in his self-admiration he loved the stone and kept creating his own images through it. Deutsch regards Ambrosi's poems as "the monologues in which the stones come to life. Using the pen to write his sonnets is for him only a complementary act of sculpting which creates the union of the timeless realities." When the poet writes "O Gott, erlaube, daß ich mit dir Zwiesprache pflege" (O God, permit me to engage in a dialogue with you) and "Du schweigst, nun reden mir die kalten Steine" (You are silent; now the cold stones talk to me—*ibid.,*6), this might indicate that Ambrosi has resurrected his father for himself, calls him God, and attempts to converse with an all-powerful father image. The multiplicity of human heads and figures created by the sculptor may also be interpreted as a constant and ultimately futile search for physical perfection.

Ambrosi's New Year's message for 1974 was in the nature of a farewell: "Im 81. Lebensjahr befindlich, ziehe ich mich gänzlich zurück in meine taube Totenstille, die schon dem Jüngling Ausbruch war zu geistigem Schaffen und nun Heimkehr ist zu sich selbst" (In my eighty-first year I am withdrawing completely into my deaf, deathly silence which represented a way out to intellectual creativity for me when I was young and now represents a return to my own self). In August 1974 he wrote to his biographer Franz Renisch: "Ich war nie ein lauter, lärmender, geltungsbedürftiger, eitler Streber, sondern einer, der tief in den Geist seines Handwerks hineinzuleiden verstanden hat und die Geduld hatte, mit welcher Planeten wachsen" (I was never a loud, noisy, self-important, vain careerist, but a man who knew how to suffer his way deep into the spirit of his handicraft and had the patience with which planets grow.) A *Leistungsethiker,* a hero of creative work in Thomas Mann's sense, Ambrosi was able to master his fate, endure his life, and feel sheltered in a homeland only through enormous strength, discipline, and productivity. When he felt his physical powers declining, realized that the naturalistic monumentality and pathos of his artistic and poetic creations were not in tune with modern tastes and sensibilities, and saw other Austrian artists, notably the sculptor Fritz Wotruba, eclipsing him in popular appeal and official favor, he committed a deed that he had repeatedly condemned in others, particularly his friend Stefan Zweig, and ended his own life by taking poison in July 1975. He was buried with due honors in Graz. But surely the meaning of his eminently heroic and productive life is better expressed in a line from the *Festprolog* that

Ambrosi wrote for the 1947 Haydn Festival in Eisenstadt: "Denn wer das Schwere seines Erdenlebens zum Segen sich umformt, lebt nicht vergebens."[15] (For anyone who transmutes the burden of his earthly life into a blessing does not live in vain.)

Notes

1. In a diary entry of October 11, 1916 Ambrosi expressed the idea of leaving mankind a museum of his works, as Thorvaldsen had done in Copenhagen, Canova in Bassano, and Rodin planned to do in Paris.
2. See the issues of April and December 1970, May 1971, August 1972, March 1973, and the memorial issue of 1976-77.
3. Franz Renisch of Vienna, the author of a multivolume picture biography of Ambrosi (1990 ff.), doubts the fiddle-smashing episode as well as the widely circulated story that the violin virtuoso Pablo de Sarasate, a friend of the elder Ambrosi, had offered to take the child to Spain for further instruction.
4. A diary entry of October 5, 1920 describes *Verzicht* (renunciation) as a great good fortune, wisdom, freedom, and happiness.
5. Renisch regards the relationship between the son and the mother as comparable to that between Peer Gynt and Mother Aase. According to him, Ambrosi's mother vainly tried to curb her son's multifarious fantasies and fabrications. She was repelled by the massive nudity of her son's creations and never accepted him as a sculptor, yet he remained indissolubly tied to her.
6. Renisch believes that this number, given out by the artist and widely accepted, is greatly exaggerated.
7. "...der Wiener Bildhauer mit der Giottogestalt und dem florentinischen Kopf eines mediceischen Fürstenjünglings...der revolutionärste Künstler Österreichs, wenn unter Revolution das gewaltsame Sichaufbäumen langunterdrückter, Neues und Großes gestaltenwollender Kräfte zu verstehen ist"—*Die Zeit,* Nov. 16, 1919; reprinted in *Ambrosi–Festschrift,* Vienna: Burgenland Verlag, 1948, p. 15.
8. Fritz Karpfen, *Gustinus Ambrosi.* Leipzig–Vienna: Thyrson Verlag, 1923, p. 70.
9. In his article "Gustinus Ambrosi—der Dichter" Rolf Engert considers it miraculous that the sonnets of Dante, Petrarca, Michelangelo, Camoens, Leconte de Lisle, Shakespeare, Gryphius, Fleming, Goethe, Bürger, Platen, Hebbel, Rilke, Labé, and Barrett-Browning form a great unity despite all differences of language, period, and personality (Catalogue of Ambrosi exhibit at Landesmuseum, Graz. Graz: Leykam, May 1937, p. 39).

10. Ambrosi, *Das Buch der Einschau,* Vienna-Stuttgart: Georg Prachner, 1959, p. 35. This collection of forty-nine poems, in which Ambrosi includes twelve of his sculptures, shows the close connection between his art and his poetry to particular advantage.
11. Ambrosi permitted me to take the sheets along and have them bound. He was actually able to make himself understood, but that was not enough for him, and so he reserved his speech only for special occasions, such as the ceremony at Eisenstadt in 1954, when Ambrosi was asked to restore Haydn's skull, which had been in the care of a 19th–century anatomist, to the coffin reposing in a church. He once wrote that he had refused to learn lip-reading, because he was not interested in determining which of his partners in conversation had false teeth!
12. Dr. Deutsch was Sigmund Freud's private physician in Vienna at the time when Freud's cancer of the jaw was diagnosed.
13. In a letter dated April 29, 1956 Ambrosi wrote Barnay: "Ich arbeite wie die alten Meister, ich verstehe unter geistigem Schaffen die *Hingabe* und die Herzensfreude, dem Nächsten einen Blick in sein eigenes wertvolles Innere zu vermitteln" (I work as the old masters did. My idea of intellectual creativity is *dedication* and the heartfelt joy that comes from giving one's fellow man an insight into his own valuable soul).
14. This and the following quotations are taken from Dr. Deutsch's letters to me and from the typescript of his talk, which is in my possession.
15. *Festprolog zur Eröffnung der Haydn-Festspiele in Eisenstadt,* spoken on May 25 and 31, 1947, by the actors Fred Liewehr and Herbert Alsen, privately printed (p. 10).

THE WIENERLIED AS THE PSYCHOGRAPH OF A POPULATION

Has there ever been a city as celebrated in song as Vienna? A city that has celebrated itself and inhabitants who have glorified themselves and their way of life to such an extent? Surely there are other old and beloved cities with a rich tradition, and there must be something to sing about "sous les toits de Paris" or "on the sidewalks of New York," "a helluva town" where once "every street" was "a boulevard." Yes, songs have been written in praise of Paris, New York, Berlin, and London, though one hardly speaks of a London song, a *chanson de Paris,* or a Berliner Lied the way one speaks of a Wiener Lied (or more properly, Wienerlied, for in theory every one of Franz Schubert's 650 solo songs could be called a Wiener Lied). But while other cities have inspired a few or a few dozen songs, thousands upon thousands of Wienerlieder, most of them in three-quarter or two-quarter time, in waltz or march tempo, and usually in both, have come into being in a rare musical-literary case of self-assertion, self-analysis, self-glorification, and even self-pity. The frequently maudlin Wienerlied is nothing short of the psychograph of a population, and it seems to embody all the widely disseminated clichés about Vienna and the Viennese which it has, in fact, helped to create. Typically given to self-doubt and feelings of inferiority, the "little people" of Vienna have used the Wienerlied as a kind of "security blanket." These songs are generally reflective of great *joie de vivre,* but the other side of the coin is the large suicide rate of the Viennese, and the "beautiful blue" Danube has always beckoned as an eminently traditional and mystical way out of life's miseries.

There is something timeless and ageless about these lovely songs which celebrate the joy of life even as they mourn its decline and yearn for the "good old days;" they are truly folksongs and "evergreens." Who knows, or cares, when or by whom "Wien, Wien nur du allein" ("Vienna, City of My Dreams": "I hear you calling me, lovely Vienna, so gay and free...") was written? This, incidentally, is one of the very few internationally known of these songs, for many of them are written in the Viennese dialect and are thus virtually untranslatable; they do not travel well and are no more exportable than the potent new wine that accompanies and indeed inspired them. "Vienna, City of My Dreams" was written in 1913 by Rudolf Sieczynski, a government official and non-musician. Perhaps it is no accident that another relatively exportable Wienerlied, the famous "Fiakerlied," reflective of a Viennese cabby's pride in his city, its traditions, and his craft, was created a few decades earlier by another non-musician, the jurist Gustav Pick (one of a number of Jews, including Alexander Krakauer and Hermann Leopoldi, who have sung the praises of their notoriously anti-Semitic city). The prolific Ralph Benatzky created his famous song about the new wine of Vienna's Grinzing district during World War I, and Robert Stolz, in his last decades perhaps Grinzing's most famous resident, contributed more than fifty songs to this genre, exulting that "Im Prater blühn wieder die Bäume" (known, though seldom performed, in English as "The Woods of Vienna Are Calling") and intoning paeans of praise to a city that is thought to become especially beautiful at night, to the Vienna Woods, to springtime in Vienna, to the city's tiny streets, its cafés, its waltzes, its lovely women, and particularly that elixir of life, its special wine. To refer to the most celebrated of Stolz's evergreens (written in Berlin!), presumably it is in Vienna that two hearts beat in three-quarter time most frequently.

The near-homonymy of Wien and Wein, with Weib (woman) thrown in for good measure (and to inspire a Wienerlied thus titled), is highly symptomatic, for Vienna has something that other cities do not have (at least in such profusion and with the same mystique) and that, in the final analysis, accounts for the proliferation of Wienerlieder: the Heurigen, the winegardens in outlying districts where the new wine is dispensed by a vintner who indicates its availability and his special privilege by affixing green branches over the entrance to his establishment. ("Ausg'steckt is" is the Viennese designation for this practice; a less colorful word is used in Germany: Buschenschenke). The wine, which is called "der Heurige" as well, is both the source and the mouth (in every sense of the word) of the Wienerlied, the river Lethe of the Viennese, a source of relaxation and a chance to forget what cannot be changed. In the shifting fortunes of the Viennese and their old city this wine has been the great constant factor; it manages to silence even the traditional "Raunzertum," the grousing and carping of the Viennese, and brings their (self-diagnosed) "goldenes Wienerherz" (heart of gold) to the fore, though anyone who has witnessed their behavior in 1938 and the succeeding years tends to believe that it is made of lesser material. The only complaint of the jolly drinkers concerns the not always optimal conditions under which the wine may be enjoyed and the decline of the vaunted *Gemütlichkeit* in an increasingly hectic and depersonalized modern age. Wine-drinking in the bosom of nature has become an almost religious rite, one that is bound to find favor in God's eyes. The Heuriger, both the wine and the winegarden (though the former may also be imbibed indoors, in a Stadtheurigen in town), provides security and self-assurance as well as therapy, inducing a euphoric and lachrymose state in its drinkers and patrons. Yet the idyllic vinicultural atmosphere also leads the hedonistic Viennese to philosophize and reflect on the transitoriness of life, to abreact certain complexes, be they guilt feelings or simply sadness about the human condition. At the Heurigen a Viennese musters his *Galgenhumor* (gallows humor) and comes to the conclusion that the situation is desperate but not serious. This is where he longs for his lost innocence, for the homely wisdom of the sentimentally recalled Biedermeier period, the early decades of the 19th century that preceded revolutionary strife and all the economic, sociological, and psychological problems of industrialization and the rise of the big cities, for the *Backhendlzeit* symbolized by the greatly enjoyed chicken roasted on a spit, for a nostalgically glimpsed golden age of stability, simplicity, and the kind of resignation that the great comic dramatist and social satirist Johann Nepomuk Nestroy once called the noblest "nation." It is not surprising, then, that despite their surface gaiety many Wienerlieder are basically elegies, melancholy and even fatalistic expressions of a sense of life rooted in the Hispanic-Catholic tradition of the Baroque Age. The lyrics are often consolatory, and the "last things"—death and sometimes even the hereafter—are presented quite artistically and aesthetically, even if this amounts to self-deception. In one of his early stories, "Der verlogene Heurige" (The Mendacious Winegarden), the Austrian-Jewish essayist and critic Alfred Polgar describes a man who takes all those Wienerlieder literally and comes to grief because he so completely identifies with the philosophy expressed in them—so to speak, the birth of tragedy from the spirit of music.

A Latin song in praise of Vindobona (the Roman name of the city later known as Wien) may be traced back to the 13th century, but "O du lieber Augustin" is sometimes regarded as the ancestor of the Wienerlied. It cannot be determined, however, whether the legendary Augustin, who is said to have slept off his inebriation in a pit full of corpses during Vienna's plague epidemic of 1679 without suffering harm, is identical with a musician named Marx Augustin, who is known to have died around 1705. The texts of Viennese popular songs were not printed until the end of the eighteenth century, but the Wienerlied as we know it today originated in the nineteenth. By 1850 these songs existed in profusion and were sung in wine cellars and courtyards, at church fairs and vaudeville palaces, and in the establishments of the Prater, Vienna's fabled pleasure ground. Of the numerous popular Volkssänger and Volkssängerinnen who performed them may be mentioned J.B. Moser, Johann Fürst, Franz Kriebaum, Wenzel Seidl, Luise Montag, Antonie Mansfeld, Edmund Guschelbauer, Hansi Führer, and Emilie Tureczek-Demel (the "Fiaker-Mili" of the Hofmannsthal-Strauss opera *Arabella*). It should be noted that while these performers were quite successful and beloved, many of them led immoderate, dissolute, unhappy lives and seemed predestined for an early grave.

During the last decades of the Austro-Hungarian empire the Wienerlied was part of the cement that held the several nations together. The tensions, strife, disputes, and resentments among them are rarely expressed in these songs, for they are basically apolitical and limit themselves to an occasional reference to certain disturbing conditions and alarming trends. A Wienerlied written in 1912 even makes a virtue of this attitude: a Viennese avers that he likes to drink his wine in peace without being drawn into political disputes and is content to let the rest of the world go by. Still, at least one Wienerlied once served political purposes: Alois Kutschera's sentimental song "Weißt du, Muatterl, was i träumt hab?," presenting a sick child's vision of heaven, was given a different text and became the "Lobtau-Lied," protesting the harsh punishment meted out to workers in a Dresden suburb in 1898 (the vision there being of the house of correction).

Visions of heaven abound in the Wienerlied. Vienna is seen as the nearby place where angels ("die Engerln") spend their vacations, for heaven is thought to adjoin the Grinzing heights. The green wreath over a vintner's gate is equated with the pearly gates. In "Du guater Himmelvoder" Alexander Krakauer (a law student who succumbed to tuberculosis in 1894 at age 28) tells the heavenly father that Vienna, apostrophized in another of his songs as his sweetheart dwelling by the banks of the Danube, is paradise enough for him.

A fresh impetus was given the Wienerlied by the founding of the Schrammel Quartet in 1878. Even though both Schrammel brothers, Johann (Hanns) and Josef, died before 1900 at the age of forty (and with such a phenomenon cirrhosis of the liver is a likely diagnosis), they had a lasting influence as composers and performers, establishing an ensemble comprised of a high clarinet (later replaced with an accordion), two violins, and a guitar as the classic accompaniment of Heurigen singing. (If there is only one instrument, it is likely to be a zither). To this day a Viennese is prepared to forego even the proverbial "schöne Leich" (sumptuous funeral) in favor of a simple Schrammel ensemble playing at his funeral. One Schrammel march, to which several sets of lyrics have been added and which can also be sung as a waltz, has gone around the world under the title "Wien bleibt Wien" ("Vienna Forever").

A performing poet who helped to rescue the Wienerlied from mediocrity and vulgarity was Wilhelm Wiesberg (originally named Bergamenter). Before his death in 1896 (at age forty-six), Wiesberg managed to write the text of more than a thousand Wienerlieder, many of which were set to music by the even more prolific Johann Sioly. One of their most enduring creations is "Das hat ka Goethe g'schriebn," an attractive presentation of the simple humanity and morality of ordinary Viennese citizens. The words of an inarticulate workingman wooing a girl, of a solicitous father, of a child praying for her sick mother, and of a man sharing what little he has with a destitute person may not be by a genius like Goethe or Schiller, but "'s klingt halt doch so voller Poesie" (yet they sound very poetic).

During the First World War the Wienerlied had a special patriotic function to perform. An outstanding example (and the bane of the existence of Karl Kraus, that vitriolic Viennese satirist and pacifist) is the mildly xenophobic "Draußen im Schönbrunnerpark" by Fritz Grünbaum and Ralph Benatzky, a Wienerlied that sings the praises of Emperor Franz Joseph and pledges the best efforts of the populace so the "dear good old gentlemen" might take it easy in his Schönbrunn palace. (Years later Ralph Benatzky included his tune in his celebrated operetta *The White Horse Inn,* sung to a different text, of his own devising, by—who else?—the dear good old gentleman himself. During World War II the exiled Benatzky wrote a nostalgic, bilingual "Wienerlied in New York").

The ravages of the war and the difficult postwar period faced by a truncated and barely viable Austria silenced the Wienerlied for a time, for it was fighting a losing rearguard action against the encroachments of new times and the blandishments of new form and tastes. (A similar fight has been going on in recent decades, for the "Austropop" scene has sometimes excluded and spurned the Wienerlied—a phenomenon observable in other countries as well; for example, in the U.S. "rock 'n' schlock" has, at least as far as young people are concerned, eclipsed the songs of Irving Berlin, Cole Porter, Jerome Kern, and the Gershwins).

In the difficult interwar years Hermann Leopoldi hymned Vienna as a "dying fairy-tale city with a friendly smile even in death." However, gifted men like Leopoldi, Stolz, Benatzky, Robert Gilbert, Ernst Arnold, and Hans Lang successfully and memorably adapted the form to a "new realism," giving it a more cabaret-like flavor and snappier rhythm. In the late 1920s Leopoldi had a "Mr. Yankee Doodle" from Michigan, who was served only "Tea for Two" and "Valencia" at the Heurigen, make a plea for more Wienerlieder, and other writers and composers addressed the "golden" Wienerlied directly, telling it not to worry, that its time would come again. It did, and the genre survived not only the troublous years between the wars but World War II and its aftermath as well. "Where has all that gone, where?" asked Robert Gilbert and Robert Stolz, both emigrants who had returned to a war-torn Europe from exile in the United States, in a doleful Wienerlied written in slow march tempo. At any rate, Wienerlieder are written even today, though a few of them reflect a Viennese's desire not to live to see skyscrapers disfiguring traditionally favored districts like Grinzing. Some of them pretend to be socially critical, anti-philistine protest songs, "Wienerlieder without schmaltz" telling it "like it is," but the frequently parodistic, hard-bitten products of Helmut Qualtinger, Gerhard Bronner, Carl Merz, Peter Wehle (the author of a book about the Wienerlied that purports to be a "satiric declaration of love"), Arik Brauer, André Heller, Peter Henisch, Karl Hodina, Erika Pluhar, Cilli Mikulik, Georg Kreisler (who claims in one of his anti-Wienerlieder that Vienna would be really beautiful without those Viennese), and many others are vintage Wienerlieder nevertheless. Many of these multiply gifted men and women have had notable careers as artists, actors, or singers, but they have not been able to escape the undeniable lure of the Wienerlied. In performing and recording the wealth of traditional Wienerlieder, the Heurigen singers, most of them with no more than average voices, were long ago joined by more serious and often internationally renowned artists like Lotte Lehmann, Erich Kunz, Julius Patzak, Richard Tauber (himself the composer of a Wienerlied, "Warum ist Wien ein Märchen?"), Heinz Holecek, Hilde Gueden, Leo Slezak, Beverly Sills, Richard Tucker, Hermann Prey, and Placido Domingo.

As long as there are Viennese (or ex-Viennese) whose "heart is a picturebook of Old Vienna;" as long as St. Stephen's Cathedral, lovingly personalized as "der Steffl," still stands and the "beautiful blue" Danube flows through (or, at any rate, near) Vienna; as long as a Viennese can view the world as "a bouquet of flowers from which Vienna peeks out;" as long as there is "a little lantern" or the "little star of Nußdorf" to guide a wine-drinker's faltering steps; as long as a Viennese can harbor hopes of being reunited, in that big Viennese café in heaven, with Sindelar and Siesta the soccer stars of yesteryear, the cabaret wits Fritz Grünbaum and Karl Farkas, and the comic geniuses Hans Moser and Armin Berg; as long as he can commune, via his magic "fiacre lantern," with great spirits of the past (Mayor Karl Lueger, the Emperor's friend Katharina Schratt, hapless Crown Prince Rudolf's whistling and singing cabby Bratfisch, the popular singing actor Alexander Girardi, and even the dear good old gentleman of Schönbrunn himself); as long as there is no shortage of music and wine and a Viennese consequently need not pack up his things and leave, there is no reason to fear that the population of Vienna will not continue to express itself in the Wienerlied and that the genre will not endure.

THE JEWISHNESS OF FRANZ KAFKA

Many years ago Professor Sol Liptzin undertook to trace the Jewishness of German writers in his book *Germany's Stepchildren,* and more recently, during the second "Dialogue in Israel," he stated that "Jewish books may be defined as books which embody Jewish wisdom of the past, Jewish insight of the present, and Jewish messianism directed toward the future, books which communicate values, visions, attitudes and aspirations of the Jewish religious, cultural, and historic community, regardless in what language these books are written."

Earlier Ludwig Lewisohn had given an equally serviceable, albeit controversial definition: "A Jewish book is a book by a Jew who knows that his ultimate self is Jewish and that his creativity and that deepest self are one...Jewish literature consists of those books, written in whatever age or tongue, whose authors knew that they were *jüdische Menschen."*

Consonant with these definitions, substantial evidence can be marshalled to justify the thesis that Franz Kafka was—to the extent that he could be anything—a *homo judaicus,* that there *is* Jewish significance in his books, that in Kafka we find not only Jewishness but something even rarer in a writer: *Yiddishkeit.*

Franz Kafka was a Jew living in Czechoslovakia who wrote in German. The ancient Jewish community of Prague has been called "the mother of Jewry." Its origin was in Eastern Europe, and the legacy of Slavic traditions in language and culture is evident in the Hebrew writings of the twelfth and thirteenth centuries. Later, the influx of Jews into Prague was mainly from Germany. Throughout the Middle Ages Prague Jewry maintained a vital connection with the Czech language and culture; the first Czech grammarian was a Talmudist from the Prague ghetto.

But there was a dual cultural stream. It is well to remember that the first German–language university was founded not in Germany, but in Prague—in 1348, by Charles IV; it was there that Franz Kafka took his doctorate of laws in 1906. Because of pressure from the Habsburg emperors, the Germanization of Prague Jewry gradually came about, particularly in the eighteenth century, at the time of Maria Theresa and the "enlightened despot" Joseph II, whose Edict of Tolerance in 1781 for all practical purposes abolished the ghetto (although the Jews did not obtain full civil rights until 1860).

The Jews now shared in German culture to an ever-increasing extent, but this coincided with the spiritual and cultural revival of the Czech people. Thus the German-Jewish population of Prague became again what it had once been: a small minority, more and more cut off from the homogeneous Czech population, oriented toward Germany, yet very different from the uncongenial Sudeten Germans, whose outlook and aspirations were not those of the Jews.

In Kafka's time, 34,000 of the 415,000 inhabitants of Prague were German-speaking, and the Jews formed but one segment of these. Like most of his fellow Jews in Prague, Kafka was a *Bildungsdeutscher* only. Lacking the vitalizing influence of a local dialect, Prague German was a curiously disembodied and sterile instrument. One detects in Kafka a yearning to transcend the limitations of this language and attain a closer communion with his Jewish roots, as witness this diary entry of October, 1911:

> Yesterday it occurred to me that I did not always love my mother as she deserved and as I could, only because the German language prevented it. The Jewish mother is no *Mutter,* to call her *Mutter* makes her a little comic; we give a Jewish woman the name of a German mother, but forget

> the contradiction that sinks into the emotions so much the more heavily; *Mutter* is peculiarly German for the Jew, it unconsciously contains, together with the Christian splendor, Christian coldness also; the Jewish woman who is called *Mutter* therefore becomes not only comic but strange. *Mama* would be a better name if only one didn't imagine *Mutter* behind it. I believe that it is only the memories of the ghetto that still preserve the Jewish family, for the word *Vater* too is far from meaning the Jewish father.

Still, in more ways than one, Kafka was an inhabitant of a ghetto—no longer a religious or a political ghetto, but a linguistic, cultural, social one. Walking through the streets of Prague with uncertain steps, Kafka felt like a spook of bygone times—so he said—for the unhealthy old ghetto was much more real within him than the hygienic new city around him; within him the dark corners, mysterious hallways, dirty courtyards, and noisy taverns were still alive.

When Kafka was growing up, the German Jew in Prague was, typically, an industrialist, a prosperous businessman, a leading bank official, a doctor or a lawyer with a large practice, or a university professor. The Jews almost monopolized wholesale merchandising, the import and export trade. Their workers and domestic servants were Czechs, and, in many cases, so were their lovers. In German-Jewish circles, Czech was spoken only to these workers, domestics, and paramours.

Next to Viennese Jewry, the Prague Jews were the cultural elite of the Habsburg monarchy. Remaining aloof from everything Czech, only marginally Jewish in a religious and cultural sense, but also repelled by German patriotism of the Sudeten variety, the German-speaking Jew of Prague (and no one felt this more starkly than Kafka) was a stranger in three senses: as a Jew by blood and creed; as a prosperous citizen in the midst of petit bourgeois and proletarians; and as a "German," but not one who was surrounded and backed up by a German nation. These people were almost exiles in their own country, and while many were never even quite conscious of their strange situation, some intellectuals did realize it and tried to escape from the Prague ghetto, out into the world.

In his book *Franz Kafka and Prague,* Pavel Eisner makes the point that Jewish men of letters fled this spiritual ghetto in various ways.

> Franz Werfel escaped through his connections with Vienna, through his cult of the Southern Baroque, through his praise of Verdi in programmatic contrast with the traditional Wagner cult of the Prague German Jews, and above all (a notable instance of sublimated erotic symbiosis) through his exaltation of the Czech nurse to the position of a saint, of a refuge from the world and epitome of all purity and meekness...Max Brod escaped through his fervent Zionism, but also through immersion in the most authentically Czech music of a man like Leoš Janáček...Egon Erwin Kisch freed himself through his world traveling and his radical socialism...Willy Haas did so by migrating to Berlin.

And so, particularly in the early part of this century, there was a veritable outpouring of Jewish genius from Prague, Bohemia and Moravia.

Franz Kafka was neither strong nor lucky enough to effect an escape except through his writing. He was a compulsive writer; he once called writing a form of prayer. He had certain things in common with the Expressionist writers of his generation, notably their rebellion against the father generation. "My writing was all about you," Franz wrote his father Hermann Kafka. "All I did there, after all, was to bemoan what I could not bemoan upon your breast." Kafka's entire work may thus be viewed as one great attempt to escape from the overt and covert tyranny of his father.

The letter to his father which Kafka wrote in 1919 and which never reached its addressee is a literary and personal document of great importance, Kafka's fullest attempt at an autobiography, an *apologia pro vita sua.* It is Kafka's sincere and presumably agonizing attempt at justifying himself to his father, a patriarchal, strong-willed, self-satisfied, healthy extrovert, basically a well-meaning person proud of his business acumen, a man whose failure to understand the genius, aspirations and problems of his gifted son had produced a serious estrangement between the two. (It should be noted that a number of Jewish writers of Kafka's generation—natives of Prague or Vienna or Berlin—encountered similar apathy and even active opposition on the part of their successful industrialist fathers; Stefan Zweig, Siegfried Trebitsch, and Franz Werfel are cases in point.)

When he wrote his letter, Kafka was aware of the things his father held against him: his writings, few of which had been published and which, moreover, his father did not understand; his failure to marry, establish a home and found a family (the subject of countless, ever-recurring, excruciating self-reproaches on Kafka's part); his timidity and obstinacy; and his seeming indifference to Judaism. This last point is a crucial one. Kafka berates his father for having passed on to him but a meaningless scrap of Judaism and for pretending that these superficial trappings of Jewishness were the genuine article, for believing "in the absolute rightness of the opinions of a certain class of Jewish business-men." Since the father disliked and distrusted all his son's occupations, he apparently resented the writer's attempts to deepen his Jewish heritage and approach Judaism on a more spiritual and meaningful plane.

Kafka had occasion to come close to the *Ostjudentum,* the Eastern European brand of Jewishness, which fascinated him with its vitality. Our best documentation of this encounter is found in Kafka's voluminous *Diaries* (1910–23). In 1910 and 1911 a troupe of Yiddish actors was installed in a Prague coffee-house, and viewing these plays and becoming acquainted with some of the players constituted a Jewish education for Kafka. His diary chronicles many evenings "*bei den Juden*." Kafka thoughtfully comments on the plays of Avraham Goldfaden (*Schulamis, Bar Kochba*) and Jacob Gordin (*Gott, Mensch und Teufel*—the Jewish *Faust*); he discusses Talmudic lore and Jewish customs like the *mikveh* and the baking of matzos; he reflects on the Hasidic tales that Georg (Jiři) Langer told him (the same man who in Marienbad took him to visit a "wonder rabbi").

The same mind is at work here that later re-examined and boldly recast some basic mythological tales of ancient Israel, Greece, the Far

East and the West. Of interest also are Kafka's impressions of his nephew's circumcision, which he attended in 1911.

> Today, when I heard the *mohel's* assistant say the grace after meals and those present, aside from the two grandfathers, spent the time in dreams or boredom with a complete lack of understanding of the prayer, I saw Western European Judaism before me in a transition whose end is clearly unpredictable and about which those most closely affected are not concerned, but, like all people truly in transition, bear what is imposed upon them. It is so indisputable that these religious forms, which have reached their final end, have merely a historical character, even as they are practiced today, that only a short time was needed this very morning to interest the people present in the obsolete custom of circumcision and its half-sung prayers by describing it to them as something out of history.

On the first of November, 1911, Kafka "eagerly and happily" began to read the *History of the Jews* by Graetz. "Because my desire for it had far outrun the reading, it was at first stranger to me than I thought, and I had to stop here and there in order, by resting, to allow my Jewishness to collect itself." There is a touch of Kafkaesque humor in the *Diaries* when he records the favorite saying of the wife of the philosopher Moses Mendelssohn (which may be taken as a valid Jewish reaction to the mainstream of European culture at a time when Jews could be part of it but found that it only brought them new problems and unhappiness): "*Wie mies ist mir vor tout l'univers!*" (How sick and tired I am of the whole universe!) Later Kafka read and took notes on Pines' *Histoire de la Littérature Judéo-Allemande,* published in Paris in 1911, commenting on the *Haskalah* movement, the Baal Shem, and the giants of Yiddish literature: Mendele, Peretz, Sholem Aleichem.

Through his attendance of the plays "*bei den Juden,*" Kafka got close to some of the actors. One of his rare public appearances took place in February, 1912, when he introduced an evening of Yiddish recitations by Isak Löwy in the auditorium of the Jewish Town Hall (next to the fabled Altneu Synagogue in the Josefstadt, the Jewish quarter of

Prague) with a perceptive little speech on the Yiddish language (which Kafka, to be sure, called "*Jargon*"): "I would have you realize, ladies and gentlemen, how much more Yiddish you understand than you think..." In one of his conversations with Gustav Janouch, Kafka said: "I should like to run to those poor Jews of the ghetto, kiss the hem of their coats, and say not a word. I should be completely happy if only they would endure my presence in silence."

It must not be inferred from the above, however, that Eastern European *Yiddishkeit* was a fountain of life and hope, the solution for Kafka. He never quite found the bridge between western Jewishness as he knew it and eastern Jewishness as he yearned for it. In 1913, for example, he chronicled a meeting with the physician-writer Ernst Weiß, whom he called "a Jew of the kind that is closest to the type of the western Jew and to whom one therefore immediately feels close. The tremendous advantage of Christians who always have and enjoy such feelings of closeness in general intercourse, for instance a Christian Czech among Christian Czechs." The same kind of ambivalence is reflected in this anguished question: "What do I have in common with the Jews when I don't have anything in common with myself?" In later years Kafka carried on a notable correspondence with his Czech translator, Milena Jesenska, whom he regarded as his soul-mate. Milena, a non-Jew, was married to Ernst Pollak, a Jew, and this inspired Kafka to many musings and expressions on Judaism and Jewishness.

It has been alleged that Kafka in later life turned Zionist and that Zionism filled the spiritual void in his life. There appears to be some truth in this, though almost any statement one makes about Kafka is bound to be fraught with ambivalence. Kafka's friends Hugo Bergmann, Felix Weltsch, and Max Brod (all of whom eventually settled in Palestine) shared their own Zionist fervor with Kafka, who avidly studied Hebrew and seems to have had a practical rather than a merely theoretical interest in Zionism. When Janouch once asked him: "Are you convinced that Zionism is the right path?," Kafka is said to have replied: "The rightness or wrongness of the path is never recognized until one has reached one's goal. In any case, we are on our way."

Kafka's last great friend, Dora Dymant, was a pious Jewish girl from Poland whom he met in 1923 at a Jewish vacation colony near a Baltic resort and with whom he lived until the end of his brief life, enjoying a modicum of happiness and hope for the future. He and Dora, whose Orthodox background stood in the way of a possible marriage, toyed with the idea of emigrating to Palestine, although by then Kafka's progressive consumption of the larynx had made such plans little but morbid fancies. Kafka once said that he had refused to grasp the last fringes of the vanishing Jewish prayer shawl, as the Zionists had done, but Felix Weltsch continued to believe that Kafka was a Zionist and that the Zionist ideal was in keeping with Kafka's striving for an uncompromisingly pure life.

The story of Max Brod's editorship of Kafka's works is by now a thrice-told tale, and Kafka's request to his friend, whom he had met at the university in Prague, that all of his unpublished writings and diaries be destroyed after his death, is as well–known as Brod's well-premeditated failure to do so. One cannot help but wonder why Kafka entrusted Brod, of all people, with this melancholy mission, when he had ample reason to believe that Brod would be the least likely man to carry it out. The Freudians may well have a field day with this, as they have had with all of Kafka's enigmatic writings. They constitute one major school within the vast canon of Kafka criticism. Another is the generally social-cultural school of interpretation, and the third is the metaphysical-religious-mystical school.

It is this last to which Max Brod himself belonged, and for many years he tried, with varying success, to superimpose his own vibrant Judaism and Zionism upon the interpretation of Kafka. Brod views the three fragmentary novels *Amerika, The Trial* and *The Castle* as one great allegorical trilogy concerned with Jewish fate in the Diaspora. "The word 'Jew' hardly appears in *The Castle,*" Brod points out, "yet K., in the novel, straight from his Jewish soul, in a simple story, has said more about the situation of Jewry as a whole today than can be read in a hundred learned treatises."

Brod is not alone in his view that *The Trial* highlights the kind of guiltless guilt a Jew incurs in the modern world. Pavel Eisner points out that Josef K. in *The Trial* is arrested by a German (Rabensteiner), a Czech (Kullich) and a Jew (Kaminer); they may well represent the population of Prague. And if Josef K. is a Jew and has certain autobiographical features (although there is no evidence in the novel that he is Jewish; in fact, his mother goes to church), he is thrice guilty and fit to be arrested: as a Jew vis-à-vis the German population; as an assimilated Jew in the face of Orthodox Jewishness; and as a German vis-à-vis his Czech surroundings. In an essay entitled "Anti-Semitism as an Issue in the Trial of Kafka's Joseph K.," Josef Waldmeier, while conceding that all allegory is ambiguous, believes the Josef K. is doomed by an anti-Semitic judgment, with all the irrationality and finality that this implies.

Another Kafka work that lends itself to a Jewish interpretation is the story "Josephine the Singer, or the Mice Nation." This may be regarded as Kafka's picture of the Jewish people in the Diaspora and an expression of his community feeling for it. In Josephine the artist we have the ambivalent figure of the prophet within the Jewish people, which appears here in humorous, ironical form as one that has but a dim memory of its religious mission but proves most durable in the face of hardship and prosecution. The mice nation displays a curious mixture of shrewdness and guilelessness, an attachment to freedom despite a long history of bondage, to dreams despite a long history of harsh reality. The presence of Josephine teaches people the existence of something higher, but they do not quite surrender to it, remaining realists, believing and doubting at the same time—the Jewish people's attitude toward its spiritual heritage. Josephine's singing is presumably God's word, but it is only a pale carbon copy of the songs heard long ago, and there is doubt as to the genuineness of her singing. The final disappearance of the singer may symbolize the end of the attempt to actualize the Jewish spiritual heritage in a forceful and forcible manner.

The search for Jewish elements in Kafka must ultimately be viewed as but one of many valid approaches to his work and his legend. As the British Germanist H.M. Waidson has put it, "The study of Kafka is something like the building of the Great Wall of China. It may be an incommensurable task to complete the work and make it impregnable, the building operations may give rise to unprovable legends, but the task is one of undeniable fascination, even if it makes unprecedented demands upon the builder's sense of responsibility."

In one of his cryptic, elliptic statements Kafka said: "Sometimes I believe that I understand the Fall as no one else." His work in its totality, after patient study, teaches Jews and non-Jews alike to understand it a little better as well.

NOTES ON A SCHOOL TEXT AND RELATED MATTERS

Werfel's Play "Jacobowsky und der Oberst"

Habent sua fata libelli ... One of Franz Werfel's more enduring creations, a work that brought him a certain amount of satisfaction but an even greater amount of heartache in his last years, is a play that has been a great favorite of mine and a *compagnon de route* in four decades of teaching German language and literature, a work that occupies a unique place not only in literary history but in the history of American publishing and of higher education as well. "Literary history will note the unusual, and perhaps unique, fact that the first edition of a significant German book appeared in the shape of a text edition for American students," wrote Gustave O. Arlt, who was both the editor and translator of Werfel's "Komödie einer Tragödie in drei Akten," *Jacobowsky und der Oberst.*[1] Lore B. Foltin commented in a similar vein: "Es war höchst ungewöhnlich, daß der Erstdruck des Werkes eines bedeutenden Dichters als Schulbuch erschien. Werfel war aber darüber gar nicht unglücklich."[2]

Arlt provided Werfel's play with a biographical introduction as well as the usual end notes and vocabulary; the hard-cover edition, which bears the imprint F.S. Crofts (later Appleton-Century-Crofts), also contains a map of the main characters' circuitous journey through France and a frontispiece photo from the American production of the play, depicting the Colonel as he offers a "Danse Macabre"-like serenade to his lady, fiddling while France burned.

"The fate of my play *Jacobowsky und der Oberst,*" wrote Werfel for an F.S. Crofts promotional bulletin,

> has been in many respects as unusual as that of its hero. It was first introduced to the public in the form of a stage adaptation which differed materially from my original text. Three months later it appeared in book form in English; it was a faithful and adequate translation, to be sure, but still a translation. Now, at long last, the play is to appear in the form and in the language in which I conceived and wrote it. I am pleased that my book will be placed first of all in the hands of students of American colleges and universities, for I know that they, reared in the atmosphere of broad humanistic tolerance, will be quick to understand the problem and the conflict between Jacobowsky and his inflexible adversary. The external factors that produced the situation in the play are now past history—the conflict remains. To resolve that conflict is the problem of the youth of the world.[3]

This school edition, intended "for late second- or third-year reading," has, *mirabile dictu,* never gone out of print and has since 1961 been available as a paperback under the Irvington imprint. Its continued availability at a time of retrenchment and declining standards, when American school editions of German works tend to be discontinued after a few years in favor of more trendy and "relevant" readings, bespeaks the undiminished timeliness of Werfel's play, and it may also have been promoted by its conversion into a Broadway play, an opera, a movie, a radio play, a recording, and a musical.[4]

Werfel's discreet reference to a stage adaptation masks years of misunderstandings, conflicts, frustration, and even litigation. The author's special concern with his play derives from the fact that it is a conflation of his own experiences and insights on his flight "from Marseille to Marseille" with the story of another Jewish refugee's odyssey through wartime France in 1940 in the company of what can only be described as a strange bedfellow. At the Hotel Vatican in Lourdes Werfel had listened to the fascinating tragicomic narratives of a fellow guest, the Stuttgart banker Stefan S. Jacobowicz, whom fate had thrown together with an arrogant, anti-Semitic Polish officer for a rattletrap ride to safety. Werfel did not forget these striking stories, and in the spring of 1941 he regaled his dinner guests in his Beverly Hills home (including Max and Gottfried Reinhardt, Mr. and Mrs. Erich von Kahler, and Mr. and Mrs. Gustave Arlt) with his spellbinding retelling of it—"in the best tradition of a Cervantes, Grimmelshausen, or de Coster," as Gottfried Reinhardt later characterized it.[5] Max Reinhardt immediately suggested that Werfel turn this story into a play (presumably as a vehicle for his own return to the Broadway stage), but Werfel demurred and his wife Alma regarded this material as too mundane and trivial, and thus unworthy of her husband's talents (though later she was not averse to the idea of accepting royalties from a successful production). Soon thereafter Gottfried Reinhardt undertook to dramatize the story in collaboration with the well-known American playwright S.N. (Samuel Nathaniel) Behrman for a production by his father. Gottfried Reinhardt later took credit for creating, together with Behrman, the character of Marianne: "I felt that we should have some love interest, so we came up with Marianne, a kind of incarnation of France."[6] Werfel may have had reason to fear that an American version of his story would be little more than a farce, a sentimental salon piece, or a drawing-room comedy, and so he may have felt that only he, an eyewitness and a survivor, could do full justice to the story. In any case, he hoped for a breakthrough on the American stage to match the success of his novel about Bernadette Soubirous, with which he had fulfilled a pledge he had made in France. He started work on a play with the working title *It's a Long Way to Saint Jean-de-Luz oder Jacobowsky und der Oberst,* writing the first scene in late July 1941, the second and third in July of the following year, and completing the play with scenes four, five, and six in his *buen retiro* at

Santa Barbara in late August 1942. In light of this fact, Werfel's reference, in a letter to Rudolf Kommer dated October 3, 1942, to a "Raimund-Märchen des größten Kollapses der Weltgeschichte" which he had "wie zum Jux in zehn Tagen hingehaut"[7] strikes one as strange. In the same letter Werfel admitted the necessity of an American adaptation—"nicht aber eines Flickwerkes fremder und in dieser Materie ahnungsloser Hände, die seinen Reiz zerstören würden.[8] By the time Werfel had finished his play, the young Reinhardt and Behrman had completed the second act of their version, but Werfel initially insisted that only a faithful translation of his own play be put on the stage. "Werfel had robbed it of most of its comedy," wrote Reinhardt, "substituting it with mysticism."[9] Reinhardt and Behrman having started legal proceedings, Werfel began to work with another noted American playwright, Clifford Odets, and in early 1943 he wrote his agent George Marton that he had been trying "einem amerikanischen Taubstummen das europäische Elend Frankreichs durch Zeichensprache zu vermitteln.[10] Soon he became disenchanted with Odets, whose version had Jacobowsky traverse France playing Mozart records on a portable phonograph while the Gestapo was lying in ambush. The situation was exacerbated when the banker Jacobowicz, who had also emigrated to the United States, heard about those dramatizations and demanded participation in the royalties. Meanwhile the Theatre Guild had appeared on the scene and suggested that Werfel collaborate with the actor-producer Jed Harris, but once again Werfel feared that this would only produce another melodramatic oversimplification. Lawrence Langner tried to mediate between Werfel and Behrman, but with little success. Transcontinental telephone calls and telegrams went back and forth, but Werfel felt increasingly helpless and fatalistic. In an undated cable to the adapter Werfel said: "I implore you not to reject every thing for what I am fighting with perhaps the last heartpower I have...I beg you on my knees to restitute the end of scene IV."[11] Werfel was especially unhappy about the omission of the scene in which Der Heilige Franziskus and Der Ewige Jude (in Arlt's translation dubiously turned into The Monk and The Intellectual) appear on a tandem bicycle and deliver themselves, with wry wit, of ecumenical wisdom that was close to Werfel's heart. Albrecht

Joseph, Werfel's trusted assistant in his last years, believes that "the upsets and strains caused by the play cost Franz Werfel years of his life."[12]

In his autobiography *People in a Diary* S.N. Behrman devotes a chapter to what was designated as *Jacobowsky and the Colonel. An American Play by S.N. Behrman. Based on the Original Play of Franz Werfel.*[13] (The title of his chapter, "Chacun à Son Goût," is a tribute to Oskar Karlweis, the stage Jacobowsky, whom Behrman had enjoyed as Prince Orlofsky in a New York production of *Die Fledermaus,* but undoubtedly it also refers to the conflicts between the Austrian and the American playwrights.) That Behrman was not insensitive to the substance of Werfel's play is indicated by the following insight: "When the conventions of property, justice, the divisions of life and death are all held in abeyance by an arbitrary God, the habits based on these conventions evidently jumble into farce, like a macabre *Alice in Wonderland.*"[14] While searching for a reason for Werfel's hostility toward him, Behrman found a friend of the playwright who explained to him that "German writers consider that no writing is any good unless it is symbolic and tragically serious. They love symbolic characters which represent profoundly somber abstractions." Behrman goes on to say that "Werfel had by this time written his own version of the play, and it was full of them. It became the libretto for a tragic German opera."[15]

"Werfel granted the [Theatre] Guild what he had denied Max Reinhardt," wrote Gottfried Reinhardt bitterly.[16] In point of fact, the Theatre Guild and director Elia Kazan started rehearsals for Behrman's adaptation without Werfel's approval in December 1943. After tryouts in New Haven, Boston, and Philadelphia the play opened at the Martin Beck Theater in New York on March 14, 1944 with Karlweis as Jacobowsky, Louis Calhern as the Colonel, J. Edward Bromberg as Szabuniewicz, and Annabella as Marianne. The music was by Paul Bowles, himself a noted writer as well as a composer. The critical and popular success of the American adaptation, which achieved 417 performances on Broadway and won the New York Drama Critics Award for 1944, must have mollified Werfel somewhat, as did the first performance by the Freie Deutsche Bühne in Buenos Aires and the

European premiere (in translation) at Göteborg (October 6, 1944) as well as the first European performance of the original at Basel on October 7, 1944. Werfel's remarkably conciliatory, but also untruthful and intellectually dishonest statement about the Broadway premiere is evidence of his resignation:

> Endlich erbarmte sich ein mutiger Mann meines Jacobowsky. Dieser Ritter war der ausgezeichnete Dramatiker Clifford Odets. Wir hatten viele Zusammenkünfte, und obgleich der Theatergott letzten Endes seine Adaption nicht auf die Bühne brachte, so verdanke ich ihm doch so manche wertvolle Anregung...Meine alte Freundin, die Theatre Guild, erwarb den würdigen Jacobowsky, und damit begann sich sein Schicksal zum Guten zu wenden. Zugleich trat ein Mann, den ich liebe, aus dem Gewölk seiner Feinfühligkeit und Scheu hervor und erklärte sich bereit, dem umherirrenden Jacobowsky, den er von Anfang an gekannt und geschätzt hatte, ins Bühnenlicht hereinzuhelfen. Es war der geistvolle und hochangesehene Dramatiker S.N. Behrman.[17]

The film version of the play, *Me and the Colonel,* was directed in 1958 by Peter Glenville and starred Danny Kaye and Curd Jürgens. George Froeschel, the Viennese-born principal author of the screenplay, won the Writers Guild Award; his collaborators were Gottfried Reinhardt and Behrman, who was credited with some of the dialogues.[18] Giselher Klebe's opera *Jacobowsky und der Oberst,* written at the suggestion of Rolf Liebermann, was premiered by the Hamburg Staatsoper on November 2, 1965 and performed by that ensemble at the Metropolitan Opera in New York on June 23, 1967. Oskar Czerwenka portrayed Jacobowsky, Gerhard Stolze played the role of the Colonel, and the American singer Arlene Saunders was Marianne. The director Günther Rennert kept the action hovering between comedy and tragedy, and Klebe was praised for his fidelity to Werfel's text and his memorable settings, as recitatives or arias, of Der tragische Herr's "Die Pariser gehn...," the bureaucratic litany of the Brigadier (in Figaro style), and Jacobowsky's presentation of the "zwei Möglichkeiten." Werfel would undoubtedly have been less pleased with the musical *The Grand Tour,* which opened at the Palace Theater in New York on January 11, 1979, with music and lyrics by Jerry Herman and a bearded Joel Grey as Jacobowsky, whose big song is "I'll be here tomorrow." The book, by Michael Stewart and Mark Bramble, includes a scene at the convent of the Sisters of Charity in which the Germans billeted there are bested by the Colonel and Jacobowsky. To elude the clutches of the SS the four refugees masquerade as performers in a carnival, and Jacobowsky acts as a human cannonball. Later the versatile man performs a Jewish wedding at Papa Clairon's café.[19]

In a somewhat simplistic interpretation of Werfel's play Anna Siemsen says "daß Werfel in diesem merkwürdigen, liebenswürdig heiteren Werk sich zurückfindet in seine alte Welt, die jüdische, und nun heimkehrend nach einer langen Wanderung Ja sagt zu seinem Judentum, zu seinem jüdischen Schicksal, zu der Zukunft seines Volkes."[20] Werfel himself was aware of possible Jewish objections to his work. In his last letter to Max Brod, who had evidently been trying to get the Habimah to perform the play, he wrote:

> Was Jacobowsky betrifft, so liegt der Widerstand gewiß in dem Mißverständnis, daß die jüdische Tragödie in meinem Stück 'unheroisch' hingestellt sei. Ich *wollte* aber gerade *das*. Deshalb habe ich einen durchschnittlichen Geschäftsjuden [!] zum Helden gemacht...Bemühe Dich aber bitte nicht länger, wenn die Einwände in tieferen Schichten des jüdischen Gefühls liegen.[21]

Two of the most thoughtful interpretations of Werfel's play are by Lionel Steiman and Alfred Klarmann, but neither is fully convincing. Steiman, a Canadian historian, describes the play as "very much the product of a latter-day Prague mystic" and "contrived and inherently implausible," because the main characters are both "actors in a drama of survival and mouthpieces for a peculiar social and theological paradigm."[22] Steiman views Jacobowsky, "no cynical, acid-tongued intellectual activist, neither... a retiring ghetto scholar nor...a culturally refined commercial magnate,"[23] as a celebration of a certain Jewish stereotype—"calculating and ingratiating...an outsider conscious of being so."[24] The play may well be a "dramatization of Werfel's theological conception of the interrelation of Jewish-gentile elements of Western civilization,"[25] but it is Steiman's fanciful notion that the function of the Jew is to induce the Christian guilt which the blood of the Savior can wash away. Surely such a static conception disregards any change or role reversal, as well as the obvious growth of the stubborn Colonel, the hedonistic Marianne, and Jacobowsky, who is initially as passive as he is resilient and resourceful.

Adolf Klarmann, the late professor of German at the University of Pennsylvania, who became Werfel's literary executor in 1945, read Werfel's play as a drama of salvation full of sacrifices and miracles. He discerns a strong metaphysical undercurrent in it and points out that "in every work he had written, Werfel had tried to state a fundamental metaphysical truth."[26] Klarmann is candid enough to say in a footnote that Werfel felt "whatever symbolism was discovered in *Jacobowsky and the Colonel* was entirely unconscious and unintended on his part,"[27] but he adds, somewhat disarmingly, "So deeply was Werfel imbued with his mission that at times he no longer realized he was writing in symbols."[28] *Oberst* surely rings up more associations than "Colonel," and "Jacobowsky" may well be read as "son of Jacob," but it is difficult to see in the name of Szabuniewicz *Szabas* (the Sabbath) plus *nie wiesc* (no knowledge), the Te Deum in Tadeusz, "the mystery of the Easter miracle"[29] in the Hotel Mon Repos et de la Rose, 333 (the house number in Saint Cyrill) as "symbolical for the triple crown of the papacy,"[30] or Deloupe, the last name of Marianne (Mary plus Anna) as denoting both a wolf (the symbol of Rome) and a magnifying glass ("which through the heavenly rays collected in her with purifying flames burns off man's earthly vanities, thus allowing him to become a true Christian"[31]). A lighter, and less controversial, touch is provided by Klarmann's insight that "whatever mental comforts [Jacobowsky] has in this play he owes to women"[32] (Madame Bouffier, Marianne, the sanctuary of the ladies' room at Père Clarion's).

To return to the school edition and translation of Werfel's play: Both represent a major achievement for the late Professor Arlt (of the University of California at Los Angeles). The play is a veritable compendium of "Aphorismen zur Lebensweisheit," to use Schopenhauer's phrase. Premier Reynaud's "La situation est grave mais pas désesperée" seems like a reversal of a typically Austrian saying (which is later quoted by Szabuniewicz as "Die Lage ist hoffnungslos aber nicht ernst").[33] The definition of democracy given by Die alte Dame aus Arras ("Demokratie, das ist, wenn die Politiker gute Geschäfte machen und die Geschäftsleute schlechte Politik")[34] is topped by Der tragische Herr, who defines it as "die Korruption der Einen dividiert durch die Korruption der Anderen."[35] "Der einzige Vorsprung, den der Verfolgte auf der Welt hat, besteht darin, daß er nicht der Verfolger ist" is dismissed by Stjerbinsky as "ein Dreh, ein mosaischer."[36] Two chilling insights of Jacobowsky are "Mut beruht auf der Unfähigkeit, sich in die Seele des Gegners versetzen zu können" and "Die Siege von gestern werden zu Niederlagen von heute."[37] "Wenn die Beine schmerzen, dann tut das Herz weniger weh"[38]—what exile who becomes a compulsive walker on a visit to places known long ago will not confirm this insight? A central theme of the play is expressed by Der Ewige Jude: "Lassen Sie Gegensätze nur alt genug werden, dann finden sie sich, wie die Parallelen im Unendlichen."[39]

Arlt the editor cannot be separated from Arlt the translator, who is said to have performed the feat of Englishing Werfel's play in eight days. A few suggested corrections might serve to make a good edition and an equally good translation even better. *Aufstoßen* is listed in the end vocabulary as "to push open; to bump into,"[40] but when Jacobowsky says, in reference to *Schneewittchen,* "Die deutsche Kultur stößt einem immer wieder auf," this is not "You can't turn around without bumping into German culture"[41] but "You keep regurgitating German culture" or "German culture keeps coming up on you." Understandably, "Act One, Part One" does not reproduce the Rilkean pomposity and Werfelian irony of "Des ersten Aktes erster Teil," and in English the Tourist (Gestapo man), who speaks a funny Saxonian dialect, has a lisp; by the time he says "We're thimply nutths about dead Jewth"[42] this grates on the reader, as do all those super-uvular r-r-rs of the two Poles. "In the first place, the monstrous dragon hasn't any claws" is simply wrong for "Zuerst hat einen der große Ichthyosaurus in den Krallen,"[43] as is the Colonel's "Who bribes by crawling meekness?" for "Wer besticht durch kriechende Sanftmut?"[44] *Bestechen* here means "captivate" or "ingratiate oneself," and *kriechen* is used in the sense of *kriecherisch,* thus: toadyish, fawning, servile, or sycophantic. *Gelegenheitsgeschäfte* is not "casual business"[45] but "occasional deals" or "odd jobs." Finally, Jacobowsky's response to the questioning of his musical judgment by Szabuniewicz, "des Todes Schammes"[46] playing a mouth organ, "Nicht musikalisch?! Kleinigkeit!," is rendered by Arlt as "Could be!"[47] For this I would suggest "Hoo-ha!," a versatile and expressive "Yinglish" term that might serve as a reaction to overinterpretations of Werfel's play and as a fitting, eminently Jacobowskian conclusion of this article.

Notes

1. New York: Appleton-Century Crofts, 1945, III. Arlt's translation: *Jacobowsky and the Colonel: Comedy of a Tragedy in Three Acts.* New York: Viking Press, 1944. Even though the commercial edition published in Stockholm by Bermann-Fischer bears the date 1944, Arlt's school edition actually came out first.
2. Lore B. Foltin, *Franz Werfel.* Stuttgart: Metzler, 1972, 105.
3. *Crofts Modern Language Notes,* December 1944. Werfel's statement also appears on a leaflet advertising the book.
4. Charles Wassermann, the son of the writer Jakob Wassermann, prepared a radio play for the Canadian Broadcasting Company. In the 1950s an abridged version of the play was recorded on the Amadeo label and under Friedrich Langer's direction, with Ernst Waldbrunn as Jacobowsky, Erik Frey as Stjerbinsky, Susi Nicoletti as Marianne, Albin Skoda as Der tragische Herr, Richard Eybner as the Brigadier, and Fritz Muliar as the Gestapo man.
5. Gottfried Reinhardt, *The Genius: A Memoir of Max Reinhardt.* New York: Alfred A. Knopf, 1979, 201.
6. Peter Stephan Jungk, *Franz Werfel: A Life in Prague, Vienna and Hollywood.* New York: Grove Weidenfeld, 1990, 298.
7. Peter Stephan Jungk, *Franz Werfel: Eine Lebensgeschichte.* Frankfurt am Main: S. Fischer, 1987, 308.
8. *Ibid.,* 309.
9. Reinhardt, *op. cit.,* 202.
10. Jungk, German edition, 311.
11. Jungk, German edition, 216.
12. *Ibid.,* 398.

13. S.N. Behrman, *People in a Diary: A Memoir.* Boston: Little, Brown, 1972, 164-177.
14. *Ibid.,* 168.
15. *Ibid.,* 168,176. Klebe's work was actually intended as a *comic* opera.
16. Reinhardt, 202.
17. Werfel, *Zwischen Oben und Unten.* Munich: Langen Müller, 1975, 625. This excerpt from "Zur amerikanischen Bühnen-Bearbeitung von *Jacobowsky und der Oberst"* appears in German in the original edition of Jungk's book (320) and in English on p. 300 of its American translation.
18. Cf. Hans-Bernhard Moeller, "George Froeschel," in *Deutsche Exilliteratur seit 1933,* ed. by John M. Spalek and Joseph Strelka, Bern: Francke, vol. 1, 1976, 725-727.
19. Clive Barnes (*New York Post*) called this musical "a happy show, full of charm and decent sentiment;" T.E. Kalem (*Time*) found it "endearing, exuberant, and poignantly humane;" Martin Gottfried (*Cue*) characterized it as "a big old-fashioned Broadway musical;" but Kevin Kelly, writing in the *Boston Globe* of January 19, 1979, called Jacobowsky "a pint-sized Job" and wrote that the musical was "like a trip to nowhere desperately stapled together by an unimaginative travel agent."
20. A. Siemsen, "Zwei Dichter der jüdischen Emigration: Franz Werfel und Alfred Döblin," *Judaica* (Zürich) 1-2, 1945–1947, 161f.
21. M. Brod, *Streitbares Leben 1884–1968.* Munich: F.A. Herbig, 1969, 72.
22. Lionel B. Steiman, *Franz Werfel: The Faith of an Exile. From Prague to Beverly Hills.* Waterloo (Ontario): Wilfrid Laurier University Press, 1985, 176.
23. *Ibid.,* 174.
24. *Ibid.,* 175.
25. *Ibid.*
26. Adolf Klarmann, "Allegory in Werfel's *Das Opfer* und *Jacobowsky und der Oberst." Germanic Review* XX, 3, October 1945,201.
27. *Ibid.,* 194.
28. *Ibid.,* 217.
29. *Ibid.,* 204.
30. *Ibid.,* 210.
31. *Ibid.,* 209.
32. *Ibid.,* 211.
33. Arlt edition, 6, 10.
34. *Ibid.,* 7.
35. *Ibid.*
36. *Ibid.,* 57.
37. *Ibid.,* 12-13,32.
38. *Ibid.,* 35.
39. *Ibid.,* 89.
40. *Ibid.,* 167.
41. Arlt edition, 83; Arlt translation, 71.
42. Arlt translation, 99.
43. Arlt edition, 102.

44. Arlt translation, 74; Arlt edition, 86.
45. Arlt edition, 96; Arlt translation, 82.
46. Arlt edition, 60.
47. Arlt edition, 60; Arlt translation, 51.

FRANZ THEODOR CSOKOR'S "ALLERSEELENSTÜCK"

3. NOVEMBER 1918

Franz Theodor Csokor was in the habit of referring to some of his more than two dozen dramatic works in a concise way that indicated their subjects. Thus *Die Gesellschaft der Menschenrechte* was his "Büchnerstück," *Der tausendjährige Traum* his "Wiedertäuferstück," *Gottes General* his "Loyolastück," *Der verlorene Sohn* his "Partisanenstück," and *Das Zeichen an der Wand* his "Eichmannstück." Most strikingly, perhaps, he called what is arguably his most famous (and certainly his most frequently performed) play *3. November 1918* an "Allerseelenstück"—"dies Allerseelenstück eines Reiches, das man erst jetzt erkennt, wo es verloren ist." The quotation is from a presentation copy of the play that Csokor sent to his friend Dori (Theodor Tagger, better known as Ferdinand Bruckner) "an einem besonders melancholischen Wiener Herbsttag (Arthur Schnitzlers fünftem Todestag), 20. Oktober 1936."[1] The appellation *Allerseelenstück* is singularly apt and more than fortuitous. The action of Csokor's play takes place on All Souls' Day, November 2, and the day after, but there can be no doubt that Csokor intended to produce a dramatic requiem for the Habsburg monarchy. In his book on Csokor, published in 1981, Paul Wimmer quotes from the typescript of the dramatist's essay "Österreichs Allerseelentag," which he describes as "bisher unveröffentlicht," apparently not realizing that this essay had appeared, in one form or another, as Csokor's foreword or epilogue (one of which is entitled "Das Heer ohne Heimkehr") to his play.[2] As Csokor mourns the carnage of the war, at least some of it avoidable, and the attendant break-up of a great empire, he also identifies lost traditional values that the present and the future ought to recapture and would ignore at their peril. With chilling prescience he wrote in a letter dated November 28, 1936: "Die Straße, auf der man uns wieder zur Humanität zurückbringt, wird uns erst noch durch Meere von Blut führen müssen."[3] Among the values mourned by the dramatist is "ein Menschentum, aus sieben Nationen gemengt oder zumindest genötigt, sich mit ihnen zu vertragen, ein erstes Paneuropa im Herzen des Kontinents. So rätselhaft in seinem Wesen, wie es rätselhaft in seinem Ende war."[4]

In this play Csokor diagnoses the demise of supranational European values and poignantly adumbrates the development of ideology. All his life Csokor concerned himself with the idea of Europe, and of Austria as an essential part of it, as much as his friend Stefan Zweig did. In an address entitled "Idee Europa," written in 1956 and published in a small collection of his writings in 1959, Csokor, who had himself tasted the bitter bread of exile, begins with this quotation from the chapter "Wo liegt Europa?" in George Saiko's novel *Auf dem Floß*: "Aber war Europa nicht mehr als seine Geschichte, der Inbegriff und die Summe seiner Ideen, eine besondere Art der Geistigkeit, die sich auch anderswo, theoretisch von jedem beliebigen Punkt der Erde aus, aufgreifen, erleben und weiterführen ließ?"[5] These are the words of a survivor (of *two* survivors, really), but unfortunately Stefan Zweig was not one.

Csokor conceived of his three-act play, which is subtitled *Ende der Armee Österreich-Ungarns,* as the first part of an "Europäische Trilogie," a loosely connected trio of political tragedies intended to highlight the apocalyptic nature of this century in concrete and specific rather than abstract and general terms.[6] It was the playwright's aim to present the disintegration of a humanistic *Menschenbild* by depicting the inner conflict between a relatively secure, unbroken, believing world and a new age beset by doubt and insecurity, an era undermined by guilt feelings and an injurious spirit of revisionism, untrammeled nationalism, separatism, and particularism, by trends and forces that tended to divide men who were once brothers and cause people to lose their identities in a faceless mask.

Michael Mitchell is undoubtedly correct when he points out, in his extensive and incisive analysis of this play,[7] that Csokor's motivation can be understood only in terms of *Zeitgeschichte.* In the middle 1930s the play was Csokor's response to, or warning against, the extreme nationalism that was so frighteningly represented by National Socialism with its ideology of a master race that must be perpetuated through selective breeding by means of *Zuchtbullen,* as it were—a term used by Csokor that is reminiscent of the *Zuchtstall* referred to in the play by Colonel Radosin.[8] *3. November 1918* had an uncommonly long gestation period. In a spoken (and recorded) autobiographical essay Csokor described his dramatic requiem for Austria-Hungary as "eine mich schon seit 1918 drängende Idee.[9] By 1935 he must have made great strides in the conceptualization of the play, but it apparently took a news item to trigger it and provide the proper setting. On July 26 of that year he wrote to Ferdinand Bruckner:

> Da las ich gestern die Notiz über ein österreichisches Kriegsgefangenenlager an der chinesischen Grenze—alle Nationen des alten Reiches befanden sich dort, ohne Ahnung, daß dieses Reich vor Jahren zerfallen sei; erst 1928 hörten sie davon. Dann gab es Selbstmorde, Streit, Verzweiflung—einem gelang es erst vor kurzem, die Heimat zu erreichen, die andern schienen alle untergegangen zu sein, sie haben die österreichische Tragödie vom dritten November 1918 dort noch einmal vollzogen. Was wäre das für ein Stoff! Hinter jeder Figur stehen Millionen. Aber man kann nicht alles schreiben![10]

In a letter to Bruckner dated December 29, 1935, Csokor refers to

> das Manuskript eines Stückes, das mir aus einer Zeitungsnotiz sich zu gestalten begann über ein Kriegsgefangenenlager in Sibirien, wo man noch 1928 nicht wußte, daß das alte Kaiserreich nicht mehr bestand...Es läßt mir keine Ruhe, Schwangerschaft im Hirn![11]

Whether this newspaper story was apocryphal or not, it did prompt Csokor to write the play—and quickly, between winter 1935 and summer 1936.

The book edition—later revised and reprinted four times in the author's lifetime—appeared in the same year, and the play was premiered at the Burgtheater in March of 1937. Csokor noted with satisfaction that the director, Herbert Waniek, and the actors playing the major roles (Otto Tressler as Radosin, Fred Hennings as Ludoltz, and Fred Liewehr as Zierowitz) had all served in World War I. In the face of an unsympathetic Burgtheater director, the Saxon Hermann Röbbeling, the *Protektion* so necessary in Austria, then as now, was supplied by Minister Guido Zernatto, himself a noted poet and an old Carinthian partisan of 1919, as well as by the Burgtheater's *Dramaturg,* Erhard Buschbeck. The success of the play and the approbation of friends and admired literary figures like Lina Loos, Ödön von Horvath (who helped supply the title, Csokor's working title having been *Die Grablegung*), Thomas Mann, Georg Kaiser, and Carl Zuckmayer greatly cheered and encouraged Csokor at a difficult time in his life and convinced him that he had written the right play at the right time—not to mention the accolade of the Grillparzer Prize which he received for it. "Was ist Erfolg?" he wrote to his friend Dori on March 15, 1937. "Eine richtige Sache kommt zur richtigen Zeit heraus: wobei es beinahe wichtiger ist, daß die Zeit die richtige war."[12] Csokor felt that in writing this "Requiem der Donaumonarchie" he had succeeded in portraying nothing less than "den Beginn der Tragödie Europas."[13] Looking back on the material of this play after World War II, which he had survived in precarious circumstances as a voluntary refugee from Hitlerism, Csokor mused: "Keinem der unmittelbaren Erben des Reiches hat sein Ende damals Segen gebracht. Zwei Jahrzehnte später rächte es sich an ihnen, im Herzen Europas ein Vakuum geschaffen zu haben, an dessen Folgen wir noch heute leiden."[14] As a sort of reward for his expressed wisdom of hindsight Csokor lived to see annual festive performances of *3. November 1918* at the Burgtheater as well as a film version made in 1965 and an abridged recording of the play.

After the *Anschluß* Csokor thought that his drama might usefully be performed overseas. On April 28, 1938 he wrote to Ferdinand Bruckner in New York:

> Ich brauche dringend die Adresse Rudolf Forsters. Vielleicht läßt er sich doch meinen "Dritten November" übersetzen, drüben, wo man Österreich (Austria) seit dem 11. März dieses Jahres nicht mehr so einfach mit Australien verwechseln wird. Und Forster, der das Stück mit Tressler in Wien gesehen hat, wäre dann als Radosin die prachtvollste Verkörperung des alten Österreich, mit dessen Ende auch der Friede in Europa untergeht.[15]

The first English translation was made by the Scottish writer Norman Cameron and titled *The Army Which Never Came Back.* Intended for broadcast by the British Broadcasting Corporation, it was lost in a London fire in the 1940s, though Cameron is believed to have retranslated it in the early 1950s before his death. In the 1960s Gerald Sharp made a new translation under the title *The Army of No Return,* but only one scene has appeared in print.[16] The third translation, published in 1994, is by Katherine Lichliter.[17]

It is no accident that the man who was born in what he termed the *Völkerkessel* of Vienna, whose paternal blood was Serbian and Croatian and whose maternal derivation was Czech, German, and Hungarian, should have written a poignant tribute to the supranational unity within the old Austro-Hungarian empire. A seemingly nostalgic war play may at first glance appear like an oddity from one of the few Austrian expressionistic playwrights of the "O Mensch!" persuasion, a pacifist, antimilitarist, and humanitarian generally, but it is well to remember that one of the great themes of the Expressionists was man's search for his true self and his place in the world. Certainly Csokor was no die-hard monarchist, but he did make one last, desperate attempt to invoke the age-old unifying mission of Austria, to give expression to his nostalgia for a world that still honored human rights and human dignity, and to call attention to his fading pan-European dream in a last-ditch effort to recapture it. Otto Basil brings out Csokor's motivation very well when he writes:

> Wenn er sich in seinem Drama *3. November 1918* schützend vor das Habsburgerreich stellt, dann nicht, weil er für die Monarchie war. Das alte Reich wird bei ihm zu einem vagen Zukunftstraum: zum paneuropäischen Staatenbund, der unter dem Szepter der Humanität und des Friedens zur idealen Gemeinschaft aufblüht. Das austriakische Reich, ein Völkerbabel *en miniature,* war eine Art Klein-Europa und darum liebenswert.[18]

3. November 1918 presents a microcosm of Greater Austrian society in its dying days. The dramatist affords us one last look at a miniature monarchy by holding a group of convalescent soldiers—mostly officers—and an army nurse in suspended animation, as it were. These people have been snowbound for three weeks in a rest home in the Carinthian Alps that was once a hotel known as the "Edelweißhof." History imposed upon Austria the task of forging seven nations into one empire, a sort of premature League of Nations, but now the last supranational army in history is becoming unglued and seems to be propelled by some mysterious centrifugal force. For many decades national unrest and discontent have undermined the stability of this great multinational empire. At the end of the ill-fated war, national interest and self-determination come to the fore and are typified by more or less subtle changes in interpersonal relationships. Csokor's military men speak the so-called "K.u.K. Armeedeutsch" flavored with each man's nationality, though some small slips indicate that the author may not have striven for absolute ethnic verisimilitude.[19] The men's colorful language reflects the tensions among them and foreshadows the impending political, social, economic, and philosophical changes in a world without empire or emperor. For instance, the greeting "Servus," so expressive of military camaraderie, now gives way to the stiff civilian "Habe die Ehre!"[20] The unifying spirit of this army is embodied in Colonel von Radosin, whose dream is "ein Vaterland über den Völkern,[21] a sort of "Österreich über alles." Career officers of his type, loyal to a supranational dynastic ideal, have held the diverging elements in the army together, just as the personality of Kaiser Franz Joseph has prolonged the symbiosis of the different nationalities. Now, however, the umbilical cord has been cut and the old order is waging a losing fight against the new *Zeitgeist.* Though the idealistic nurse, Christina, is aware that men will always invent something new to die for, she believes in the enduring legacy of Radosin—indeed, in the indestructibility of this type of man—and dreams of a "Reich, das aus Menschen gebaut wird und nicht aus Nationen und Grenzen."[22] In the end she prefers service to many to a liaison with one man. The only other true Austrian patriot, a man who does not feel the pull of the new political entities, is the regiment's Jewish physician, Dr. Grün (called "Doktor Jod" by the men, though he is aware that they really mean "Doktor Jud"). This figure is an illustration of an insight expressed by Joseph Roth and others: that the only people the Habsburgs could fully rely upon were the Jews; they simply *had* to be Austrian patriots.

In an atmosphere of disintegration, Oberst Radosin tries to derive inspiration from a reading of Xenophon's *Anabasis:* "Je weiter die weg waren von ihrer Heimat, desto mehr sind sie richtige Griechen geworden, nicht Athener, Spartaner oder Thebaner!"[23] He attempts to inspire his men by proclaiming their convalescent home "die Grenzschanze unserer Heimat...Wenn dieses Österreich einmal aufhört zu sein—dann kommt in die Welt niemals Friede."[24] In an effort to cure his men of their "eigenes winziges Heimweh" he reminds them of their past triumphs and their blood-brotherhood in the service of a supranational ideal, and he implores them not to give in to their atavistic impulses:

> Wir waren doch mehr schon als eine Nation! Gerade weil es uns immer gemischt hat, weil wir uns immer nur ausgleichen müssen: Jahrhunderte schon...deshalb zaubern wir jeden Fremden zum unsern, deshalb haben wir unsere große Musik—eins sind wir aus sieben gewesen—und ihr wollt das zerhacken, zerreißen, wollt euer fröhliches Menschentum wechseln in Worte von Stämmen, von Völkern und Rassen—ihr wollt aus der hellen Wohnung zurück in den Zuchtstall?[25]

One answer is given by Ludoltz:

> Herr Oberst—das ist mir zu bunt! Was ahnen denn Sie von uns Jungen—ob wir in Kärnten sind oder in Ungarn, in

> Polen oder aus Trient, oder Slowenen oder aus Prag—wir wollen ja alle viel mehr, ihr Aktiven, als euch je geträumt hat! In dem Frieden, der unserer sein wird, gibt es nur mehr Soldaten: Soldaten in Waffen, Soldaten am Werkplatz, Soldaten am Motor, Soldaten am Acker...es lebt keiner für sich allein mehr, es stirbt keiner allein mehr für sich, unser Dasein wird Pflicht, unser Tod erhält Sinn in der Welt, die wir aus der Bluttaufe heben, aus diesem Krieg.[26]

Radosin cannot prevent these men's "Abmarsch aus Österreich-Ungarn,"[27] however ill-advised and unpromising it may be, any more than he can stop the march of history. Though one may have reservations about the description "helle Wohnung" when one thinks of the scenes of pandemonium in the Viennese parliament, the repressive measures against the restive nationalities, and the other iniquities and absurdities of the Dual Monarchy, the ideal conjured up by the playwright seems doubly attractive when one considers the bleak postwar fate of the successor states.[28]

The revolutionary strife of the coming era is strikingly symbolized by the appearance of Pjotr Kacziuk, a deserter from the flagship *Viribus Unitis,* which is like the incursion of a barbarian into a relatively civilized environment. His powerful map-slashing scene is a stark reflection of Kakanian cacophony and chaos. With compelling peasant logic and in the language of Marxism, Kacziuk tells the men "die noch immer nicht ahnen, wo Gott wohnt"[29] that Austria-Hungary is finished and that its fighting forces have been reduced to a "Landstreicherarmee." There can be no doubt that the predominant color of the "farbenvoller Untergang" glimpsed by Stefan George is red. Though the men generally are not ready to swear allegiance to Kacziuk's new "Feldherren" Engels and Marx, it is evident that, for better or for worse, ex-Maschinenmaat Pjotr Kacziuk represents the wave of the future. Colonel Radosin's fate is only the most extreme of many personal tragedies. "Wohin soll der Herr Oberst auch wirklich?" asks Lieutenant Vanini between hemorrhages. "Er ist kein Kroate, kein Deutscher, kein Ungar..." "Ein Österreicher ist er," says Rittmeister Orvanyi. "Ja—eigentlich wohin soll er da wirklich?"[30] Their poignant, unspoken answer is "In den Tod." At the improvised grave of the suicide the men are united for the last time as they throw symbolic handfuls of earth from Hungary, Poland, Carinthia, Slovenia, Czechoslovakia, and Italy into it. There is also Dr. Grün's haltingly announced contribution of "Erde aus Österreich."[31] In 1937 this line, which shows a sensitive understanding of Austrian Jews in 1918 as well as twenty or more years later, was cut by Director Röbbeling, ostensibly out of fear of demonstrations by the "Illegalen," the Austro-Nazis, to whom the idea of an independent Austria was anathema.

Csokor's play ends with an anticipation of the *Kärntner Nachkrieg* on a poignant personal plane. The Carinthian Ludoltz and the Slovene Stevo Zierowitz (who now insists that his name be pronounced Zjerschowitz), natives of the same village and old friends, remain behind to fight for the soil on which they are standing—a somber and sobering premonition of what the new Europe will be like and yet another disquieting literary confirmation of Franz Grillparzer's breathtaking dictum that "der Weg der neueren Bildung geht von Humanität durch Nationalität zur Bestialität."

Notes

1. This copy, a gift from the recipient's son Peter Tagger, is in my possession.
2. P. Wimmer, *Der Dramatiker Franz Theodor Csokor.* Innsbruck: Universitätsverlag Wagner, 1981, p. 181.
3. Csokor, *Zeuge einer Zeit: Briefe aus dem Exil, 1933–1950.* München-Wien: Langen Müller, 1964, p. 130.
4. Csokor, "Das Heer ohne Heimkehr," epilogue to *3. November 1918.* Wien: Danubia Verlag, 1949, p. 93.
5. Csokor, *Du bist gemeint,* ed. by Erhard Buschbeck. Graz-Wien: Stiasny-Bücherei, 1959, p. 110.
6. The other plays are *Besetztes Gebiet* (Wien: Zsolnay, 1930) and *Der verlorene Sohn* (Wien: Ullstein, 1947).
7. "'Aus der hellen Wohnung zurück in den Zuchtstall': An Examination of F.T. Csokor's *3. November 1918.*" *Modern Austrian Literature* 16, no. 1, 1983, pp. 37-52.

8. Csokor, *3. November 1918,* in *Zwischen den Zeiten* (series Österreichische Dramatiker der Gegenwart), Wien: Österreichische Verlagsanstalt, 1969, p. 196. All subsequent references are to this edition.
9. Csokor, *Ein Leben im Werk* (series *Die prominente Stimme*), Preiser-records, Vienna.
10. *Zeuge einer Zeit,* p. 109
11. *Ibid.,* 116.
12. *Ibid.,* 135.
13. *Ein Leben im Werk.*
14. *Ibid.*
15. *Zeuge einer Zeit,* 178.
16. Adolf Opel, ed. *Anthology of Modern Austrian Literature.* London: Oswald Wolff, 1981, pp. 100–105.
17. K. Lichliter, *A Critical Edition and Translation of Franz Theodor Csokor's "Europäische Trilogie,"* Dissertation, Brandeis University, 1979, published in 1994 by Peter Lang.
18. O. Basil, "Panorama vom Untergang Kakaniens," in *Das große Erbe,* Graz-Wien: Stiasny-Bücherei, 1962, p. 83.
19. For example, the heroic epic poems mentioned in the play are Serbian rather than Slovenian, and Zierowitz's "Videtjemo se!" (*op. cit.,* p. 209) is not Slovenian but Serbocroatian. The name of Lt. Kaminski's orderly, Josip Braz, bears a striking resemblance to the real name of Marshal Tito, Josip Broz.
20. *3. November 1918,* p. 198. In her dissertation (pp. 33-34) Katherine Lichliter recounts an incident revealed by the actor Fred Hennings in an interview conducted in Vienna in February 1977: "Hennings had described to Csokor a confrontation at the conclusion of World War I. In 1918 he was a young Carinthian first lieutenant who had fought for Austria-Hungary during World War I. After the collapse of the empire, the newly instituted provisional government in Carinthia had put Hennings in charge of a group of fellow Carinthians and instructed the first lieutenant to conduct Field Marshall Boroevic to its capital, Klagenfurt. With Austria-Hungary's defeat, Hennings had identified with his native Carinthians and replaced the Habsburg and imperial insignias on his uniform with the Carinthian shield. By contrast, Feldmarschall Boroevic, although of Yugoslavian descent, remained staunchly loyal to the empire. When the two men met, the Feldmarschall immediately noticed the Carinthian shield on Hennings's cap and stared disdainfully at the first lieutenant as he stood in front of his fellow Carinthians. Then, instead of saluting Hennings in the usual military manner, Boroevic responded, 'Ich habe die Ehre,' a civilian greeting. In Boroevic's eyes Hennings had forsaken his country and army, which was an act of considerable disrespect and dishonor. The Feldmarschall no longer looked upon Hennings as a soldier. Csokor linked the newspaper article about the prisoner-of-war camp with Hennings' experience and combined these two tales with his own dramatic ingenuity and sense of loss at the passing of the Habsburg empire."
21. *3. November 1918,* p. 198.

22. *Ibid.,* 215.
23. *Ibid.,* 177.
24. *Ibid.,* 195, 194.
25. *Ibid.,* 196.
26. *Ibid.,* 197. K. Lichliter writes (*op. cit.,* 44-45): "The Burgtheater actor Fred Hennings's description of his relationship to Csokor's drama illuminates the great extent to which the attitudes of Ludoltz and Radosin are intertwined with the Austrian experience of those years. Hennings acted the roles of both Ludoltz and Radosin in the Burgtheater productions of *3. November 1918* and admits that he has a unique personal understanding of both characters. This closeness arises from his encounter with Feldmarschall Boroevic and also from his personal identification, at different points in his life, with the political and social values of Ludoltz and Radosin. In the 1937 premiere of the play Hennings...played the role of Ludoltz. Like many Austrians at that time, Hennings's sympathies fluctuated between the memory of the imperial and royal Habsburg monarchy and a longing for a closer association with the German Reich. He feared it was impossible for the Austrian Republic, a tiny remnant of the former empire, to exist as an independent state. However, the debacle of World War II and the birth of the Second Republic convinced Hennings that a free, independent Austria could be a political reality. In an intriguing shift in roles, which paralleled his own life, Hennings no longer acted Ludoltz, but empathically played Radosin in Burgtheater productions of the drama after World War II. In his autobiography *Heimat Burgtheater* Hennings recalls that his performances in *3. November 1918* were the rare occasions in his long and varied theatrical career on which he did not suffer from stage fright. In contrast to his usually acute awareness that he was performing a role, in these performances the actor felt he was simply reenacting his own personal life."
27. *3. November 1918,* 209.
28. Cf. Ernst Trost, *Das blieb vom Doppeladler: Auf den Spuren der versunkenen Donaumonarchie.* Wien-München: Verlag Fritz Molden, 1966.
29. *3. November 1918,* 185.
30. *Ibid.,* 198.
31. *Ibid.,* 202.

THE AUSTRO-AMERICAN JEWISH POET ERNST WALDINGER

In a lecture delivered in 1960 at Skidmore College in Saratoga Springs, New York, the Viennese-born poet and American college professor Ernst Waldinger described himself as a "confirmed maverick, a hybrid poet with scholarly inclinations, an inveterate and ardent teacher (who knows how little can be taught), a conservative liberal—a cosmopolitan, and, at the same time, an Austro-American."[1] Waldinger was also aware that he was a "double-faced creature, a highly suspect animal, a person called a hyphenated American."[2] While he was engaged as a cultural mediator and literary and psychological bridge-builder between his old and new homelands, Ernst Waldinger, the poet and the man, remained very conscious of his Jewishness, which to him meant the urge and the obligation to preserve a great heritage and to lead a life of high moral standards, as well as chosenness for suffering and bearing witness. In his poem "Aus Davids Geschlecht" he refers to Jesus as a suffering Jew: "...bin ich nicht wirklich auserwählt, als Jude, leiderprobt, das Kreuz zu tragen, gleich jenem Jesus, der von David stammt?"[3] (Am I not truly chosen, as a Jew tried by sorrow, to bear the cross, like that

Jesus who was descended from David?) He expressed the same insight more powerfully in another poem:

Quam Olim Abrahae Promisisti

Als ich zum ersten Mal als Bub dies lernte
Hebräisch und mit Gleichmut, wußt ich erst
Nur halb, was dies bedeutet: auserwählt!
Es wog noch leicht auf meinen Knabenschultern.
Als mir's im ersten Jahr des ersten Weltkriegs
In Mozarts Requiem im strahlend-hellen
Konzerthaus nun lateinisch und fugiert
Entgegendröhnte, dies, was meinem Stamme
Seit Abraham versprochen ward, erahnt
Ich's besser schon, obwohl der Neue Bund
Gemeint war, nicht der meine, und obwohl
Dann Christi Leidenslast vier Schreckensjahre
Wir teilten. Doch als ich das Requiem
Heut hörte nach dem unvergeßnen Grauen,
Nach jener Schmach der Nazisintflutzeit,
Da wußt ich, daß zum Leiden auserkoren
Nur wir, das wirklich auserwählte Volk, sind,
Obschon das Leid der Dinge Wesen ist—
Nur wir verkörpern seit der Kreuzigung
Die Imitatio Christi, wir allein![4]

When as a boy I learned it, hardly yet
With interest, in Hebrew at that time,
I only grasped half of the words' importance.
This "chosen" was no load yet on my shoulders.
When it reverberated in my ears
At the beginning of the First World War,
In Mozart's Requiem once in Vienna,
In Latin and as a fugue in the bright light
Of our concert hall, what has been promised
To our tribe since Abraham already
Was better rooted in my mind, although
It was not our covenant, although
We shared Christ's burden four bitter war years,
But when I heard that Requiem today,
The unforgotten horror in my heart,
The shameful age of brown barbarity,
I knew: to suffer *we* are chosen only,
Though suffering be the essence of all things.

And since the crucifixion we alone
Have represented the "Imitatio Christi."

Translated by the poet

No limitation of Waldinger's stature in modern literature in the German language is intended if one calls him the most distinguished Austrian poet who found a new home in the United States after 1938. The list of such lyric poets, after all, includes such notable figures as Guido Zernatto, Heinz Politzer, Franz Golffing, Berthold Viertel, Friedrich Bergammer, Max Roden, Margarete Kollisch, Alfred Farau, and Mimi and Norbert Grossberg. (Richard Beer-Hofmann, the patriarchal figure among the Austrian writers exiled in the United States, was not primarily a writer of verse.)

Waldinger was one of the great "adepts at self-portraiture," "Dichter ihres Lebens," to use Stefan Zweig's phrase. About his romantic name with its sylvan connotations ("forest-dweller") he wrote two poems—one in which he muses on the way in which one of his ancestors might have been given that name ("Der Name Waldinger"[5]) and another ("Mein Name"[6]) in which he credits his name with implanting the spirit of poetry in him. Even though Waldinger's only published autobiographical work is an essay entitled "Darstellung einer jüdischen Jugend in der Wiener Vorstadt," which he contributed to Josef Fraenkel's compendium *The Jews of Austria* (London: Vallentine, Mitchell, 1967), and which is a warmly evocative description of a Jewish boyhood in Neulerchenfeld, part of one of the outlying districts of Vienna, his life was "no more and no less than the history of our time," and many aspects of it are preserved, interpreted, illuminated, and transmuted in his poetry.

Ernst Waldinger was born in Vienna on October 10, 1896, as the oldest of four children. Both his parents were natives of Galicia. His father's Orthodox background became somewhat attenuated over the years, but Ernst did receive a good Jewish education and later remembered, in addition to joyous Seder evenings, his studies at a Beth Hamidrash in the Leopoldstadt, Vienna's largely Jewish second district, giving warm though far from uncritical pen portraits of various religious leaders and teachers. Waldinger's mother, who had recognized the dreamy nature and rather impractical bent of her oldest son at an early age, hoped that he would become a rabbi. Waldinger's childhood was not exactly idyllic, but it was full of relationships, ideas and images, sights and sounds that he later used in his poetry. After graduating from the Gymnasium, Waldinger volunteered for military duty in 1915. While serving as an officer in Rumania, Waldinger received a head wound in August, 1917 which paralyzed his right hand and the right side of his face and temporarily deprived him of the faculty of speech; this injury constituted a lifelong, albeit comparatively minor, physical impediment. Waldinger was hospitalized until 1919 and then studied German literature at the University of Vienna, where he was awarded a doctorate in 1921. Two years later he married Rose Beatrice Winternitz, an American-born niece of Sigmund Freud.

Even though Ernst Waldinger had written verse since the age of seventeen, he was "An Unknown Poet" when he was visited in 1926 by the noted Berlin-born American-Jewish critic Ludwig Lewisohn. The American wrote about the Austrian in the influential weekly *The Nation;* the essay was subsequently included in Lewisohn's collection *Cities and Men* (New York: Harper, 1927). Lewisohn found Waldinger "sweet and indomitable and incorruptible," (p. 214) and was delighted to discover in his work "a union of precise fidelity to fact with plasticity of contour and musical resonance of texture" (p. 219). He described one of Waldinger's poems, which he saw in manuscript form, as being "as severe as a canto of Dante and as rich in vowel-music as a sonnet of Rossetti, and yet there blows through it a bleak wind of modern life" (p. 220).

Waldinger's first collection of poetry did not appear until 1934 and bore the title *Die Kuppel* (The Cupola); it secured for the poet the Julius Reich Prize of the University of Vienna. A second collection, *Der Gemmenschneider* (The Gem-Cutter), was published three years later.[7] Waldinger's early publications already stamp the poet as a consummate craftsman, a cosmopolite of experience, whose work is imagistic, rhythmic, and infused with a profound sense of ethics and an abiding humanitarianism. In making "music for our time" (*Musik für diese Zeit* is the title of a collection issued in 1946), Waldinger is aware that, in the final analysis, it is the inner music that will prove to be the most enduring. Because of his inherent realism, Waldinger never was a mere aesthete, not even where he cast his poetry in strict and artful forms, trying his hand at a ghazal or a *Siziliane*, or writing cycles of sonnets about colors, flowers, and months. The majority of his poems are rhymed, and again and again he used the sonnet form, which gave him "the intellectual bliss of a strict, clear order" and which, to him "can encompass everything, even simple things." In a letter to Ludwig Lewisohn dated May 19, 1946, Waldinger described as his aim "the subtle simplicity of the [Matthias] Claudius type to which German poetry is so perfectly suited." One of his poems is entitled "Die Heilkraft der Sonette"[8] (The Curative Power of Sonnets). On numerous occasions the poet availed himself of what he characterized as the "kelch-kristallene Kraft" of this form, and in "Warum ich Sonette schreibe" (Why I Write Sonnets), a poem included in the collection *Gesang vor dem Abgrund* (1961), he wrote: "Ich kehre zum Sonette stets zurück / In unsrer Zeit, die aller Helle bar, / Zur Form, die meine erste Liebe war, / Zur scharfen Schau und zum Gedankenglück."[9]

If some of Waldinger's earlier poems, bearing such titles as "Ode to International Traffic," "The City Dweller," and "Song of the Mythical Threshers," are expressionistic in outlook and style, many of his most characteristic lyrics are eminently musical, expressing the spirit of music, reflecting on the special quality of an instrument or on the meaning of a musical form, communing with the great masters of music, or interpreting specific compositions by Schubert, Mozart, Tartini, Vivaldi, or Chopin. Beginning in 1929, Waldinger gave himself a foretaste of his future homeland by translating, over a period of two decades and under the title *Prairie and Skyscrapers,* about one hundred poems by such eminent American poets as Edwin Arlington Robinson, Robert Frost, E.E. Cummings, Edna St. Vincent Millay, Emily Dickinson, Marianne Moore, and Archibald MacLeish.[10]

Having earned a living in a commercial establishment in Vienna for many years, Waldinger emigrated to the United States with his wife and two children in September, 1938. While living in New York City, he had a variety of occupations, working as a librarian, in a department store, and as a government clerk before being appointed, in 1947, to a full professorship at Skidmore College in Saratoga Springs, New York. During his tenure there, Waldinger published four collections of his poetry (*Glück und Geduld*, 1952; *Zwischen Hudson und Donau*, 1958; *Gesang vor dem Abgrund*, 1961; *Ich kann mit meinem Menschenbruder sprechen*, 1965). He gave numerous public lectures and readings at home and abroad, and was awarded several prizes and decorations by the Austrian government, including the Goldenes Ehrenzeichen für Kunst und Wissenschaft in 1962. Following his retirement from his academic position in 1965, Waldinger and his wife lived in New York City again. The last year or two of the poet's life brought him untold sorrow: the untimely death of his daughter Ruth, a talented artist, and the illness of his wife and her death during an Austrian vacation a few days after Waldinger himself had suffered a stroke. The poet's death came in a New York hospital on February 1, 1970.

If the First World War had been the decisive experience that gave Waldinger his poetic voice after a period of speechlessness, his expulsion from his homeland and the necessity to fashion a second homeland for himself was an equally decisive experience, one that was as difficult as it was fructifying. Waldinger became a cultural mediator "between the Hudson and the Danube," and surely there were few in his generation who had such a positive attitude toward America, while preserving vivid memories of a nostalgically cherished native land, in particular the mellow, idyllic beauty and comforting solitude of the Danubian and Alpine regions. At first Waldinger was somewhat repelled by the boundlessness of the American landscape and the seeming formlessness of American life, but later he wrote perceptively and even lovingly about his new homeland—even though an occasional elegiac tone indicates that he regarded America as the land of his old age in contrast to Austria, the nostalgically evoked land of his youth. In the "insular heat of Manhattan" he longed for "the cool rooms in the farmhouses" of Austria (*Die kühlen Bauernstuben* is the title of a collection issued by the Aurora-Verlag, New York, in 1946); a room in his Saratoga Springs home was a replica of such a *Bauernstube.* In the Berkshires or the Canadian Rockies he dreamt of the Semmering. With equal empathy and zest he wrote about a cemetery in the mountains of the Eastern Tyrol and a village in New England, the Golden Gate Bridge and a summer afternoon in Lower Austria, a choral society in Neulerchenfeld and a Quaker Meeting in Haverford, the Wolfgangsee and Saratoga Lake, a horse on 47th Street in New York and a blackbird in Salzburg, a beach in Santa Barbara and a swimming pool in Sauerbrunn, the Musikvereinssaal in Vienna and Lewisohn Stadium in Manhattan. Even as he was alive to the sights, the sounds, and the spirit of his new homeland, he kept recalling a Vienna that really no longer existed, a city which, as he put it, he had saved and preserved by taking it to another country and enshrining it in truth itself, in his heart. He revisited his native city for the first time in 1958, and, predictably, with mixed emotions; his attitude may be summed up by the title of one of his poems: "Verzeihen, aber nicht vergessen."[11] As late as 1967 Waldinger described himself as "noch so stark in Wien verwurzelt, daß diese schicksalshafte Anhänglichkeit alle verständlichen Ressentiments überwunden hat und daß mir allgemein versichert wird, daß in meinen Versen Wiener Wesen und Landschaft in Wort, Bild und Melodie stets mitschwingt." As he intoned poetic paeans of praise to his mother tongue, Viennese German, an idiom that shaped and colored even his utterances in English, he was careful to point out that he was "a son of the German language only" ("Ich bin ein Sohn der deutschen Sprache nur…").[12] Elsewhere he apostrophized the German language as "O great, good spiritual motherland."

Many of his bittersweet poems reflect poignant memories of his childhood, but Waldinger had the rare faculty of endowing a personal, local experience with universal, timeless significance. Moreover, throughout his work it is evident that Ernst Waldinger was not only a *homo austriacus* and a *homo americanus,* but a *homo judaicus* as well—a constellation rare enough among German-Jewish writers. Waldinger never forgot that he was a member of the People of the Book, that his background and his gifts inextricably bound him to the word. In his poem "Kol Nidre" he writes about "diese menschlichste der Bitten" (this most human of all supplications) and says about the haunting melody: "Selbst in der banalsten Tätigkeit wie die alltägliche Rasur ermahnt sie mich an unsrer Sendung Judenschicksal."[13] Waldinger's poem "Der Handlee" memorializes what was once a familiar figure in the streets of Vienna, the Jewish peddler, who was referred to by his cry, which means "I trade (in old clothes)."[14]

Der Handlee

Der Mann mit dem alten Schlapphut,
Ausgefranstem Kragen,
Fettigem Rock und verbeulten Hosen,
Vertretenen Schuhen,
Der Handeljud, der durch die Höfe zog
Und durch die engen Wienergassen:
Sein Kaufruf durchgellte die Luft
Wie ein Peitschenschlag.
Daß das Echo fast die Fenster erklirren ließ:
Handlee!

Als Junge schämte ich mich seiner sehr—
Aber dann wußt ich,
Daß er zu meinem Stamme gehörte,
Unwiderruflich, der bescheidensten einer.

Vielleicht saß er allein am Abend
Über Thora und Talmud
Und holte sich Trost in den guten Legenden,
Und an der Sabbattafel
Fühlte er sich wie ein König.

Mit Tausenden seinesgleichen
Erlitt er das Martyrium in Auschwitz und Mauthausen,
Auf daß der Name des Herrn geheiligt werde.
Aber wollte der Herr wirklich dieses Opfer?

Wenn ich seiner gedenke,
Schäme ich mich, der ich entkam,
Und neige mich in Ehrfurcht
Vor seinem Schatten

Und verfluche seine Mörder,
Denen ich vergeben muß,
Weil das Unheil und ihre Schuld
Zu gewaltig sind, daß sie gesühnt werden könnten.

The man with the old broad-brimmed hat,
With the frayed dirty collar,
Greasy jacket and rumpled pants
And the worn, shapeless shoes,
The peddler who moved through the courtyards
And the narrow lanes of Vienna,
His trade call whizzed through the air
Like the stroke of a whip
That its echo almost rattled the windows:
"Handlee...!"
As a boy I was ashamed of him,
But then I knew
That he belonged to my people,
Irrevocably, as one of the humblest of my people.

Perhaps he sat alone in the evening,
Bent over the Torah and the Talmud,
And was consoled by the good legends.
And at the Sabbath table
He felt like a king.

Together with hundreds and thousands of his faith
He suffered the martyrdom of Auschwitz and Mauthausen
That the name of the Lord be sanctified.
But did the Lord really demand this sacrifice?

When I recall him
I am ashamed for having escaped
And bow in awe and reverence
Before his shade
And curse his murderers
Whom I have to forgive
Because the evil they committed and their guilt
Are too tremendous ever to be expiated.

Translated by the poet

"Wenn ich auch nicht die alten Psalmen summ' / Ich wandle auf der Ahnen Tränenspur" (Even though I do not hum the old psalms, I walk along my ancestors' trail of tears), Waldinger wrote.[15] A poem of consolation and encouragement in dark times is entitled "The People of Millennial Hope:"

Das Volk der tausendjährigen Zuversicht[16]

Wenn soviel Jammer auf der Erde ist,
Wie soll ich da mein eignes Los beklagen!
Laß mich gefaßt die Bürde weiter tragen,
Soweit das Schicksal meinen Pfad bemißt.

Als kleines Kind schon—was man nicht vergißt—
Hört ich des Todesengels Schwingen schlagen;
Mich traf das Schwert in meinen Kriegertagen;
Ich stöhn, weil Schwermut mir am Herzen frißt.

Und Lahmheit schlug mich, Armut und Exil,
Und wie im Mächtespiel der Würfel fiel,
Fast immer stand ich, wo ich mitverlor—

Doch flüstert eine Stimme mir ins Ohr:
"Kannst du denn nicht die Zuversicht bewahren?
Dein Volk hat sie seit dreimal tausend Jahren."

Seeing all earth so overwhelmed with woe,
I cannot stoop my own lot to bewail
Nor let the strength to bear my burden fail
As long as destiny will have it so.

My unforgotten childhood felt the low
Pinions of death's dark angel near me sail;
The sword of war struck me and left me pale.
Shall my sad heart not fill to overflow?

Shattered, exiled, in need—I paid the price.
Whenever the insensate powers played at dice
I was where losers were, where losers lie—

Yet in my soul a whisper will not die:
"Cannot *that* faith master thine own poor fears
Which kept thy people firm through thrice
a thousand years?"

Translated by Ludwig Lewisohn

Waldinger's most comprehensive collection of poetry, truly his poetic testament, characteristically entitled *Ich kann mit meinem Menschenbruder sprechen,* and published in Vienna in 1965, contains a section entitled "Aus Davids Geschlecht" (From the Line of David), including such poems on Jewish themes as "Hebräisch" ("Nicht meine Muttersprache, dennoch heut gesprochen vom Volk, dem ich entstamme, heilig-herbe Sprache...Erzväterzunge"[17] /"...not my mother tongue, yet spoken today by people I spring from, holy and acerbic language... patriarchal tongue of my forefathers"), "Siebenarmiger Leuchter" ("So versöhnend wie der Regenbogen...widerlegst du des Verneiners Wut"[18] / "as conciliatory as a rainbow...you refute the negator's rage"), "Sabbatausgang," "Die Leopoldstadt" ("fand...das Judenviertel gänzlich judenrein...und dünkte sich so grenzenlos allein"[19] / "...found the Jewish district completely *judenrein*...and felt so boundlessly lonely"), and "Anläßlich des Auschwitz–Prozesses" (concerning T.W. Adorno's dictum that after Auschwitz it is no longer possible to write poetry: "So meine ich, daß es gerade deshalb notwendig ist, Gedichte zu machen, damit dem Unmenschlichsten in jedem von uns das Menschlichste, die Sehnsucht nach dem, was der Mensch sein sollte, entgegengehalten wird."[20] (I think it is necessary to write poems to confront what is most inhuman in all of us with our most human quality, the yearning for what a human being ought to be.) Other poems memorialize Maidanek, Lidice, Theresienstadt, and the Warsaw Ghetto fighter Simon Feigenblatt.

Waldinger's lighter side and his vibrant sense of humor are illustrated by his charming versification of a little conversation reported by Marion Mill Preminger in her autobiography *All I Want is Everything:*

Albert Schweitzers Kravatten

Als sie ihm lächelnd einen Vorwurf machte,
Daß zwei Kravatten doch zu wenig seien,
Altväterische schwarze Schlipse, die er
So lange trug, bis sie ins Grüne spielten,
Erstaunte er: "Wieviele sollt' ich haben?"
Drauf sie naiv und leicht kokett versetzte
(Der weise Mann, geduldig, wie sichs ziemt,
Gab er ihr Recht der Dummheit): "Manche Herren
Vermögen zwischen hunderten zu wählen
Wenn sie am Morgen vor dem Spiegel stehen,
Um ihre Toilette zu vollenden.
Sie tragen freilich nicht die Dreieckschlipse
Wie die Gelehrten von vor anno Schnee."
Doch kurz und kehlig sagte Albert Schweitzer:
"Was, hundert Schlipse? Und für *einen* Hals?"

When, smiling and reproachful, she told him
That two neckties were not nearly enough,
Old-fashioned black cravats which he
Kept wearing till they were faded and threadbare,
He was astonished: "How many am I supposed to have?"
Whereupon she naively and a bit coquettishly replied
(While the wise man, in seemly patience, conceded
Her the right to be stupid),
"Some gentlemen I know have hundreds to choose from
When in the morning they stand before the mirror,
Completing their toilette.
Of course, they don't wear the stocks
That scholars used to wear way back when."
But pithily and throatily said Albert Schweitzer:
"What, a hundred ties?! And all for one neck?!"

Translated by Harry Zohn

A revealing statement about Waldinger's conception of himself is contained in a letter to the author of this article dated June 26, 1964, and referring to a reading by a celebrated contemporary novelist sponsored in Cambridge by the Goethe Society of New England: "Ich bin zwar keine Kanone wie Günter Grass...aber in meiner altmodischen Art glaube ich mehr dem, was mit dem Namen Goethe symbolisiert ist, zu entsprechen." Waldinger was a poet's poet and strove to remain in the literary mainstream, though he was aware that he was fighting a rearguard action, as it were. In many of his poems he communes with or apostrophizes an array of intellectual-spiritual *compagnons de route,* such great figures of the past and present as Franz Kafka, R.M. Rilke, Freud, Thoreau, Bertrand Russell, O.M. Graf, Ernst Schönwiese, Hermann Broch, Mark van Doren, Theodor Kramer, Joseph Weinheber, and Max Mell (the last two, to his consternation and poetic disapproval, sometime adherents of Nazism).

The eight volumes published during Waldinger's lifetime were joined in 1982 by *Arabesques,* a selection in German and English edited and translated by the poet's cousin, Rudolph Lindenfeld and in 1990 by *Noch vor dem Jüngsten Tag,* a selection of poems and essays edited by Karl-Markus Gauß.[21] Both before and after his death, Ernst Waldinger has increasingly attracted critical attention, although he has yet to be recognized on both sides of the Atlantic in his full stature. In an article written on the occasion of the poet's sixtieth birthday and published in *Books Abroad* (Winter, 1957, p. 28), Jacob Picard hailed him as "one of the foremost representatives of all the pure poets writing in the German language in exile and, in fact, in some respects the voice of his former compatriots who found refuge in America." The Viennese critic Otto Breicha wrote that, along with Theodor Kramer, Waldinger exerted the greatest influence on the post-World War II generation of Austrian poets. Writing in *The German Quarterly,* in January 1972, Alexander Kallos discussed the poetry of this "defender of literary tradition" under these rubrics: Permanency and Healing Power of Nature; Preservation of Tradition in Art; Purity of Language; Musicality; Metaphysics; Religion; and Death. Kallos discerned in Waldinger's work "a Horatian buoyancy, evenness and clarity, the healthy and down-to-earth simplicity, hiding some deep thought, reminiscent of Robert Frost" (p. 102). Frederick Ungar, who published collections of Waldinger's poetry both in Vienna and in New York, wrote in 1984: "Waldinger's clear and pure voice was the noblest of the Austrian and German emigration. It is our own fate, poetically heightened, that we confront in his work."[22] Waldinger's literary remains repose in the Dokumentationsstelle für neuere österreichische Literatur in Vienna and include much unpublished material: three to five thousand poems, fourteen autobiographical essays and an equal number of other articles, a memoir of Sigmund Freud, a great deal of material on the situation of exiled writers, and over a thousand letters from such correspondents as Albert Einstein, Thornton Wilder, Hermannn Broch, Kurt Pinthus, Franz Theodor Csokor, and Ernst Křenek. It is to be hoped that scholars will not neglect this valuable material and that some of it will appear in print.

Ernst Waldinger will be remembered as a man of letters who sought to stem the tide of rampant materialism and combat the dehumanizing tendencies of modern life by reasserting, in the face of "modernity" and untrammeled subjectivity, the great traditions of Western civilization, a man who defined his ideal of *Gestalt* as "the humane synthesis of emotion and reason." In a poem entitled "Programmatisch" he said: "Auch ich könnte von den Waben der Verwirrung schwarzen Honig saugen."[23] (I, too, could suck black honey from the honeycombs of confusion.) Instead, however, he chose to place himself in ideological and formal opposition to the mainstream of contemporary poetry, which is informed by cynicism, despair, and nihilism and often makes a cult of egotism, hedonism, formlessness, alienation, dissolution, absurdity, and atavistic brutishness. A foe of obscurity, esotericism, and opaque symbolism, Waldinger strove to achieve his poetic effects through lucidity and communicativeness. "In this age of withdrawal, anarchy, and extreme conformity," he said in *Tradition and Poetry,* "tradition may be a strong counterbalance to the overpowering forces of leveling—*if* we can revive it. Our period, the most revolutionary since man learned to tame the flame and to make tools, is also one of rapid disintegration of all values which we were accustomed to deeming essential for civilization."[24] Beyond this conservatism, which stamps this child of the Austro-Hungarian empire as one of the great classicists in modern Austrian letters, Waldinger deserves recognition and wider dissemination as a poet who poignantly chronicled Jewish fate in our time and touchingly articulated the feelings of many of those whose taste of the bitter bread of expulsion and exile led them to a reaffirmation of their Jewish heritage.

Notes

1. "Tradition and Poetry," *Bulletin of Skidmore College,* Vol. 46, No. 1, September, 1960), p. 13.
2. *Ibid.,* p. 2.
3. *Ich kann mit meinem Menschenbruder sprechen* (henceforth referred to as *Menschenbruder*), (Wien: Bergland Verlag, 1965), p. 136.
4. *Ibid.,* p. 152.
5. *Glück und Geduld* (New York: Frederick Ungar, 1952), p. 117.
6. *Zwischen Hudson und Donau* (Wien: Bergland, 1958), p. 31.
7. Both works were issued by F. Ungar's Saturn Verlag in Vienna.
8. *Menschenbruder,* p. 14.
9. *Gesang vor dem Abgrund,* ed. by Ernst Schönwiese, (Graz: Stiasny, 1961), p. 63.
10. Some of these are included in *Gesang vor dem Abgrund.*
11. *Menschenbruder,* p. 150.
12. *Glück und Geduld,* p. 8.
13. *Menschenbruder,* p. 44
14. *Ibid.,* p. 146.
15. *Glück und Geduld,* p. 8.
16. *Die kühlen Bauernstuben* (New York: Aurora Verlag, 1946), p. 90.
17. *Menschenbruder,* p. 135.
18. *Ibid.,* p. 139.
19. *Ibid.,* p. 145.
20. *Ibid.,* p. 147.
21. Santa Cruz: Bayshore Press; Salzburg: Otto Müller Verlag.
22. *Encyclopedia of World Literature in the 20th Century* (New York: Frederick Ungar, 1984), Vol. 4, p. 581.
23. *Menschenbruder,* p. 22.
24. *Tradition and Poetry,* p. 6.

NOTES ON A SCHUBERTIADE

The term Schubertiade originally referred to the convivial meetings, often in the form of outings, of Franz Schubert and his celebrated *Freundeskreis,* the literary, musical, and culinary activities of his circle of friends, men and women who seem to have been as bibulous as they were gifted. These events were frequently recorded in memoirs as well as on drawings and paintings. In recent times the term has been used to designate cyclical performances of Schubert's works, such as the ongoing series in New York and the concerts in Boston that were willed into being by Henny Bordwin. Elly Ameling has used it for some of her Schubert recitals and recordings.

My first experience of Schubert was not literary and only marginally musical. Two books that I acquired not too many years ago stirred memories of a Schubertiade of monstrous dimensions and dubious orientation that took place in my native Vienna when I was barely five years old. One of these books is lighthearted and grotesquely amusing, but the other is altogether humorless and represents what was at the time a grim foretaste of tragedies to come as well as an unheeded warning.

One of my earliest childhood memories is the centennial commemoration of Schubert's death in 1928, when every train seemed to bring a fresh *Schub* of Schubertians (in the way one might speak of a "batch of bachelors" or a "list of Lisztians") to Vienna and Schubert's music was in and on the air day and night. One concert was estimated to have had five million listeners on what was then a new toy, and not only for a child: the radio. Groups of men, some of them clearly in their cups, sang Schubert melodies in the street, foreshadowing the dire economic straits that would soon force many fine musicians to take to the streets and practice their craft for handouts.

I may well have walked on the Schubert-Ring (then as now part of the majestic circular boulevard called die Ringstraße, or der Ring), and I am almost certain I washed with Schubert Soap, played with Schubert Balloons, and noshed delicacies like Schubert-Ringerln, Schubert-Rollen, and the chocolate Schubert-Roulade that aroused the ire of the satirist Karl Kraus. The case of the culinary kitsch at Schubert's expense was soon rendered nougatory (*sic*), whereas another delectable confectionery continues to bear the name (and likeness) of Mozart, though the rotundity of those bite-sized Mozartkugeln suggests the roly-poly Schubert rather than Mozart, whose embonbonpoint (*sic*) was considerably less. At any rate, I am sure I didn't wear a Schubert-Brille (a replica of the kind of eyeglasses the composer wore) or walk in Schubert Shoes with durable Doppelgänger Soles (the reference being not only to extra mileage, but also to the Romanticists' notion of a "doubleganger" or double, as immortalized in the Schubert-Heine song bearing that title). In those days a *Konditor's* crowning creation of commemorative kitsch was a sugar Schubert, but one must wonder about the mentality that spawned a reported *Schweineschmalz* Schubert, a sculpture made of lard, and the sight (and smell) of it melting in the summer sun.

I don't remember whether a Schubert Coffee Mill was used in our household, nor was I aware at the time that there was a certain connection between Schubert and various mills. The legend that Schubert composed his Müllerlieder (his settings of the poems of Wilhelm Müller —the song cycles *Die schöne Müllerin* and *Winterreise*) at the Höldrichsmühle in the Hinterbrühl near Mödling seems to derive from an operetta written by Hans Max and Franz von Suppé in 1864.

The year 1928 brought not only commercial kitsch, to be sure. 1189 out of 3122 items in a Schubert bibliography covering the first 100 years after the composer's death bear that date, and there was even a musicological *cause célèbre.* Professor Robert Lach of the University of Vienna delivered an address in which he discussed certain limitations of Schubert's art and polemicized against the prevalent idolization, glorification, and trivialization of the composer. His remarks were widely regarded as lese majesty and decried as a "Lach-Salve gegen Schubert" (*Lach-Salve:* Lach salvo; *Lachsalve:* burst of laughter).

The more amusing book referred to above is Robert Werba's *Schubert und die Wiener,* published in 1978 and subtitled *Der volkstümliche Unbekannte* (the popular unknown). The author points out that Schubert has long been misunderstood despite (or because of) the fact that of all the great composers who lived in Vienna, Schubert has always been the one to whom the average Viennese has felt closest. Werba is not so much concerned with a critical analysis of Schubert's music, though he does write perceptively about the nature of his genius and the fluctuating fortunes of his works, as with separating fact from fiction and life from legend in chronicling Schubert's popularity in its myriad manifestations. It has always been the fictions that have captured the imagination of the Viennese, and the purveyors of the multifarious legends about Schubert have not left very much to the imagination. The obfuscation started with Schubert's *Freundeskreis,* and it took a long time for the composer to emerge in his full stature from under the shadow of Beethoven. One of my favorite anecdotes about Schubert (which is not retold by Werba, possibly because it may be apocryphal) involves a pun in the Viennese dialect, which turns *einer* (one) into *aner* or *-aner;* an English equivalent for the latter would be the suffix -ian or -ean. When he was asked whether he was a Mozartianer or a Beethovenianer, Schubert is said to have replied, "I bin sölber aner"—meaning that he was his own fan, or perhaps a charter member of a Schubert school.

Literary treatments of the composer have ranged from rhymed obituaries via works of fiction and operettas to screenplays for color films. There is scant information on the three women whom Schubert may have loved—Therese Grob, Pepi Pöckelhofer, and Countess Karoline Esterhazy—but this has only spurred the mythmakers to action. In his immensely popular 1912 novel *Schwammerl* ("Mushroom," Schubert's nickname) Rudolf Hans Bartsch created the long-lived legend of the "Dreimäderlhaus" (Hannerl, Heiderl, and Hederl Tschöll) on the Mölkerbastei, just off the Ringstraße. This served as the basis of the equally popular operetta *Das Dreimäderlhaus* (1916) by Heinrich Berté (Schuberté?), adapted a few years later by Sigmund Romberg for the American stage as *Blossom Time* and for British audiences as *Lilac Time.* In these concoctions Schubert melodies are made to serve purposes for which they were clearly not intended. One novella about Schubert presents a symphony of the birds at the composer's grave. No fewer than six silent films dealt with Schubert, four of them dating from 1928. The first sound film was *Leise flehen meine Lieder* (its title was derived from a setting of Ludwig Rellstab's poem that is known as Schubert's *Ständchen,* or Serenade), and this was followed three years later by *Mölkerbastei Nr. 3. Dreimäderlhaus,* one of several postwar films about Schubert, starred the aptly named Hannerl Matz. Werba points out that modern research has filled in many gaps and eliminated numerous misconceptions, but even in Vienna a *Marktschreier* ("market crier," a shill or huckster) will always have more listeners than a Peter Schreier, and an operetta Schubert singing his own melodies made up as schmaltzy Wienerlieder (Viennese winegarden songs) with suitably sentimental texts is such a beguiling figure that Rudolf Hans Bartsch is likely to continue to have more readers than Otto Erich Deutsch, who was to Schubert what Köchel was to Mozart.

The more alarming book mentioned above is the "official" album commemorating the tenth German Sängerbundfest in Vienna, July 19 to 22, 1928), which used Schubert for nefarious ideological and political purposes. The gargantuan dimensions of this centennial celebration were relatively harmless: A wooden Sängerhalle was built in the Prater especially for the occasion to accommodate 100,000 people, including an audience of 60,000. Among the 200,000 delegates, divided into regional and ethnic associations, that paraded down the Ringstraße were groups from Austria, Germany, Switzerland, Hungary, Czechoslovakia and Rumania, but also from Africa and the United States, including Indians from Brooklyn and "Sängergirls" from San Francisco. Colorful floats bore such names from Austrian history and culture and Germanic folklore as Walther von der Vogelweide, Andreas Hofer, O du lieber

Augustin, and Rübezahl. As the printed public addresses indicate, Schubert the *Liederfürst,* Prince of Song, was portrayed as the quintessence of the Germanic soul. Amid cries of *Heil!* the word *deutsch* was used constantly, though never in reference to Otto Erich Deutsch, presumably because as a Jew he was considered "un-German." The slogan "Liedgemeinschaft sei Volksgemeinschaft" (meaning that those united in song should be united ethnically and politically as well) indicated that Schubert was used as the great symbol of the longed-for unification of Germany and Austria. Ten years after the first campaign for such unification and ten years before Hitler's army accomplished it, the word *Anschluß* was used unabashedly and liberally, and the prominent participation of the Ostmärkischer Sängerbund adumbrated the coming reduction of Österreich to the Ostmark (eastern region) of the Third Reich. Richard Strauss composed a special fanfare for the occasion, and Viktor Keldorfer made an arrangement of *An die Musik* for men's chorus and brass band. (The words of that Schubert Lied are by Franz Schober, a namesake of Vienna's chief of police, Johannes Schober, who had exactly one year earlier been responsible for the first police riot in modern European history, an outrage that claimed ninety lives and was excoriated by Karl Kraus and commemorated in literary works of Elias Canetti, Heimito von Doderer, and Manès Sperber). With the wisdom of hindsight one reflects that rarely has a great cultural figure been misused and politicized in such ominous and chilling fashion as Schubert was in his native Vienna in 1928.

OUR FIRST HALF-CENTURY

The Austro-American Association of Boston was founded in 1944 by a group of "thirty-eighters"—that is, mostly Jewish refugees from Nazi Austria who had started a new life in the Boston area. Several persons can lay claim to having been the founding fathers (and mothers). Paul Hayek, who had been an attorney in Vienna but worked as an accountant in the United States, is generally credited with having taken the initiative, but Paul and Greta Mueller, Leo Hayek, Theo and Claire Waldinger, Frank Orne and Martha Brunner-Orne, Joseph and Minna Brand, and Frederick and Eugenia Bauer may be regarded as having been the co-founders and, in several cases, early officers of the Association. The author of this brief history is one of the few surviving charter members. Many of the original and later members of the A–AA also belonged to the Immigrants Mutual Aid Society (IMAS), which had been founded in the late 1930s by German-Jewish immigrants and, as its name indicates, was more of a self-help organization. As World War II was drawing to a close and the independence of Austria was likely to be restored, it was felt that Austrian cultural traditions should be fostered in a spirit of camaraderie and an attractive social setting. As more and more native-born Americans joined the Association, they developed a greater appreciation of this heritage. After the war the A–AA provided a matchless forum for visitors from Austria. In July 1970 the Association became incorporated as a non-profit organization in the Commonwealth of Massachusetts and was confirmed in its original purpose of furthering interest in Austrian culture and fostering Austro-American friendship. The Austro-American Association of Boston is one of the oldest organizations of its kind and the only one in the New England states. Its greater scope and breadth of purpose is indicated by the very names of other groups, such as the Austrian Ski Club , the Burgenländische Gemeinschaft, the Steirer Damenchor, the Pro-Mozart Society, and the American Friends of Austrian Labor.

Over the years the A–AA has presented eight to ten programs annually between September and June: lectures in English and German, readings by Austrian writers, concerts, art exhibits, films, discussions, dramatic performances, receptions for visiting artists, and social gatherings. The highlight of the last-named has been the Association's annual meeting coupled with a dinner dance.

No records have been preserved of the earliest years. However, some old-timers remember that the programs often featured talented members and local artists, but also presented such distinguished exiled writers as Berthold Viertel and Ernst Waldinger. While very few "thirty-eighters" returned from Boston to Austria after the war, the Association's charter flights to Europe were very popular in the late 1940s and 1950s.

In the early decades the International Institute of Boston, located on Beacon Street and later on Commonwealth Avenue, provided the Association with a regular meeting place, though some programs took place at the Brighthelmstone Club in Allston, the Goethe Institute on Beacon Street, the Busch-Reisinger Museum in Cambridge, the All-Newton Music School, and the historic Lyman House (The Vale) in Waltham. Numerous programs were presented in collaboration with academic departments at Harvard University, Suffolk University, and Brandeis University. These programs often featured such Massachusetts artists as the singers Mary Sindoni, Karol Bennett, Hanni Myers, Ann Jeffers, Marjorie McDermott, Patricia Metzer, Friedl Haberler, Elsa Feinberg, Joseph Igersheimer, and Frederick Destal; the scholars, scientists, and journalists Victor Weisskopf, Philipp Frank, Charlotte Teuber, Otto Ehrentheil, Richard Geehr, Katherine Lichliter, Otto Zausmer, Eduard Sekler, Leo Gross, Robert Spaethling, Stanley

Hoffman, Sara Lennox, Rudolf Zuckerstatter, Martin Orne, Ernest Pisko, and Arthur Burkhard; the Suburban Singers; the Romanul Chamber Players; the art historians Konrad Oberhuber, John Coolidge, and Julia Phelps; the musicologist Karl Geiringer; the opera director Sarah Caldwell; the composer Alan Hovhaness; the photographer Egon Egone; the actresses Leni Fromm and Miriam Varon; the pianists Edith Vogl Garrett, George Zilzer, Frederick Popper, Erwin Bodky, and Minuetta Kessler; the world traveler Ann Tibbetts; the critic Alta Maloney; and the novelist Ingeborg Lauterstein. In 1966 the Association presented the first American recital of the Hungarian-born German violinist Denes Zsigmondy, and in 1981 the American violinist Louis Krasner reminisced about his commissioning of the Alban Berg violin concerto. Austrian-born performers and scholars who visited from the New York area included the actresses Lilia Skala, Greta Hartwig Manschinger, Dolly Haas, and Evelyn Solann; the singer and film star Marta Eggert-Kiepura; the historian Alfred Tyrner-Tyrnauer; the musicologist Fritz Kramer; and the psychologist Alfred Farau. Representatives of the Austrian government in America who addressed the Association included Wilhelm Schlag, Gottfried Heindl, Thomas Nowotny, Otto Zundritsch, and Walter Greinert. Art exhibits presented the work of Helmut Krommer, Ernst Degasperi, and Georg Kirchner. Another artist, the witty Hans Herbatschek-Hansen, also emceed a number of entertainment programs. As for visitors from Austria, their roster constitutes a veritable Who's Who in Austrian Culture: The writers Hilde Spiel, Christian Wallner, György Sebestyén, Florian Kalbeck, Lotte Ingrisch, Peter Stefan Jungk, Gitta Deutsch, Ernst Jandl, Friederike Mayrocker, Paul Kruntorad, and Frank Zwillinger; the actresses Angelika Schütz and Brigitte Antonius; the library director Josef Stummvoll; the filmmaker Ruth Beckermann; the psychologist Walter Toman; the men's chorus Die Steirer; and the historians and political scientists Norbert Leser and Erik von Kühnelt-Leddihn. In 1982 Herbert Lederer brought his one-man Theater am Schwedenplatz to Brandeis with "Playboy Nestroy," and the singing couple Joan Kiefer and Joseph Maschkan presented four programs of Viennese light music between 1961 and 1973. In 1980 Margarita Pazi came from Israel to speak on Franz Kafka and his circle. The A–AA also hosted post-concert receptions for the Vienna Philharmonic, the Johann Strauß Orchestra, the Vienna Choir Boys, and Paul Badura-Skoda. In 1975 a fund-raising "Ball in Vienna" was held at the Harvard Club of Boston. Among the most memorable programs enjoyed by members of the Association (all at Brandeis University) were readings by Burgtheater actors on their 1968 world tour (Susi Nicoletti, Achim Benning, Otto Kerry, Andreas Wolf, Richard Eybner) and a Grillparzer matinee with Judith Holzmeister and Heinz Moog two years later; the American premiere of Alfred Farau's Grillparzer play "Schatten sind des Lebens Güter" in 1962; and a "Kakanian Festival" (1976) which included the second performance by A–AA members of the hilarious skit "Goethe im Examen" by Polgar and Friedell.

Film showings have always been popular with the Association, and these have ranged from the silent film "Die freudlose Gasse" via such screen classics as "Maskerade" and film versions of plays by Nestroy, Raimund, Schnitzler, and Kraus to contemporary documentaries like "Vienna, the Mask of Gold" and "Wien Retour." Attempts to replicate the atmosphere of a Viennese café, a Grinzing winegarden, or a Fasching celebration usually took the form of a wine tasting or a cabaret evening, but there also were autumnal costume parties with the revealing punning title "Hallo Wien!" Lectures, readings, exhibits, and concerts commemorated anniversaries of Schubert, Beethoven, Mozart, Stefan Zweig, Martin Buber, Karl Kraus, and Albert Schweitzer. Such observances culminated in the annual Beethoven birthday concerts sponsored by the Orne sons and their families in memory of their father, an outstanding player of chamber music. For many years members of the Association arranged and staffed a Viennese booth at the annual ball of the International Institute in Boston, and the Association also participated in the City Hall festivities connected with the 350th anniversary of the City of Boston and in United Nations Day at the State House. More recently members of the Association have enjoyed the Boston Aria Guild's New Year's Eve performances of "Die Fledermaus" at Sanders Theater in Cambridge.

Since 1976 the A–AA has each year awarded a stipend to a person working on a project dealing with some aspect of Austrian culture. In the past these scholarships have facilitated such diverse pursuits as the translation of plays by Franz Theodor Csokor, the preparation of song recitals, a biography of the Burgtheater actress Jenny Gross, a doctoral dissertation on the Nobel laureate Elias Canetti, a study of the architect Adolf Loos, and an examination of organs in Austrian churches.

The acid test of any voluntary association and its activities concerns their uniqueness and utility. Whom does an association benefit and what is the spirit informing its programs and projects? Is the association really needed, and would there be a loss to a wider community if it did not exist? In all these regards the A–AA, with its cultural mediatorship and its mix of European and American elements, the old and the new, ranks very high. The rich menu of Boston's (and New England's) culture would have been, and would be, immeasurably poorer without it. Under the long-term presidencies of Paul Mueller, Martha Brunner-Orne, Kurt Toman, Wolfram Jarisch, Karl Hormann, and (currently) Elisabeth Holubar-Davies, not to mention the devoted efforts of other officers and friends too numerous to list here, the Austro-American Association of Boston has enjoyed remarkable stability and has repeatedly rejuvenated itself by attracting not only American-born members but also younger Austrians who have come to Boston temporarily or permanently in search of greater professional opportunities. The IMAS, which experienced no such renewal, dissolved itself in 1994, but there is every reason to believe that the cultural and social mediating activities of the Austro-American Association, informed by an unflagging sense of purpose, will continue well into the twenty-first century.

PART TWO

Translations

INTRODUCTION

Many of the short prose pieces that are presented here in my translation are perhaps best characterized as feuilletons, and what they have in common is their description of life in *fin-de-siècle* Austria. Feuilleton, the word and the concept, has never had as great a currency in the English-speaking world as it has had in western and central Europe. In 19th century France, *feuilleton* (derived from a word meaning "little leaf") denoted the Sunday supplement or rotogravure section of a newspaper that usually featured a serialized novel. In Germany and Austria, however, the word denoted something broader—namely, the entire cultural section of a newspaper. It began on the front page "*unter dem Strich*" (under a line) and consisted of short fiction, a travel report, a review, or a critical, evocative, stylistically notable essay (often a "think piece") on literature, art, music, education, or manners. Heinrich Heine is widely regarded as the father of this literary or journalistic form; for this the Viennese satirist Karl Kraus excoriated him in an essay published in 1910, blaming him for turning journalism into an unwholesome intermediary between art and life as well as a parasite on both, for creating a facile pattern that beguilingly blended substance with form in a linguistically and aesthetically deceitful manner.

"Beard of the Prophet" is a chapter, slightly abridged, from Raoul Auernheimer's autobiography, *Das Wirtshaus zur verlorenen Zeit* (Vienna, 1948). Auernheimer was born in Vienna on April 15, 1876, as the son of a German Gentile father and a Hungarian-born Jewish mother. After obtaining a doctorate of laws from the University of Vienna, he became a prolific writer of stories, novels, comedies, and essays. He contributed to many newspapers, including the *Neue Freie Presse,* and edited several books in the field of cultural history. Auernheimer is generally grouped with the "Young Vienna" circle of writers, which also included Hofmannsthal, Bahr, Beer-Hofmann, Stefan Zweig, Altenberg, and Salten. In 1911 Auernheimer edited a two-volume collection of Theodor Herzl's feuilletons, a form in which Auernheimer also excelled. In 1938 Auernheimer spent five months in the Dachau concentration camp. After his release he came to the United States where he published *Prince Metternich, Statesman and Lover* (1940). A psychological biography of Grillparzer and his autobiography were his last works. Auernheimer died at Oakland, California, on January 7, 1948.

In *fin-de-siècle* Vienna Theodor Herzl was one of the foremost practitioners of the feuilleton, a form successfully practiced even today. Stefan Zweig has characterized Herzl's short prose pieces in these words: "His essays are still enchanting in their wealth of sharp and ofttimes wise observations, their stylistic animation, and their aristocratic charm. Whether light or critical, they never lost their innate nobility; they were the most cultivated in journalism and were the delight of a city that had schooled itself to every subtlety."

"The Menorah" is of definite autobiographical significance. It must not be inferred, however, that Herzl completely identified with the artist in the story. He was not an observant Jew, and ritual practices interested him only when he encountered them in aesthetic, symbolic, or artistic form, when they appealed to his sense of style. Compare this with Herzl's diary entry of December 24, 1895: "I was just lighting the Christmas tree for my children when Güdemann [the Chief Rabbi of Vienna] arrived. He seemed upset by the 'Christian' custom. Well, I will not let myself be pressured! But I don't mind if they call it the Chanukah tree—or the winter solstice" (*Complete Diaries,* vol. 1, p. 285). Like so many of Herzl's writings inspired by his preoccupation with what he called the Jewish cause, "The Menorah" has a marked prophetic quality. In the form of a parable about a *baal teshuvah* ("master of the return," a Jew who returns to the fold) Herzl meant to highlight the progressive growth and acceptance, the symbolic beauty of his Zionist idea, with the darkness of suppression and a ghetto mentality gradually giving way to the splendor of Jewish auto-emancipation and a new Zionist fervor lighting the way to a Jewish State.

"The Bell on the Left," one of Herzl's "philosophical tales," dates from 1901, and "July Sunday in the Prater," written in 1899, presents a picture of the city of "wine, women, and song" that differs markedly from other, uncritically and nostalgically roseate accounts. "Trudel's Tear" was written in 1899 about the Zionist leader's youngest child, named Margarete (or Gretherl) but called Trude or Trudel. Some of the poignancy of this piece derives from the sad fate of Herzl's children. Pauline and Hans Herzl both died in 1930 after short and unhappy lives, the son committing suicide. After many years of mental instability, Trude was deported from Vienna by the Nazis and died in Theresienstadt in 1943 at the age of fifty, her husband, Richard Neumann, having predeceased her there.

Peter Herz (1895–1987) is best known as the man who wrote the lyrics of many of Vienna's most successful and most fondly remembered popular songs. He was a noted wit and a prolific author of poems, essays, revues, radio plays, and operetta libretti. His wise and conciliatory autobiography, *Gestern war ein schöner Tag,* appeared in 1984, three decades after Herz had returned to his native Vienna from seventeen years of exile in London. Herz was a frequent visitor to Baden. His feuilleton "The Cholent War," published in 1986 in the *Neue Illustrierte Welt,* a Vienna journal that considers itself as the successor of Herzl's Zionist publication *Die Welt,* is a lighthearted reminiscence of the Zionist endeavors of the author's near-namesake. Cholent, a delicacy poetically celebrated by Heinrich Heine as "kosher ambrosia," has been defined as "a stewed or baked dish, especially of meat and beans, served on the Sabbath but cooked the day before or overnight on a slow fire."

At the turn of the century the poet, dramatist, storyteller, and essayist Richard Beer-Hofmann (1866–1945) was the only *homo judaicus* in the distinguished circle of writers known as Young Vienna. He achieved fame in 1897 with his "Schlaflied für Mirjam" (Lullaby for Miriam), written at the cradle of his firstborn and widely admired as a philosophical poem that affirms Jewish continuity and hope in the midst of evanescence and uncertainty. Beer-Hofmann's magnum opus is a grandly conceived cycle of poetic plays about King David, of which only *Jaakobs Traum* (*Jacob's Dream*) and a stage prologue were completed. In the 1920s Beer-Hofmann collaborated with Max Reinhardt on various theatrical projects, and in 1936 he visited Palestine. Three years later he emigrated from Nazi Austria and reached the United States via Switzerland, where his wife had died. From November 1939 to his death in September 1945 he lived in New York with his daughters Miriam and Naëmah.

The *Gedenkrede auf Wolfgang Amadé Mozart* is a rhapsodic evocation of the surroundings and impressions that miraculously shaped the composer's life and art. It was written for the 150th anniversary of Mozart's birth, in 1906, at the behest of the *Frankfurter Zeitung.* The editors requested that Beer-Hofmann not write directly about Mozart's life and works, and this restriction, paradoxically, freed the author's fantasy: "Since all had been forbidden me, I found that all had been vouchsafed me." The result was this "fairy tale of the wondrously beautiful young music-maker from Austria who was not allowed to grow old." The address was first published as a booklet by S. Fischer Verlag in 1906 and was reissued in 1926.

"In the Snow" is one of Stefan Zweig's earliest pieces of short fiction; it appeared as "Im Schnee" in the *Jüdischer Almanach,* a literary and artistic publication edited by Berthold Feiwel in Berlin between 1902 and 1904. Zweig did not include it in any of his later collections. It is hardly "vintage Zweig," but it already bears some of the earmarks of the author's sensitive and evocative but somewhat overheated style, and his early preoccupation with a Jewish theme foreshadows such masterpieces of Jewish content as the play *Jeremiah* (1917) and the haunting legend *The Buried Candelabrum,* published in 1937, which Sol Liptzin has called "as sad an affirmation of Jewishness as ever was penned in our century." "The Legend of the Third Dove" is a vibrant expression of Zweig's pacifism, and "Thanks to Books" is an enduring tribute to the author's bibliophile pursuits. "The Tower of Babel," which appeared in the first issue of *Le Carmel* (Geneva, April-May 1916), was one of the pieces through which Zweig strove to reestablish the community of European intellectuals during the war. It reveals its author as somewhat of a European chauvinist, for he rejects America and Asia as places where a spiritual regeneration of mankind might take place. The story clearly shows that Zweig's religion was Europe and that he viewed God as the jealous, inexorable Old Testament deity. It also poignantly foreshadows his suicide at a time when he felt that the Tower of Babel had crumbled beyond repair and could never be rebuilt.

Z.F. Finot was the pen name of Dr. Z.F. Finkelstein, who was born in Lvov (Lemberg) in 1886. For many years he was a resident of Vienna, where he was editor of *Die Stimme* as well as a correspondent of the Jewish Telegraphic Agency. Long active as a Zionist, he wrote a book about Theodor Herzl, *Schicksalsstunden eines Führers* (A Leader's Hours of Destiny). In 1938 Finkelstein-Finot emigrated to Jerusalem, where he worked as a free-lance journalist and founded the Austrian Settlers' Association. He died in Jerusalem in 1959.

This is hardly the place for extended remarks on the 300-year history of that venerable Viennese institution, the Kaffeehaus. Cafés, particularly those frequented by the literati and other creative people, have flourished in other cities as well, but nowhere else have they acquired such a mystique. The three legendary cafés that existed in Vienna from the late nineteenth century to the 1930s were the Griensteidl (razed in 1897), the Central (pronounced Tsentraal, with the stress on the second syllable), and the Herrenhof, all of them located within a few steps of one another on the Michaelerplatz or the Herrengasse, in the heart of the city. Alfred Polgar (originally Polak, 1873-1955) became the "theorist" of the Café Central, where he regularly met such noted fellow writers as Peter Altenberg, Egon Erwin Kisch, Egon Friedell, and Anton Kuh. Among the many other notables who frequented this legendary café were Mayor Karl Lueger, the architect Adolf Loos, and an inveterate chess player named Lev (Leib) Bronstein, known in history as Leon Trotsky. In recent years the Café Central has been reconstituted at its old location, and it is even possible to join Altenberg in effigy for coffee at one of its tables. The witty and prolific Alfred Polgar, who was active as a dramatist, storyteller, essayist and theater critic in Vienna and Berlin, spent relatively unproductive and unhappy years in the United States (where his dream of being published in *The New Yorker* was unfulfilled) before returning to postwar Europe, where he died in Zurich.

The writings of the prolific Jewish thinker Martin Buber, who was born in Vienna in 1878 and died in Jerusalem in 1965, include a novel, a play, and numerous essays. "Bücher und Menschen," written in 1947 for a volume in honor of the merchant, publisher, and philanthropist Salman Schocken, brings this book to a fitting close.

Raoul Auernheimer:

BEARD OF THE PROPHET

Besides my father's another beard hovered over my youthful years while I was growing up leisurely on the fringe of literary Vienna. It was an entirely dissimilar beard, however, as inky as my father's was corn-blond; and thus the counterpoint of the blood which dominated and agitated my entire life found here an early, distinct, and decisive expression.

This silky-black Flying Dutchman beard with its fairy-tale aura of dark shadows encircled the eloquent mouth of a celebrated Viennese writer who had "won his spurs," to use the ever-chivalrous journalese of the time, as the Paris correspondent of the *Neue Freie Presse*. In a word—it was the beard of Theodor Herzl, who was my mother's nephew.

My memories of the great Jewish leader go back to a time when he was not the new Moses as yet and his barely sprouting beard was still anything but famous. I am one of the few people who knew Theodor Herzl when he was still smooth-shaven—with a chin, in fact, on which there was nothing to shave off. He was 21 years old and I was barely six when mama took me along to visit her cousin, Theodor's mother. I was shunted off into his room, and suddenly, looking up at a 45-degree angle, I faced my cousin, three times my size, who was studying in his room, pacing up and down among books and papers.

The first thing he asked, smiling down at me, was whether I wanted anything. One of the most charming traits of his personality was his understanding of a child's psyche. Yes, I replied with a composure that bespoke a tacit prior preparation, I did have a big request to make: I wanted a pen knife. Whereupon my eloquent cousin silently took me by the hand and led me down three flights of a stone staircase that smelled of abrasives.

Presently we stepped into a nearby shop whose paltry window looked promising and whose interior did indeed teem and gleam with knives of all kinds. Uncle Theodor—bathed in the glow of the knives, the cousin had suddenly been promoted to uncle—had two knives placed before me for my selection: one in a mother-of-pearl case, the other encased in horn. "This mother-of-pearl one," he said with a wink at the sympathetically smiling sales clerk, "costs 95 kreuzer, and that one" (he pointed at the somewhat longer horn case) "is one guilder fifty. Which one would you like?" Modest by upbringing, I decided on the cheaper one. "This one," I said, pointing to the mother-of-pearl knife. It was the more expensive one, however; my good uncle, who in his youth sometimes had too low an opinion of people in general, had simply wanted to put me to the test by switching prices. Thus, rising above my baseness, I carried off the more beautiful knife after all.

My cousin Theodor liked to subject me to such tests of character. Many years later he told about one of them in the house of the Berlin journalist Lewisohn where he had taken me. When I was two—so he said—I was delightfully stupid. He used to test me by placing a lump of sugar under the piano. I crawled after it, put it in my mouth, and proudly stood up, banging my head against the rather unprepossessing underside of the piano. "That stupid boy," cried my cousin, joining my mother in the enjoyment of my unspeakable stupidity. But when, a week later, he repeated the experiment for the umpteenth time, something quite unexpected happened. I crawled under the piano and put the lump of sugar in my mouth, but instead of straightening up as expected, I crept, sucking away at the sugar, to the opposite side of the room, and only there did I carefully resume my vertical position, slowly and shyly looking upward. "And that, my dear Raoul"—so my cousin concluded his narrative in his friend's house—"is how you will always fare in life." This whimsical philosophic conclusion was already Theodor Herzl at his best and most genuine. It sounded the key-note of his enchanting children's feuilletons which drew on his own experience and for a time delighted countless young Viennese mothers. "The Century of the Child," as predicted by the Swedish pioneer Ellen Key, was already making itself felt, and, like Victorian England, the Vienna of Franz Joseph loved to chat about children. When I was twenty, I wrote—surely under Herzl's influence—a little story of that kind, "Stanniol" [Tinfoil]...

My big cousin—our relationship always reminded me a bit of Andersen's fairy-tale, "Big Claus and Little Claus"—was a Viennese celebrity, and his fame extended to Paris, which at that time was the Mecca of European letters. From there he wired daily columns of reports on the Dreyfus affair to his newspaper, which we read every day, and at regular intervals he published his Paris feuilletons, which scintillated with wit and life and quickly made him famous. With comic grace he followed in Heine's footsteps, just as Heine had followed in Lawrence Sterne's, offering variations on his *Sentimental Journey:* everything in literature and life is interconnected and mutually dependent. Apart from this, Heine's Viennese successor displayed from the very beginning an unmistakable tendency toward greater depth. Here was a Heine who had also read Maupassant and, like the French Naturalists, spurning all cloudy Romanticism, constantly patterned his style after reality.

My cousin came to Vienna but once a year, usually in early spring, and then he regularly drew up before our little house in an open hansom cab—the height of elegance in those days. The dogs barked and I rushed up to the garden door to let him in. It was always a joyous surprise, and once, when I was 18 or 19, this surprise was so sudden that I didn't have time to put away a volume of Maupassant in which I was engrossed. My tall, dark-clad cousin took the book—it was *Bel Ami,* no less—out of my hands and twisted his ivory-pale features with the blue-black silky beard, which now solemnly covered his chin, into the face of an offended Arab sheik. He thought, not unjustly, that it was too soon for me to be reading such things. But my mother, who had little taste for preachments, stood up for her son—militantly, as was her wont in intellectual matters. She parried his reproach that this was not proper reading matter for a young fellow of my age with this nonchalant question: "Well, did *you* always read only what was proper for you?" "No," my avuncular cousin had to admit, and with a droll smile he added: "That is why I am so much against it."

Herzl possessed to a high degree this talent for clever conversational dodges and lightning-quick remarks—what the French call *saillie.* It was a talent of the Viennese theater, the quintessence of which was the Burgtheater, and Paris, the real home of the *mot heureux,* had an active share in it. I remember many of these felicitous and gratifying remarks from his short articles and essays, which were always dramatically alive and often were little works of art. For example, he wrote about Biarritz—the "Coast of Dandies," as he titled the feuilleton, using *Geck,* an old word which meant both "dandy" and "fool." He wrote it; but it was anything but a description: it was a picture, with color and atmosphere. It contained a dash of social pessimism—which was very popular, even indispensable at that time—but the smell of the landscape, the breath of night, and the primeval sounds of the sea were in it as well. The *flâneur* in his white flannels spoke about the gambling casino and closed with this sentence: "The Biarritz casino is built on a foundation of indestructible granite: human stupidity." And in the end everything is summed up in the vision of a young navy officer who is on deck watch on his warship. He sees the lights of Biarritz flash through the night from afar and smiles a smile of remembrance and possibly expectation: "Ah, Biarritz!" Gambler's luck, women, the joys of the senses—this "Ah, Biarritz!" says everything and lets one guess even more. Like a good ending of an act.

My cousin had this talent for "last lines" in great measure, and on occasion he even had the courage to turn such last lines into first lines. When Daudet suddenly died in Paris, his obituary began with this unforgettable phrase: "A charming mouth has closed forever." When Mitterwurzer, a great actor and possibly even greater comedian, left the stage, Herzl began: "With one of his sudden turns he has slipped away from us." It was like a flashlight which lights up the features of a dead man, not unraveling his secret, but shedding light on it. Hofmannsthal pursued this secret in one of his most beautiful poems which contains the immortal line "But what was he, and what was he not?" To be sure, that was not conceived and written for a newspaper. But Theodor Herzl, who did write for newspapers, dared nevertheless to explain Anatole France to the Viennese and to give a definitive characterization of the great writer—a pillar of our age of culture who had everything but Nature—with this final sentence, which sums up his essence: "The muse of Anatole France has the beautiful neck of sterile women."

That is what we called brilliant in those days. And we called it witty and clever when this fine critic captured the glory of an autumn day with these words: "Autumn has come like a young colonel. He is still out to make conquests, but secretly a shudder runs down his spine." *Geistreich,* and even more than that. That word, incidentally, is untranslatable into English. The closest word would be "thoughtful;" but "thoughtful" means only that one has thoughts, whereas *geistreich* means not just having thoughts, but being able to play with them.

This is what my big cousin did for some years in Paris and Vienna to the indescribable pleasure of his many readers. But then he suddenly stopped playing and became serious; Paris had something to do with this, too. One day it had been Herzl's journalistic duty to describe the degradation of the Jewish captain Dreyfus, who was still avowing his innocence (which was later proved) while they were tearing the epaulettes off his uniform. This event had two consequences in world history. It gave rise to neo-European anti-Semitism, which was to blossom into the poisonous plant of Nazism a quarter of a century later. But the self-confident defense of Jewry, Zionism, also stems from this experience of mankind. And Theodor Herzl, an idealist of high calibre even in his stylistically elegant journalism, became its prophet. Even before Dreyfus had arrived at Devil's Island, the witness of his degradation had given the world a pamphlet in which he demanded the program of Zionism, including "a home for the Jews in Palestine secured under international law."

A great deal could be said about Zionism which would transcend the confines of this book. Its *raison d'être* as a countermovement, an eternal countermovement, has been justified a millionfold by the heinous deeds of Nazism. Nor can there be any doubt of its historical logicality. The nineteenth century was the century of nationalism, with one nationalism arising out of another, from the French to the Jewish kind. Jewish nationalism was the last link in the chain. It is not surprising that this national movement of protest arose in Austria, where it had been preceded by Hungarian, Czech, Polish, Yugoslavian, and Italian asseverations of national independence—not to mention the German ones. Thus, if nationalism was the course of history, the pioneer of Zionism could not have chosen a more practicable one. It would be different, of course, if nationalism should turn out to be but a byway of history from which the twentieth century will have to find its way back to a supranational world citizenship—which is in keeping with this author's views. But even then the answer which Herzl gave to anti-Semitic presumptuousness would have been the only correct one, because it was the only dignified one. What he had in mind was the replacement of the deficient national feeling on the part of the Jews by an ever-latent national pride. His answer was that of *Uriel Acosta:* "You may curse me, because I am a Jew!"[1] And at the same time it was the answer to a German nationalism emerging threateningly on the horizon, a nationalism about whose danger the thinker and politician Theodor Herzl was under no illusion. He once wrote down a sentence which is memorable in its determined resignation: "German anti-Semitism is everlasting; German fairy-tales and German folksongs are anti-Semitic."

This, to be sure, the German-oriented liberals refused to see, for they believed in the legend of assimilation. The publisher of the *Neue Freie Presse,* a stronghold of cosmopolitan Jewish intellectualism, once told me in these words: "I am not *pro*-Jewish; I am not *anti*-Jewish; I am *a*-Jewish." This is an intellectually unexceptionable view, and it is also in keeping with the American philosophy, although its practicability in America has yet to be shown. In Europe, at any rate, it proved to be unfeasible, and it remains to be seen what attitude the other continents will take.

---

[1] Translator's note: From Act 2 of Karl Gutzkow's tragedy *Uriel Acosta* (1846/7).

Herzl died at the age of 44, much too early for his own generation and for future generations to whose attention the prophetic feuilletonist, and the fine writer too, has a claim. A short time before his death he was in Breslau, at the grave of Lasalle to whom he paid homage as a kindred spirit in intellect and convictions. There is also an unmistakable similarity of character, although Herzl had better manners. Both men displayed the same blend of ambitious romanticism, diplomatic realism, worldly wisdom, and fiery idealism, and if Lasalle's irresistible dynamism as an agitator exceeded that of the younger man, Herzl made up for it through the princely demeanor of an instantly captivating personality. His blue-black beard, his dark, dreamy eyes, his full glance, his well-proportioned tall figure, his face with its noble pallor and the expressive features as though engraved in wax impressed themselves upon all who met him as the most beautiful portrait in an art gallery does. On my tortuous path through life I have never encountered a person of greater magic, nor anyone whose magic was embellished with so much grace. "Epaphroditus" is what the Romans called the darling of the gods—so Herzl reminds us in one of his *Philosophical Tales,* which were obviously inspired by Anatole France. He himself was Epaphroditus; the title fits the author.

Only days before his death he said goodbye to one of his last visitors on the terrace of the sanitarium where medical skill was hopelessly attempting to make his ailing heart serviceable again. It was evening, at sunset, and the transfigured Austrian countryside once more spread before him its early-summer magic in the light of the waning day. He smiled, looked into the eyes of his guest, and said, pausing at the threshold before he stepped into the darkness: "*Le soir—mon soir—bon soir!*" In his figure there was a strange blend of the prophetic and the French eighteenth century when people always kept a pretty saying in readiness for their last breath. But the prophetic element made him enigmatical. "When Herzl comes into my office to report on the manuscripts that have come in," said his editor-in-chief Moriz Benedikt, "I never know whether it is my literary editor or the Messiah after all." He said this with a smile; but he really didn't know. Nobody did.

Theodor Herzl:

THE MENORAH

There once was a man who had felt deep in his soul how hard it was to be a Jew. His external circumstances were satisfactory enough. He made an adequate living and was fortunate enough to have a vocation in which he could create what his heart impelled him to. You see, he was an artist. He had long ago ceased to pay any attention to his Jewish origin or to the faith of his fathers when the age-old hatred asserted itself again under a fashionable slogan. Like many others, our man too believed that this movement would peter out soon. But it kept on getting worse instead of better, and those attacks pained him over and over again, even though he was not directly affected by them. Gradually his soul became one bleeding wound.

This excruciating psychic torment had the effect of steering him to its source, namely his Jewishness, and something came about that he might never have achieved in better days, because he had become so alienated from it: he began to love Judaism with a great fervor. At first he did not fully acknowledge this wondrous affection, but finally it grew so powerful that his vague feelings crystallized into a clear idea to which he gave voice: the thought that there was only one way out of this Jewish distress—namely, the return to Judaism.

When his best friends, whose situation was similar to his, found out about this, they shook their heads and thought that he had gone out of his mind. How could something be a remedy that meant only an intensification and deepening of the malady? He, on the other hand, thought that the reason for the acuteness of their moral situation was that the modern Jews had lost the counterpoise which our strong forefathers possessed in their hearts. People ridiculed him behind his back, some even laughed right in his face, but he did not let the silly remarks of people whose judgment he had never before had occasion to value throw him off his course, and he bore the malicious or good-natured jests with equanimity. And since his actions were anything but unreasonable, people gradually let him indulge in his whims, although some used a stronger term, *idée fixe,* to describe it.

In his patient way our man repeatedly displayed the courage of his convictions. There were a number of considerations which he himself had a hard time with, although he was stubborn enough not to let on. As a man and artist of modern sensibilities he was deeply rooted in many non-Jewish customs, and he had absorbed ineradicable elements from the cultures of the nations among which his intellectual pursuits had taken him. How was this to be reconciled with his return to Judaism? This gave rise to many doubts in his mind about the soundness of his guiding ideas, of his *idée maîtresse,* as a French thinker has called it.

Perhaps the generation that had grown up under the influence of other cultures was no longer capable of that return which he had discovered as the solution. But the next generation would be capable of it, provided it was given the right guidance early enough. Therefore he tried to make sure that his own children, at least, would be shown the right way, that they would receive a Jewish education from the very beginning.

In previous years he had let the festival which has for so many centuries illuminated the wonderful phenomenon of the Maccabees with the glow of small candles pass by unobserved. Now, however, he used it as an occasion to provide his children with a beautiful memory for future days. An attachment to the ancient nation was to be instilled early in these young souls. A Menorah was acquired, and when he held this nine-branched candlestick in his hands for the first time, a strange mood came over him. In his father's house, too, the little lights had burned in his youth, which was already remote, and there was something intimate and homelike about it. This tradition did not seem chill or dead. The custom of kindling one light by another had been passed on through the ages.

The ancient form of the Menorah was food for thought as well. When was the primitive structure of this candlestick devised? Ostensibly its form was originally derived from that of a tree: the sturdy stem in the center; to the right and to the left four branches, one below the other, each set being on the same level and all eight of equal height. A later symbolism added a ninth, shorter branch which juts out in front and is called the *shammash* or servant. What mystery this simple artistic form, taken from Nature, has been endowed with by the successive generations! And our friend, himself an artist, wondered whether it would not be possible to infuse new life into the rigidified form of the Menorah, to water its roots like those of a tree. The very sound of the name, which he pronounced in front of his children every evening now, gave him pleasure. It sounded especially lovely when the word came from a child's mouth.

The first candle was lit and the origin of the holiday was recited along with it: the wonderful phenomenon of the little lamp which was long-lived beyond all expectations, as well as the stories of the return from the Babylonian exile, of the Second Temple, of the Maccabees. Our friend told his children all he knew. It was little enough, to be sure, but it served. When the second candle was lit, they repeated what he had told them, and although it had all been learned from him, it seemed to him quite new and beautiful. In the days that followed he could hardly wait for the evenings, which became ever brighter. Candle after candle was in the Menorah, and the father mused on the little candles with his children, till at length his reflections became too deep to be uttered before them.

When he had resolved to return to the fold and to acknowledge this return openly, he had only intended to do an honorable and sensible thing. But he had never dreamed that on his way back home he would also find gratification of his longing for beauty. Yet nothing less than that was befalling him. The Menorah, with its growing brilliance of lights, was a thing of beauty indeed, and it inspired lofty thoughts.

So he set to work and sketched with his practised hand a design for a Menorah which he wanted to present to his children the following year. He made a free adaptation of the motif of the eight arms of equal height which project from the central stem to the right and to the left on the same level. He did not consider himself bound by the rigid traditional form, but created directly from Nature again, unconcerned with other interpretations, which, of course, continued to be no less valid. What he was aiming at was vibrant beauty. But even as he brought new motion into the rigidified forms, he still observed their laws, the refined old style of their arrangement. It was a tree with slender branches; its ends opened up like calyxes, and it was these calyxes that were to hold the candles.

With such thoughtful occupation the week passed. There came the eighth day, on which the whole row of lights burns, including the faithful ninth candle, the *shammash,* which otherwise serves only for the lighting of the others. A great radiance emanated from the Menorah. The children's eyes sparkled. But for our friend the whole thing became a parable for the enkindling of a nation. One candle at first; it is still dark and the solitary light still looks gloomy; then it finds a companion, then another, and more and more. The darkness must retreat. The young and the poor are the first to see the light, then the others join in, all those who love Justice, Truth, Liberty, Progress, Humanity, Beauty. When all the candles are burning, everyone must stop in amazement and rejoice at what has been wrought. And no office is more blessed than that of a Servant of the Light.

Theodor Herzl:

THE BELL ON THE LEFT

There was nothing festive about Mr. Wendelin's return. He had been away for some 20 years, and now he simply was there again. He had grown older and the town younger, but there was still many a corner left from the old days and the weeds of memory grew there between the cobblestones. Since his return Mr. Wendelin dreamed a lot; he could not get over the old times. The old days came around every corner. An excessively fat lady came waddling along and Mr. Wendelin's heart skipped a beat, like in the old days, because he could see from afar that it was the mother of sweet little Eva. Oh no, it was Eva herself. Then came a skinny graybearded man, the Financial Counselor whose son Fritz he had beaten up in school. Oh no, it was Fritz himself. Thus Mr. Wendelin received graphic evidence of the passage of a generation. He could see all of them slowly walking toward the cemetery.

People paid attention to him for only a few days, and then he gradually lost the attraction of novelty. He lived with his cousin, whose wife had died a short time ago. No one knew how long Mr. Wendelin intended to stay there. Someone asked him, and he replied: "Until I am ready to go away again. Just as I stayed out there till I was ready for my hometown..."

Still, he did not seem to be in a hurry. Was he able to take that much time off from business, or had he already feathered his nest? But the local snoops had trouble finding out how Mr. Wendelin had fared "out there." He had become a taciturn person, and his exterior revealed nothing. It was not even possible to infer anything regarding his circumstances and past history from his clothing. For when he arrived, the weather suddenly turned cold and he wore an old coat of his father's until the tailor at the main square had finished his new winter coat. And then Mr. Wendelin looked exactly like the other solid citizens of the town. Only his brown summer hat betrayed the rigors of his journey somewhat. Still, a slight aura of mystery surrounded Mr. Wendelin and made him appear so refined that he was welcome at any table when he came into the Rathskeller in the evening. But he usually went to the back room where the "Table of the Fortunates" was located. This was a wag's appellation for the regulars' table, and there was envy and scorn as well as reverence in it, for anyone who wanted to hold his own there had to be someone, have something, or represent something. Mr. Wendelin had calmly sat down at this table on the very first day; after all, he had known almost all those men from the days when they were throwing snowballs, stealing apples, and secretly smoking pipes behind great rock piles.

The fact that Mr. Wendelin had joined the Fortunates without much ado predisposed people in his favor. He, however, at first did not know what company he was in. When he gradually found out, he preferred to sit at the tables of other acquaintances, for around the Fortunates there was an atmosphere that he found disagreeable in the long run. They were so sure in their judgments and the self-confidence of each individual was so great that Mr. Wendelin felt intimidated and more and more of a stranger. But once he had started associating with them he could not easily stay away from them. He had to have an excuse for doing so, and that presented itself one evening during a conversation.

Kauer, a steel manufacturer, said: "Oh, I'm tired of hearing about those who have fallen by the wayside. It's always their own fault. I won't deny that a capable fellow can run into some bad luck occasionally, but he always fights his way out of it. That's what I think."

The others murmured their approval, and then they suddenly looked at Mr. Wendelin. His voice sounded strange as he said: "If you want me to, I will tell you a little story that is pertinent here. I was a participant in those events myself."

Of course they wanted to hear his story. Now, perhaps, they would learn something about Mr. Wendelin's veiled past. Some quickly emptied their glasses and asked him to wait until they had been refilled. He watched these preparations with a smile and then stared into space. Some cigar ashes had fallen on the table; he smoothed out the gray mass with his finger and then made marks in it.

Now the fresh glasses had arrived, the men were all ears, and Mr. Wendelin began his story.

> In the first years after I had left here, things were not rosy for me. If I hadn't been ashamed to come back, I would have returned. It's a peculiar kind of local limitation, evidently something akin to local pride. It was all right for me to be badly off elsewhere, but not here. Today I ask you: Why? I wanted to achieve something. I wanted to show you. Show whom? You, Kauer, or you, Martin, or the man who was mayor then, or my first love, or my teacher? In short, I was an ass. But asses can find themselves in a desperate mood, and I was in such a mood when the turning point of my fate came.
>
> I happened to be in a coastal town. I was anxious to emigrate to America, and I considered applying for work as a stoker, for I didn't have the fare. There I was on the pier, looking at the Wilhelm Wielemann, which was being scoured for the voyage. It was a handsome steamship named after its owner, the big merchant. Every child knew Wilhelm Wielemann's story. He had started quite small—some say as a stoker or waiter on a mail boat—and now he was the foremost shipowner. Ships bore his name, he owned the finest mansion, and wherever one glimpsed something

magnificent or luxurious in town, he had a share in it or was its sole owner. In a word, "*Kannitverstan!*"[1]

From the harbor I walked downtown, toward the business district, vaguely hoping to find some way of earning a livelihood. I kept thinking of Wilhelm Wielemann, who had probably had to experience similar feelings before he became such a big man. And while I was thinking of him, suddenly, as if in my hungry dream, I heard someone speak his name. Two young people were walking past.

"That's Wilhelm Wielemann's carriage," said one of them.

The other one emitted a whistle. "This one? Well, it's nothing to brag about."

The carriage stopped in front of an ordinary gray office building. The vehicle in which the famous businessman made his calls really did not look like much. I was still staring at it when suddenly a little old man stood next to me and asked me: "What's so special about this carriage? Is anything broken?"

This reminded me of my earlier thoughts, and I said in jest: "No, but it's Kannitverstan's carriage."

There was a gleam in the old man's intelligent eyes. My reply had amused him. And now something strange happened; I cannot tell it as quickly as it happened. The old man stepped behind the carriage with me, and in two minutes he had learned all about me and my plans. Never again have I met a man who was so quick about asking, guessing, and comprehending. After two minutes he knew me inside and out as though he were my doctor and had palpated me and listened to my heart. And in the manner of a doctor he finally took out his billfold, wrote something in pencil, and handed me one of his cards.

"Take this and deliver it on the second floor of this building," he said. He quickly climbed into the carriage, the door was closed, and while I was still staring at him speech-

---

[1] The reference is to Johann Peter Hebel's celebrated story by that title (1809) in which a German in Amsterdam who inquires about the owner of sumptuous properties and finally about a person being buried always receives the answer "*Kannitverstan*" (Can't understand you) and thinks it is the name of a man.

less, he was already gone. For it had been Kannitverstan in person—Wilhelm Wielemann.

The following words were written on the card under the name Wilhelm Wielemann: "...is interested in the young bearer of this card and asks that he be employed if he is qualified."

I immediately appreciated this stroke of luck. A recommendation from Wilhelm Wielemann was bound to work wonders; it might be a kind of royal command for business firms. I instantly rose to the occasion, and with the gait of a gentleman I entered the building and climbed the stairs to the second floor. This was the extent of my instructions and my wisdom, but suddenly I faced a dilemma. In the corridor, next to each other, were two identical doors with two identical bellpulls. Though it happened more than a quarter of a century ago, I can still see these off-white doors and can still visualize the two bellpulls. In the fashion of that time they were thin iron rods with wooden handles, and at the top of the doors were two identical holes in the wall through which wires ran inside, where the bells rang when someone pulled them.

Oh, but which of the two wooden handles was I supposed to grasp? They were hanging close to each other, the one on the left to the right of its door and the one on the right to the left of the doorpost. And I was supposed to choose without any clue! For the names of the two firms that I was able to read above the doors meant nothing to me; it said Weißenried & Co. on the right and Eberhard Krause on the left. I knew neither Weißenried & Co. nor Eberhard Krause. My unexpected patron had not given me any name, and there was no further information on the card. I had to decide in favor of one bell or the other. I chose the one on the right, and this, too, happened a lot faster than I am telling you about it. After all, it was nothing special, the kind of thing that happens every day. I had no inkling that it was the most important moment of my life. Nor did I have the feeling that I was making a decision when I activated the bell on the right. And that is why today I would seem foolish to myself if I said: Oh, I was efficient, or I was smart, I pulled the right bell.

The door of Weißenried & Co. opened. Soon I stood before the head of the firm, a friendly elderly gentleman.

Wilhelm Wielemann's card worked its magic. Mr. Weißenried interviewed me amiably, my answers satisfied him, and I was hired. To Kannitverstan I wrote a letter of thanks which he probably tossed in the wastebasket unread along with a hundred others. I never had any further contact with him. But some time later I was permitted to visit Weißenried's house. My boss had a daughter, a dear, demure creature. In his family I re-encountered the salutary, sound spirit of peace and labor I had already become familiar with at the office. All the virtues of the solid, modest bourgeoisie were assembled in this house. It became my aim in life, and when after a few years of hard work I had become indispensable to the business, Mr. Weißenried made me a partner and gave me his daughter for a wife. This is an ordinary story of the kind that happens a hundred thousand times, isn't it? And it's a good thing. Children come, fill the house with play, laughter, song, and growing seriousness. One knows what one lives and toils for, and one is not cheerless in one's old age.

But the bell on the left is part of my story as well. Naturally, in due course I also learned what was behind that bellpull. I found out more and more details, and as the years came and went I grew more pensive as I beheld the two bellpulls which once had meant nothing to me. Of course, I did not have time to stand before my door every day. But as I obtained greater insight into the nature of things and as certain events occurred, I sometimes stood in front of the two bells and thought to myself: If you had pulled the other bell that day…

Eberhard Krause was an elderly, sickly man who had a young, pretty, flirtatious wife. Around that time Mr. Krause hired a new bookkeeper, and this man also soon became a visitor to his boss's home. The young man was musical, Mrs. Krause was no less so, and—to cut a long story short—they took a liking to each other. Mr. Krause's health deteriorated, and when he died his widow very soon knew how to console herself. After the proper mourning period the two got married, and henceforth the firm bore the truthful name Eberhard Krause's Successor.

Eberhard Krause's successor was not a happy man. That woman tormented and deceived him as well. To be sure, for a long, long time he knew only about the torment

> and not about the deception. Others knew it, the whole house and the whole street, and only the successor was in this respect the way Eberhard Krause had been. His wife dominated him. She had spendthrift moods, and he had to supply the money. Eberhard Krause's poor successor consumed himself with cares and toil, and by making a superhuman effort he endured this for many years. But one day he simply could not go on any longer. He had a strange feeling of relief, like a worker who has toiled away with fever wracking his body and then is finally felled by his sickness like a little child.
>
> So the man was truly glad that his sufferings were over. He immediately wanted to tell his dear wife that prestige and high living were now things of the past, that they would now have to stand aside, that there would be no more costly clothes and ostentation. He hated the woman because of all the torment she had caused him all those years. At an unaccustomed hour he ran home from the office to tell her these things—and found her in the arms of a lover. Eberhard Krause's successor took a deep breath as if he had gone bankrupt again...But it so happened that this lover was a rich man and wanted to bail his firm out of its financial difficulties. Yet he had reckoned without Eberhard Krause's successor. He caused a fine, great, double scandal and refused to hush up the breakdown of his marriage and of his honor. For he told himself that the disgrace would be no smaller if it were covered up... There you have the story of the bell on the left.

During the narrative Mr. Wendelin's face had become slightly flushed. Now he stood up to leave, but they detained him for a moment longer. Someone wanted to know whether things had really happened like that.

Mr. Wendelin smiled in his ironic, pained manner.

"Exactly like that. I told you the story of my life the way it was and the way it might have been. It all depended on whether I pulled one bell or the other at a moment which nothing marked as anything special. This is my answer to the claim that a capable fellow can always make his way. He has to pull the right bell, then he will have been a capable fellow. For the rest, you can ask my cousin whether or not I have told the truth."

The cousin, however, waited until Mr. Wendelin had closed the door behind him. Only then did he slowly say, "It certainly is the complete truth—only as told from the other point of view. Wendelin did not ring Weißenried's bell but Eberhard Krause's. He pulled the bell on the left."

Theodor Herzl:

JULY SUNDAY IN THE PRATER

I believe it was Théophile Gautier who said that one should go to Russia in winter and travel south in summer. But to the Prater[1] you must go on a Sunday. Not on a fine Sunday when the high pavement of the Hauptallee is crowded with carriages, when the elegant or the merely wealthy whiz by on rubber wheels and watch one another with mixed feelings. To the Prater you must go on a Sunday in midsummer, on a beautiful, hot, dusty Sunday afternoon when the stillness of despair seems to lie over the exhausted city and no one is to be seen in the deserted streets.

To be sure, someone who loves rare moods will be more attracted to the forsaken city at that particular time. Everything is so strangely dead; in the stony stillness one sees many a house that one has frequently passed for the first time, just as the appearance of a corpse seems very strange to us even if we have known the living person well. The inhabitants have been gone for who knows how long, gone with their love and their hatred. Through gates that are open, as though there were nothing left to guard, one can look into sinister, silent courtyards. In one of these old courtyards there is a well with a crooked pump-handle. Between the stone walls grows green grass. The hole in the ground over there may be a cistern, and if you looked way down to its deep bottom, you would see in the water the reflection of terrible or lovely secrets of the great stillness. Any moment now one of the small doors to the yard will open and some unexpected animal or fabled creature will come out and tell you about this astonishing enchantment. And a door does turn on its hinges; a little old woman in felt slippers comes tottering out with an enormously long blue stocking over her arm, sits down in front of the gate, and starts to knit.

The city is not really dead; it is simply that its inhabitants have escaped from its confines for a while, trying to enjoy the summer air. So let us go after this summer air, too. How about using the Stadtbahn?[2] A nice little trip from our western suburb via Heiligenstadt to the Prater. At the station there is a young female cashier who with obvious sadness sells tickets to the enviable people who are now able to hurry to the Prater. The traveler is almost ashamed of his happiness when he sees such a poor thing in such dreary confinement; after all, this girl would also like to get out, taste some of the joys of living, and be conscious of her youth. But she still has a lot of time left; there will be many such Sundays, a whole lifetime, before she too can sit down in front of the gate and knit a stocking with rough blue yarn, like that old woman who has given up wishing.

The trip to the Prater is a real journey. At first it goes fast; after a few minutes we are in Heiligenstadt, but there we have to get out and wait for another train. When does it leave? Nobody knows for sure. Five or ten minutes more will not matter now. We do have some traveling companions whom we can watch to while away our waiting period. First of all, there is a young couple—slim and goodlooking, obviously lovers. Between them they have three dimples. He—and you may find this a bit much—has a dimple in each cheek when he laughs; she has only one, on the left. But her single dimple is much to be preferred to his two. And they keep laughing and chatting, so all three dimples are constantly in view. Waiting is not hard for them; they already *are* in the Prater, for they walk up and down arm in arm, snuggling close to each other. Then there is a family: a father, a pale mother, and three skinny boys under ten years of age. They are more in a hurry. Soon it will be evening. When will they get to that green meadow where the father and the pale mother plan to take a load off their feet while the three boys perform somersaults? There is also a married couple to be seen—still young but already sullen. He is wearing an uncomfortable dresscoat and has good, large, red workingman's hands that seem to consist of all thumbs. These hands would seem to indicate a butcher or a grocer, and almost automatically one thinks of a ham on which all these thumbs rest as the man cuts off some artistically thin slices. His young wife is morose and loaded with jewelry that tries to look like more than it actually is. These golden things cannot have been bought from savings, but they have another characteristic, too: they have not been pawned yet. Since this woman is not pretty and is ill-humored to boot, it may be surmised that she married beneath her rank. He was an assistant in her father's butcher shop, saw her every day, and got used to her appearance; and because she was the only daughter, she seemed charming to him as she sat at the cash register. Two hearts beat in three-quarter rind.[3] They became man and wife, and this is their Sunday relaxation.

We have been waiting for a quarter of an hour now. Someone has the bright idea of asking, at the top of his voice, when the Prater train will be leaving. The answer is crushing: In an hour and four minutes! A harsh fate, having to sit at the station in Heiligenstadt for an hour and four minutes on a Sunday afternoon in July when one is trying to get to the Prater. This news has various effects. The jewel-studded wife of the man with all the thumbs turns her back on him with unspeakable disgust, as though *he* were responsible for this foolish summer timetable of Heiligenstadt. The slender lovers become serious for a moment and all three dimples disappear, only to reemerge a moment later amidst joyful laughter. This is an adventure, something unexpected, the charm of the march of time. To them, this wasted hour will be a memento of one day in their love. Five or ten years later, when they are far apart and hear the name of this station, they will remember this delightful experience. That will be the only thing left of an entire Sunday of their love.

She will think: "Heiligenstadt!...In those days he was still so nice. He would never have thought of leaving me. Or—could he have had that in mind when he smiled at me, the mean fellow?..."

He is going to think: "Who was I with when I was there? Was it JoJo or Betty? No, it was...what's-her-name. The one with the dimples! We had to wait in Heiligenstadt for an hour. A sweet hour...It'll never return..."

But it is a bitter hour for the family with the three skinny boys. The mother sits down feebly on a bench. Even on a Sunday, even on an outing there is no end of disappointment. If she had her way, she would go right back. Shyly she makes such a suggestion, but the skinny boys, all three of them, won't hear of it and start crying. The father tries to do a little jesting to cheer his enfeebled family up, but he chokes on the jokes. Well, so they will have some extra time to look forward to the enjoyable train ride. This almost makes sense to the skinny boys, but the mother says voicelessly: "Go on, what's so enjoyable about it?!"

And the wait becomes leaden. Gradually a motley crowd gathers on the platform—Sunday misery in various hues. They are lost in silent daydreams. Most of them have forgotten what they are really here for—just as in life generally. Finally, after everyone has become apathetic, the train comes and people rush aboard as though it were taking them to some desirable destination. Evening is already descending on the landscape. There is an opalescent gleam on the Danube and a light haze over the meadows. The excursionists gloomily sit down in outdoor restaurants, no longer expectant and not yet inebriated. And soon they will have to think about the return trip. The three skinny boys start to get sleepy. But the Heiligenstadt lovers walk arm in arm toward quiet bushes.

If one roams through the green meadows, one frequently encounters such couples stepping along blissfully in their dual dream. There are always new performers in the midsummer night's comedy, and they all regard themselves as extremely original. Outside the Krieau, near a pigeon coop, two military cadets with two adolescent girls are taking an innocent walk in the woods. As they stroll past, one of the cadets says something meaningful: "*La tourterelle roucoule.*" This is elementary French and elementary love. How terribly simple it all is! The dove coos, boy loves girl—where have we heard it, seen it, read it before? And how it grabs people over and over again!

But this is not peculiar to a midsummer afternoon in the Prater. The turtledove coos everywhere, even on weekdays, and such happy, romantic young cadets with their green girls go wandering through other meadows, too. In fact, they seem to have gone astray if they move through the general melancholy of the place with their unexpressed, rosy feelings. For there is nothing more melancholy than a July Sunday in the Prater.

In the great Rotunde there is a big fun fair. Without any apparent need to do so, strong men lift very heavy weights. People admire them because it is a useless effort. No one admires a furniture mover who pants as he carries a heavy load. Near the ceiling, tightrope walkers do their stuff. The attraction for the spectators can lie only in the mortal danger to which these poor fellows up there expose themselves. Illogically, people clap their hands when a rope walker gets safely to the other side. So they did not want the performer to break his neck. Then why did they not hiss when he climbed up there? At booths, fancy goods of poor quality are offered for sale by badly dolled-up young ladies. Anyone who buys something there must already be tipsy from the new wine, and he is only buying tomorrow's regret. Along with the beer and the sourish wine, a sort of squeaky music is dispensed, and people listen to it because they want to get their money's worth. But the footsteps of the celebrants who wander about tirelessly and peevishly among the cheap attractions raise ever thicker clouds of dust, and in the end one would gladly buy a ticket of emission to be allowed to get out in the open again.

There is the Hauptallee. Great throngs of people walking up and down, up and down. There, too, the dust and the gloom. The air under the trees is thick as in a closed room and barely fit for breathing. People know this from the previous Sunday, and yet they are here again, walking up and down, up and down, like prisoners in a prison courtyard. What must their dwellings be like and why don't they go out to the real freedom, Nature? One can almost understand why the well-behaved girls from good, impecunious homes participate in this sad parade. They have to be seen, for otherwise they will never attract a suitor. But unless they are flashily dressed, they are lost in the crowd. And if they are all dressed up, no one dares to approach them. Who is brave enough to pay for such beautiful clothes? Of course, experience shows that such strange fellows do exist. That kind may be seen slinking along at the side of their victorious ladies, their brows wrinkled with sorrow. And that is why the foolish virgins, followed by their anxious parents, walk up and down, up and down. Until it gets dark and they once again drag their Sunday sadness home.

By now there are a lot of lights in the Wurstelprater as well as a jumble of sound from all sorts of relentlessly obtrusive music. One hurdy-gurdy man does not spare his competitors, and each bandmaster tries to drown out the tunes of the others. They sink one another like battleships. People roam about intimidated and finally crawl into some inn. The open-air restaurants with the worst lighting do not always have the smallest number of customers, for many people like to have their supper in darkness after proudly strolling along the tree-lined avenues.

There is noise from the booths, the old, well-known, mysterious booths where curiosity costs money. The best business is done by the proprietors who count on the vanity of the esteemed public—those who sell tests of skill and strength. There are short rifle-ranges where you can extend your arm and touch the target with the barrel of your rifle, and there are enormous hammers that a little tailor can bang down and that make him think he is as strong as a blacksmith. But things are really popping at the meting places of all curiosities and vanities, the dance halls.

For five kreuzer, a dance and all that goes with it. These are not the refined, restrained dance steps of the salons. In these mute dramas there are struggle and passion, wooing and defeat. The powerful, elemental meaning of the plot is not disturbed by any dialogue. A tempestuous festival is celebrated in honor of Dionysus. These are mostly country folk, peasant boys and farm girls who are adrift in the city, disguised as servant girls and soldiers, and when they dance they surely are less unhappy than they usually are. And they have an intoxicating effect on one another, to the point of unconsciousness, as they listen to the miserable sound of the music in the painful, steamy air of this hall. You have to see their faces—the half-closed eyes of the girls, the ardor of the fellows, all expressions of surrender and romanticism. And when a male dancer finally bends over his female partner and kisses her—no, drinks the sweat from her cheek—this is probably a greater love than a sweet-smelling countess can inspire. For here illusion has more repugnant things to overcome. But there is a long-range purpose to this: In twenty years more servant girls and soldiers will be needed.

Only when the intoxication of the dancing, the noise, and the kisses is over are their hearts seized by sadness again, and this sadness is presumably mixed with remorse. Then two of them may be seen sitting over a single glass of cheap beer and hanging their heads.

Thus a July Sunday in the Prater is composed of melancholy. And yet there is something refreshing about it: It teaches those who labor and are heavy laden to love their hard weekdays again.

Notes

1. The Prater is Vienna's celebrated pleasure-ground. The Hauptallee, a long, tree-lined boulevard, runs through it, and the part known as the Wurstelprater is an amusement park. The section called the Krieau is the site of a race track. The Rotunde, a large hall built for the World Exposition of 1873, burned down in 1937.
2. The Vienna Stadtbahn, part elevated railway, part subway, was built between 1895 and 1903 and has only recently been replaced by an increasingly extensive subway system. The suburb of Heiligenstadt, made famous by Beethoven, has since 1892 been part of Vienna's sprawling, viniculturally notable 19th district. Herzl was living in Währing, the 18th district, when he wrote this feuilleton.
3. Herzl's sentence, *Er schnitt es gern in jeden Schinken ein,* is a punning reference to a line from "*Ungeduld,*" the seventh song in the Schubert-Müller song cycle *Die schöne Müllerin: "Ich schnitt' es gern in alle Rinden ein...*" (I would fain carve it in every bark...that my heart is yours). Herzl substituted *Schinken* (ham) for *Rinden* (bark). The translation puns on an "evergreen" by Robert Stolz and at least preserves the Viennese ambiance, which is more than can be said for another possible rendition, "To him, love was a many-rendered thing," a reference to another popular ballad that was written even later than Stolz's song, in the 1950's.

Theodor Herzl:

TRUDEL'S TEAR

Trudel can write, too. Just five more letters, including the difficult k, and she'll have the whole alphabet. It is a strange chapter in her life and I am only now beginning to understand it. Pauline and Hans learned this skill some time ago. Two or three years ago they were at the point where their sister Trudel is now, but that wasn't so surprising, because at that time it wasn't easy to distinguish their previous state from the stage which they were entering.

Grown-ups are separated from the world of children by so many thousands of miles. It may be that we know even less about them than they know about us. The mysterious and magnificent events in their development take place before our eyes, and yet we hardly notice them, or at most we notice the very obvious things: that their pale blue eyes become brighter and bigger, that their little hands reach for things more surely, that their babbling changes to more distinct sounds, that they learn to talk, to stand, to walk, that they are growing. And now they keep growing, constantly and without stopping, catching up with us, acquiring our knowledge as they mature, hurrying to have our experiences, experiences that all our love could not spare them even if we knew what goes on inside the children. But we haven't any idea, even though we ourselves once passed through these lovely areas.

Forgetfulness is a blessing for us earthlings, for we forget life no less than we forget death. The stages of a development which we have gone through physically and mentally become so strange to us that if our attention happens to be drawn to something commonplace, we face it in astonishment, as though it were a discovery.

When Pauline began to write the famous letter i in her first brown notebook, we secretly felt sorry for her. A year later, when Hans courageously approached that i, this event was still not fully appreciated. I believe that when we watch our children learn, we regard that which even all our love cannot save them from as a hardship—simply because we are strangers to them. Learning to write—what a horror! If we weren't already able to write, we certainly couldn't get the hang of it today.

It is a shrewd arrangement that children are forcibly educated at a time when they still can't fight back. Having to choose between making letters and being punished, they have to decide in favor of the former as the lesser evil. And before they know what is happening, they have been pushed out of the paradisiac state of ignorance. How cruel of us to end for them this happy age, which we long for all our lives, so quickly and violently.

These are some of the thoughts with which parents accompany the first lessons of their children. But one must not let the poor little ones become aware of one's sympathy, because otherwise they would rebel as one rebels against a government that is too weak. The way things have been arranged, paradise presumably is always here, but we also keep losing it.

Well, Trudel has arrived at the exit of this beautiful garden, and the other day she shed a tear—one small round tear that did not fall on the floor but on the page of a book, which means that a trace of it will be preserved for some time. This is a whole story, and it does not lack a moral. From it you can see how much a grown-up may learn from a child if he keeps his eyes and ears open.

During the past two years Trudel's position in the nursery has been a strangely despised and envied one. She was the only person in the house who had no duties. All she was asked to do was to eat well and fall asleep promptly. In everything there was freedom, the Garden of Eden. She was a charming barbarian, tolerated and spoiled. Even the older children referred to her—half disdainfully and half benevolently—as "the little one." Fortunately she was not yet sensitive enough to be aware of the humiliation that lay in this friendliness. She enjoyed a succession of cloudless days. When the other children sadly sighed over their assignments, she played to her heart's content. They had to toil over horrible arithmetic, while Trudel just let her imagination roam freely.

We shall never know, and she will forget, what wonderful adventures she had in her mind when she sat with her doll on a little stool in the corner or wound a long piece of string around a log of wood or cut strips of paper and made them into a wreath which she put on her locks like a queen in a fairy-tale. For her that period was full of songs that moved through her soul without a sound. This sort of thing exists only in children and in spring in poets who are too proud to write verses for publication. Sometimes, when there was a pensive gleam in her eyes, it was possible to have an inkling of this.

But did she really know how fortunate she was? No matter how small a human being may be, this universal law applies: We don't recognize good times while they are here. Because of the contrast it was easy for Trudel to appreciate her more pleasant situation. Only *she* played so marvelously, while the others were bent over a dictation exercise and received the harshest reproaches because they were always making mistakes. For writing probably is one of the most excruciating things in the world.

Even the most excellent condition has its drawbacks, and of course Trudel soon realized this. When she wanted to send birthday wishes to someone, she had to make use of someone else's hand. When she wanted to have a story read to her, she had to beg the governess, Pauline, or Hans to do so, and sometimes she could not bribe them even with the biggest decals and chocolate cigars from her treasury. In her despair she would read stories to herself—that is, she would go through the motions of reading though she didn't know how. She pretended to be reading from an open book in which she turned a page from time to time, droning along in a voice that imitated the intonations of fluent reading. There were memories of things she had heard, but also much that was freely invented, and anyone who listened with only half an ear might really think that everything was in the book. The sentences were not any sillier than those to be found in many a children's book. Now and then she would confuse the names of her heroes; she would have a person who had just died return, and do other things that are perpetrated by careless storytellers, even greater ones than Trudel.

It sounded something like this: "'But Edith,' said mother, 'you must have been sliding around on your knees again. I see that you have a hole in your stocking. A big girl of five; that's not nice.' The little girl listened to her mother's reproaches with tears in her eyes, and she was closer to crying than to laughing. Thereupon father said: 'We must break her of that habit; our Elsbeth is wilder than a boy.' Soon thereafter the father went away on a trip, and when he returned after a few weeks, Elsbeth was no longer sliding around on her knees. By the way, she darned her stockings herself if they had holes, just like a grown-up seven-year old girl. But she was only six-and-a-half. Her parents were very pleased."

A child's narrative skill is reminiscent of a child's paintings—these heads with handle-like ears which have no neck but rest on square rumps, or those houses that are smaller than the men shown entering them. But no matter; such a representation tells children more about life than many a perfect work of art tells us. From this it may be seen how much more powerful and more magnificent the imagination of children is than our blunted, aging imagination.

So Trudel had many compensations for that which was denied her. If no one wanted to do her the favor of reading a story to her, she took a book and declaimed a story of her own invention, even though she occasionally held the book upside down. Surely the book didn't contain all that she found in it. In addition to that, she had the freedom which the older children lacked. Wasn't that a very rosy period?

Well, anyone who made that assumption was mistaken. Trudel wasn't happy. To put it succinctly, she didn't appreciate her paradise. She felt rejected, humiliated, and shamed, and she regarded her ignorance as a great burden. She felt inferior and not happier, because she wasn't learning what the other children were learning.

One evening, when I stood by her little bed and had her tell me about her day's activities, she made a sorrowful confession. "The children are nasty to me," she said. "They always have secrets, and that makes me sad. Today they didn't want to read to me again. I was so sad that I sang so they shouldn't notice, but my voice cracked."

And really, her voice was still shaky from her repressed emotions. For a nursery has its dramas, too, though we pay no attention to them, because they are so inconsequential and slip by so quickly. For these little hearts they are weighty and great enough to squeeze sighs out of them. In short, Trudel was yearning to be able to read and write like the others. She, too, wanted to leave paradise.

Of all the wishes one has in life, this one is the most certain to be fulfilled. This is how it went with Trudel, too, and that tear in her book proves it. It is a thin, gray book, one that is called a primer. At the bottom of page two there is a little circular spot with a slightly jagged edge. That's the tear, Trudel's bitter tear. It may be seen under the word "fish." Why did the child cry at that place? Because she had to study? No, the psychology of children isn't that simple. After all, Trudel did want to learn. She was glad when someone opened up that book for her. And did she lose interest so soon after the beginning? Surely that cannot be, and it wasn't. It wasn't interest that she lost on the second page; it was courage. C-a-t cat, n-e-s-t nest—that much she understood. But f-i-s-h fish—that was more than she could grasp. She felt so helpless and so lost, and she thought that she would never learn it, that she would be the only person in the world who could not read—she, of all people, who enjoyed fairy-tales and stories so much. At that point a child's despair made the little tear drop on that page.

That happened a few short weeks ago, and already the incident is in the dim past. Day after day Trudel sits bent over her school notebook and makes letters and numbers which become more and more legible. She already wants to use her knowledge for purposes of daily living, because her courage has returned and has even grown after she overcame those initial difficulties. Recently she committed a rather serious crime. After saying her evening prayer she took it upon herself to lower the bars of her bed and to climb out. The next morning the air was heavy with punishment to fit the crime, and Trudel was crestfallen. Then she got the idea of drafting a letter of apology. Resolutely she sat down, drew some rather crooked lines on a sheet of paper, decorated it on top with a flower decal, and began writing: d-e-e-r m-u-m-y, deer mumy. That's as far as she got; she lacked a few letters for the expression of her full remorse.

A bit of childishness, of course. But what is more human than childlike things? Many things that appear important to serious people vanish into insignificance next to these young shoots of burgeoning life. It is the springtime of education—touching and cheerful, enchanting like every spring. A child cried with impatience because she could not get out of the beautiful garden soon enough, the garden to which no road leads back.

Some day when the children are big and all the wonderful events of this simple period are past and seem like one single dream, it may happen that Trudel will poke about among old books and find that primer. She will open it and discover the faded trace of a tear on page two under the word "fish." And it may also happen that a second tear will join the first one on the page. Progress was too slow—that's what the first tear says. No, says the second tear, it went too fast.

Peter Herz:

THE CHOLENT WAR

No history of the world has ever taken cognizance of this war. Let me express the hope that this very first account of it will make enjoyable reading. There were, after all, no victims, no bloodshed, and no tears. No battles were fought in that war, and no decorations were awarded. Instead of laurel wreaths there were herbs and vegetables in soups, and meatballs took the place of cannonballs.

The Cholent War took place at the turn of the century in Baden near Vienna, when that place was one of the most frequented international health resorts. In the summer months visitors came from all over the world, and disproportionately large numbers of these were Jews. Baden became an international meeting place for Jews, and because they particularly enjoyed the likable little town on the Schwechat River that was blessed with so many natural beauties, they kept flocking to it. Yes, Baden was especially attractive to Jews, and one of its many attractions was the fact that it provided excellent kosher food.

There was the venerable Rausnitz Restaurant on Annagasse that occupied a large Biedermeier building and had a fine garden. It also featured desirable guest rooms and was excellently managed by dear Herr Rausnitz. Those who took their seats in the cozy garden under the tall trees were assured of true culinary delights. "Rausnitz, Baden" was a name to conjure with, and the restaurant certainly was a summertime favorite with its Jewish customers. Rausnitz, however, was not the only gastronomist in Baden, for diagonally across the street there was Schey's Restaurant, a favorite with Orthodox Jews because it really offered outstanding specialties of kosher cuisine. It was only natural that in the course of time a certain rivalry between the two restaurants should have developed, and so their proprietors did not greet each other when they met—in the synagogue on Grabengasse, for example. The situation was exacerbated when it became known that the resident restaurateurs were going to get powerful competition. You see, the world fame of the spa and the number of those frequenting it kept growing, and the increasing number of Jewish visitors heightened the demand for kosher food. Thus one day Rausnitz and Schey received the disturbing news that the best-known Jewish restaurant in Vienna, Tonello's at the Marienbrücke, had decided to open a branch in Baden. This meant the keenest competition, for Tonello's was known far and wide for its kosher cuisine, and tourists from the four corners of the earth had heard of it. On Antonsgasse, a few steps from the Rausnitz and Schey establishments, Tonello found a fine house with a garden, and his Baden branch was promptly installed there. This meant that now there were *three* Jewish restaurants in Baden within a stone's throw of one another. Was it any wonder that this really heated up the competition among them? Certainly, at that time there were enough Jews taking the waters in Baden to sustain even three restaurants, but the ambition of the three gastronomists was such that a veritable war, the so-called Cholent War, broke out among the three combatants. Now Schey and Rausnitz really cut each other, for a third competitor, Herr Tonello, had appeared on the scene, and he ruled his summer empire with a firm hand. The mild summer air of Baden was abuzz with gossip and wild rumors of mutual abuse and degradation as well as with jokes directed against one or another of the hostile hosts. The Cholent War was in full swing. People retold the last joke of the comedian Eisenbach. A guest at Tonello's Restaurant was said to have complained to the owner: "Herr Tonello, your sauerkraut isn't sour enough!" Whereupon the frightened innkeeper is supposed to have exclaimed: "But for heaven's sake, Herr

Samek, that's not sauerkraut, these are poppy-seed noodles!" Samek was said to have replied: "Poppy-seed noodles? *Nu,* if they're poppy-seed noodles, they're sour enough!"

Another story was told about old Rausnitz reprimanding a guest who put his fingers—and spittle—in all the bowls, noisily smacked his lips, and belched. "My dear sir," said Rausnitz, "your table manners are atrocious. Look, I have a refined clientele, there are a lot of tourists here—and you eat like this?! If you behaved like that at Tonello's, you'd get the boot!" But the guest thus rebuked refused to be intimidated: "Don't laugh, Herr Rausnitz—this is just how I ate at Tonello's. They didn't throw me out, but simply told me that this is how I could eat at Rausnitz's!" Another guest, a man who wanted to be served as early as half past eleven and was told that the kitchen wasn't ready yet, is said to have grumbled: "You're not serving yet?! *Some* service! At Schey's they're already belching!"

With such a choice of kosher restaurants there were, of course, a number of guests who ate at all of them and spread all sorts of wild rumors about the atmosphere and culinary quality of these rival eating places. This, of course, kept the prevailing competition—the Cholent War—among them boiling. One week, for example, Dr. Bloch's *Jüdische Wochenschrift* praised Rausnitz's Restaurant; the next week the *Sonn- und Montagszeitung,* which also had a Jewish orientation, ran a report about the marvelous meat dishes at Schey's; and finally Tonello managed to get an editor of the prestigious *Neue Freie Presse* to print a story according to which the famed Wonder Rabbi of Sadagora, who was vacationing in Baden with his retinue, had expressed a desire to dine at Tonello's there as well, whereupon the proprietor of the most famous kosher restaurant in Vienna had decided to open a branch in Baden.

That did it! The contest in Baden was already raging with tremendous force, but it was to get even worse, for the climax of the Cholent War was yet to come.

In those days the efforts of Dr. Theodor Herzl to create a Jewish State in Palestine were the focus of everyone's attention. The greatest Jewish leaders of the time banded together to help Herzl's Zionist idea gain acceptance and translate it into reality. An important Jewish

Congress in Basel was in the offing, and all the complex aspects of the Jewish Question were being discussed. This Congress required both extensive and intensive preparations. Dr. Herzl, who had sacrificed his private life and his entire journalistic career at the *Neue Freie Presse* to his idealistic Zionist idea, was under great time pressure. As a good son he had promised his parents, who were taking the cure in Baden, to spend at least a few days with them during the summer, but the important discussions in preparation for the Zionist Congress were claiming all his time. Dr. Herzl managed to persuade the participants to hold these discussions in Baden, for this would enable him to spend a little time with his parents after all. The gentlemen were glad to go along with their intellectual leader, for the beautiful international spa Baden was very attractive at that time of year, and so these Jewish leaders and their large families went to Baden. Dr. Herzl's office had the task of securing good accommodations for these people and seeing to it that the proper kosher cuisine was provided. When this became known, the Cholent War heated up again. Each of the three warriors wanted the privilege of feeding the participants in the Zionist discussions.

Another factor that sparked the cholent championship was a newspaper report according to which the well-known Ischl restaurant Sonnenschein had decided to open a Baden branch in that summer of Zionist zeal. The Baden restaurateurs boiled with rage. Sonnenschein of Ischl was world-famous and would offer keen competition. Julius Bauer, the famed Jewish editor and humorist, had once coined this *bon mot:* "Ischl is a strange place; from rain you catch cold and from Sonnenschein [sunshine] you get an upset stomach." Well, this fear of competition turned out to be groundless; the local authorities protected the established restaurants by refusing to issue another license. Nevertheless, Dr. Herzl's office could hardly cope with the onslaught of the three rival restaurateurs, each of whom was eager to obtain the exclusive right to feed the Zionist guests. Finally the sorely pressed Herzl had a saving idea.

Having ascertained that a large number of Jewish dignitaries were coming to Baden to participate in the preliminary discussions for the Zionist Congress, the Zionist leadership after heated debates devised a plan that finally led to a solution—and this was only logical. A common denominator had to be found for Jews from all over the world—but should three restaurateurs in Baden fight a Cholent War? No, that was out of the question, especially in view of the Zionist Congress. Thus Dr. Herzl's suggestion finally brought about a peaceful solution of the culinary question. In midsummer the municipal restaurant of the health resort was not so busy and could therefore be placed at the disposal of the Jewish guests. The head chefs of the three Jewish restaurants—Rausnitz, Schey, and Tonello—were invited to give joint demonstrations of their culinary skills in the enormous, newly koshered kitchen of the spa's central restaurant. Thus they all participated in the feeding of the guests, and once this compromise had, after a great deal of back and forth, been accepted by all three sides, a sweet peace ended the Cholent War, a conflict in which there had been neither victors nor vanquished.

Henceforth both friend and foe of the bygone war again dined peacefully under the chestnut trees of the Baden municipal park. The farfel soup was piping hot, the beef chine with ritschert (barley, beans and bits of smoked meat) was as delicate as ever, the pepper carp was delicious, and the kreplach and seven-layer cake were as scrumptious and fattening as they had always been...In contrast to the ancient Roman *non olet,* there was no *non cholent.* No, the diners once again enjoyed cholent, the symbol of the recently concluded war—*b'sholem,* in peace...

Richard Beer-Hofmann:

MEMORIAL ADDRESS ON WOLFGANG AMADEUS MOZART

From high mountains a stream flows down to deep valleys below. It breaks forth from a glacial lake; wildly raging waters from adjoining valleys rush to join it, and plunging and falling from level to level, gaining in volume and richness, it seeks its way. Confluent brooks bear revealing evidence of hoarded treasure slumbering secretly deep in the stark mountains roundabout; and if one grasps the sand from its banks in the hollow of one's hand, there sift though the fingers, with the sand itself, dark iron ore, red copper, gray cobalt, and gold and silver from the Rauris.[1] And should one dip a hand in the rushing stream, even where it descends to the plain, one will still feel that this turbulent flood, whose destination is the sea, comes from the heights.[2] Fed by glaciers that adjoin the primordial ice, the surging stream leaps forth bright-eyed. Deep below is the mist of the valleys.

From the Venetian coast a highway rises to the snow-covered passes of the Tauern mountains and seeks the slopes where once the Ambisontians and Alauni guarded the sacred salt deposits.[3] Laden with oil and dark wine, mules first trod the trail; the marching feet of Roman legions widened it; and before the ancient gods retired to their final rest, their sacred nudity still illuminated the mountains.

Where these two meet—the stream from the snows of the Noric Alps and the highway from the sea coming up from the south—a city is located. There Mozart is born!

Music is around this child when he wakes: the heavy bells of many churches, bright and somber, vibrating like human voices, and alongside them smaller chimes, braided together in the graceful songs of the Residenz glockenspiel;[4] and above all this, greeting the hours of the day from the mountain, the Hornwerk of the Hohensalzburg fortress.[5]

No alien sounds waft down to the child from above. The organ-like tones from the mountain that now resound through the precincts of the city were in his father's house before him—resounding only for him, inaudible to others. But now there resound from above, so that all may hear, Leopold Mozart's shepherd's minuet in May, a hunting song in September, and in February a carnival piece. And mornings and evenings they have captured the wind up there in mighty bellows; and the wild morning wind that rends the mountain mists and the gentle evening winds—they are all in the service of music!

And when the bells of the city fall silent, its streams murmur to the lad, and not just those of the marble fountain where above the dolphins, which are enticed by music, Triton blows his horn.[6] A road leads to the castle of Marcus Sitticus, where brightly gushing fountains are harnessed to provide power for ingenious displays.[7] There he will first see the radiant god flay the bungler Marsyas;[8] in a stone grotto Orpheus will stand, his hand raised, ready to play on his violin the song that will open for him the way to the land of the dead; a door will spring open and on a colorful stage, crowded about a house under construction, laborers will bang and hammer away as they perform their work, burghers will go about their business, and noblemen will bow to one another from their windows. And in the midst of this noise and the comical haste of the animated figures there sounds a chorale: the water that drives this mechanism also powers the organ that is now heard. Here, by means of an allegory, the boy may first perceive what is conferred upon him as upon all those whom God has summoned to creative work: to observe the continual hustle and bustle, the daily toil, the evanescent pleasure and ultimate pain of people, while smiling gently and enjoying their colorfulness—and at the same time to listen to the song of praise that solemnly ascends from the noisy restlessness of their activity, and to know that one source activates both.

Yet he outgrows this city before he is able to comprehend all that. Other children may listen to fairy tales in which kings and emperors, remote and magical, pass by like fabulous beasts and good fairies. But early on, to this child's wonderful fingers was given the power to turn the pages of the world like a book of fairy tales. Far behind him now are the city and the Untersberg, where the ancient emperor of legend sleeps.[9] His Imperial Majesty, the ruler of the Holy Roman Empire, sends him gold-trimmed clothes and invites him to his court.[10] The emperor's daughters lead him by the hand through its mirrored halls; the empress kisses him on the mouth; the emperor himself stands next to him and grows speechless when he begins to play.[11] And here is the city of Paris, and when the descendant of St. Louis sits down at table, this child stand near the queen, who offers him fruit from golden plates.[12] And now he is on the British Isles, and when the king rides in the park with his queen, he bows to this boy from his royal carriage and waves to him.[13]

Is this a fairy tale?

A tablet is affixed as an enduring memorial to the organ on which he once played. The pope in Rome hangs the Order of the Golden Spurs around this childish neck. Upon meeting the child, a famous old musician sees the labor and the fame of a lifetime crumble to dust: "This child will cause all of us to be forgotten!"[14]

If this a fairy tale?

If it is not, then what more can he experience who has experienced this? Indignities? They glance off the man who wears the proud memory of such a childhood around his hips like a golden armor. Poverty? He will bear it smilingly, the way one wears the costume of a carnival evening. And death? Orpheus knows this: when he dies, his lyre will flame in the starry heavens as an eternal constellation!

And so this youth can fearlessly reach for the reins of his realm. And what is not within his realm? The elements are ranged about him; they bubble up from the streams; all the fires of the deep yearn to come up to him; from the atmosphere something comes down to him. And all the transitory passion and grief of created things rise up to woo him, demanding to become eternalized in music. He touches them—and a reflection of his countenance is on everything! Bright, uncorrupted, childlike eyes look at the world, and these lips have tasted neither bitterness nor disgust.

All that moves us grows from richly fertilized, ancient, blood-soaked soil. May it not be that the unassuaged yearning of many ancestors demands fulfillment upon these lips and no others? Does not perhaps the unexpiated torment of the dead flare up from our hatred? That which mysteriously gropes about with icy fingers in the dark—is it a resurgence of the scarce-forgotten terrors of a primeval night?

But this master's tones resound from the quietly sun-drenched meadows of mountain-locked valleys. From virgin nature spring certain elemental forces, and, as in the innocence of nature, their various aspects may unfold next to one another. Hatred and smiles, sweet rapture, brutish greed and noble grief rise on tender stalks, their roots laved by clear paradisiac streams, and the serene breezes of blissful gardens blow brightly about their calyxes.

Here the master stands and beckons!

And on the coasts of Crete the sea foams and threatens. Has Idomeneo broken his vow?[15] Recede, sea, behind your shores, and make way for the procession! Masks, you think? No masks! For where could there be more truth than in the face that he gave everyone? Ghosts? But feel how their hearts pound! Listen to Leporello, how he shivers with cold after a sleepless night, how he plucks up his courage to give notice to his master—yet, bragging, cowardly, gluttonous, and thrashed, he will remain with him to the end. Let him take Osmin with him—reeling Osmin[16]—and Monostatos, the lustful ape (but on a chain)! And let Papageno bring up the rear![17]

But let us go on. You two, clinging to each other, are Belmonte and Constanze, the faithful lovers;[18] things that trouble you pass quickly, like a shower on an early summer night. And the voices that now intermingle I recognize too. Make way, you peasants, that I may see your masters! Are you changing your costumes, are you hiding behind bushes, and are you using the darkness as a mask before your faces to conceal your love games? And everything is really but the jolly confusion of a crazy day, the light-hearted love of a rollicking day.[19] Do you see Don Giovanni's white plumes gleaming through the darkness?[20] That woman who glides behind him like his shadow—behold, she is in love! Even though she warns against him, threatens and maligns him, beneath all her veils her cheeks flame crimson with memory. Greet Donna Anna: black crepe flutters about this pure brow, but if you think she is bowed low with suffering, watch out! She will snap back to her revenge like a fine steel blade.[21] Are there more, crowding forward? Is the procession without end? Strange costumes and priests and incandescent fire and steam—are they gathering into a cloud? You who burst forth from the clouds like shafts of light, you blessed boys—are you the last?[22] Is no one behind you? Do not speak; I need no answer. For even someone who has never seen him recognizes the eyes of him who now steps behind you. The master has given a voice even to you, somber one, who concludes every procession.[23] It resounds from dark choirs when he sings himself to eternal peace!

Thus the master stands at the border of two epochs, placed there by destiny. To him, as to no other, was it given to make known to all future generations the face of his own time before it changed, and to be the blessed harbinger of that which remains eternally sheltered behind the changing face of time.

Behind golden garden gates his prisoners may still breathe the free air of the sea, and the name of the man who guards them is Osmin. The time will come when their flesh will rot away in the darkness of a damp stone prison, and their master's name then will be Pizarro. At Don Giovanni's feasts is still heard the jubilant choir of masks in a hymn to freedom; the time will come when choirs of prisoners in dismal dungeons will moan to heaven for freedom.[24] The master's Masonic funeral music may still mourn the death of noblemen in pious melodies. Blood and more blood will have to flow before the track will be clear for the funeral march of a hero.[25]

Our souls do not always wish to tarry with you, Wolfgang Amadeus Mozart! Too long have we been taught to mine the most secret quarries of our souls, and we know far too much of suffering. We turn our gaze away from the white and carefree forehead of Jove to seek the deep, compassionate eyes that dwell under the painfully knitted brow of Prometheus.[26]

But in spring and on days of happiness, when we step into our gardens in the early morning and, with limbs still relaxed from sleep, enjoy the moist air of early spring and the fragrance of the earth, and high above us a bird, its earthly bonds eased by flight, thrusts itself against the sky, pouring out the happiness of its life in song—then we salute you, Wolfgang Amadeus Mozart! And our souls flow toward the spring and to our happiness and to you—irresistibly, as the water flows from the high mountains above down to the deep valleys below.

Notes

1. The Rauris is a valley in the Tauern mountain chain.
2. The Salzach River springs from the Salzach Cap, at a height of almost seventy-five hundred feet.
3. The Ambisontians and their kindred Alauni (who mined the mountains for salt) were Noric tribes of Celtic ancestry.
4. In 1703 Prince Archbishop Johann Ernst Count Thun commissioned the clockmaker Jeremias Sauter to build a Dutch glockenspiel for him.
5. The Hornwerk, also called the Salzburger Stier (bull), is the mechanical carillon built in 1502 during the incumbency of Prince Archbishop Leonhard von Keutschach. Leopold Mozart, Wolfgang Amadeus' father, assistant kapellmeister of the ducal orchestra, composed six pieces for the Hornwerk. The sound it makes before it starts playing suggests the bellowing of a bull.
6. The palace fountain is in the center of the Residenzplatz (castle grounds), erected by Antonio Dario in 1664 under Prince Archbishop Guidobald (Thun).
7. The chateu Hellbrunn was built by Prince Archbishop Marcus Sitticus between 1613 and 1619. In the park are the Kunstbrunnenwerke, fountains that include grottos with figures set in motion by water power.

The "mechanical theater," built between 1748 and 1752 by Lorenz Rosenegger, contains more than a hundred marionettes.

8. In Greek mythology, the flute-playing faun or satyr Marsyas challenged Apollo to a musical contest and was severely punished after he lost.
9. According to an old legend, the emperor Karl will sleep inside the mountain until his beard has encircled the table twice and will awake on Judgment Day (according to another version, when twenty-four ravens have flown around the mountain three times).
10. Mozart received a lilac-colored cloak with wide gold borders that had been made for Archduke Maximilian, and he was painted wearing it.
11. The empress was Maria Theresia, in September 1762, at Schönbrunn.
12. Louis XV received Mozart on New Year's Day, 1764, at Versailles.
13. The king and queen were George III and Sophie Charlotte, in St. James's Park.
14. Johann Adolph Hasse was the husband of the famous singer Faustina Bordoni and the most celebrated composer of operas in Europe before Mozart's time. When he heard the fourteen-year-old boy play in Milano, the seventy-two-year-old musician exclaimed, "Questo ragazzo ci farà dimenticar tutti!"
15. In Mozart's opera *Idomeneo, King of Crete* (1781) the king promises the sea god Poseidon to sacrifice to him the first person he meets upon his safe return home, but that person turns out to be his son, Idamante.
16. Osmin is a character in *The Abduction from the Seraglio* (1782).
17. Monostatos and Papageno are characters in *The Magic Flute* (1791).
18. Belmonte and Constanze are characters in *The Abduction from the Seraglio.*
19. Beaumarchais' play *The Marriage of Figaro,* which furnished the basis for Lorenzo Da Ponte's libretto to Mozart's opera (1786), bears the subtitle *A Rollicking Day.*
20. The opera *Don Giovanni* dates from 1787.
21. Donna Anna is a character in *Don Giovanni.*
22. These are references to *The Magic Flute.*
23. The reference is to Mozart's *Requiem,* his last major work, which remained unfinished at his death.
24. The reference is to Beethoven's opera *Fidelio* (1805).
25. The third movement of Beethoven's Piano Sonata in A♭, op. 26, bears the inscription "A Funeral March on the Death of a Hero."
26. Mozart's Symphony no. 41 in C is known as the *Jupiter; The Creatures of Prometheus* is a ballet by Beethoven.

Stefan Zweig:

IN THE SNOW

Picture a small German town in the Middle Ages, close by the Polish border, with the square-built massiveness characteristic of fourteenth-century edifices. The colorful, fluid picture normally presented by the town is reduced to a single impression, a dazzling shimmering whiteness that lies high over the wide town walls and weighs on the tower tops around which night has already woven its lusterless veils of mist.

Darkness descends rapidly. The noisy, tangled hustle and bustle of the streets, the activities of many busy people are muted into a sound that dies away and seems to reverberate from a distance, a noise pierced only by the monotonous pealing of the evening bells at rhythmic intervals. Day's end begins its dominion over the exhausted workmen craving sleep; lights become more and more sparse, at last disappearing entirely. The town lies in a deep sleep like one single mighty creature.

All sound has died away; even the trembling voice of the heath wind has dwindled into a gentle lullaby; all that is audible is the soft lisping of the drifting snowflakes when their wandering has found a destination...

Suddenly a soft sound becomes audible. It is like a distant, hurried hoofbeat approaching. The astonished, drowsy watchman at the gate goes in surprise to the window in order to listen. And indeed, a horseman approaches at full gallop, heading straight for the gate; a minute later, a raucous voice, rusty with the cold, demands admittance. The gate is opened and a man enters, leading a steaming horse which he immediately turns over to the gate-keeper, quickly silencing his protests with a few words and a handful of money. With quick, sure steps which reveal his familiarity with the locality he then hastens past the deserted, white-shimmering market-place through quiet lanes and snow-covered paths to the opposite end of the town.

Here there are located a few small houses, closely crowded together as though they were in need of mutual support. All are unadorned dwellings, inconspicuous, smoke-stained and ramshackle, and all stand in perpetual stillness in those obscure lanes. They look as if they had never known any festive occasion, gay and brimming over with mirth, as if there had never been any joyful jubilation to rattle their blind, hidden windows, as if no gleaming sunbeam had ever reflected its glittering gold in their window-panes. Lonely, like timid children who are afraid of the others, they press together in the narrow enclosure of the ghetto.

In front of these houses, the biggest and relatively most imposing, the stranger stops. It belongs to the wealthiest man of the small community and also serves as a synagogue.

From the slits of the drawn curtains there escapes a bright glimmer of light, and from the illuminated room resound voices in religious chant. It is the festival of Chanukah that is being peacefully observed, the Feast of Lights commemorating the victory of the Maccabees, a day which reminds a people exiled and enslaved by fate of its erstwhile fullness of strength, one of the few joyful days which law and life have granted it. But the chants have a melancholy and yearning sound, and the bright metal of the voices is tarnished with a thousand shed tears; like a hopeless wailing chant their song penetrates to the lonely street and drifts away...

For some time the stranger remains motionless in front of the house, lost in thought and dreams, and heavy, gushing tears choke his throat as he involuntarily joins in the age-old, sacred melodies that well up from the depths of his heart. His soul is full of profound reverence.

Then he pulls himself together. With hesitant steps he goes up to the closed gate and the knocker descends heavily upon the door, making it shake with a muffled sound. And this shaking vibrates through the entire building...

Immediately the chanting upstairs ceases, as though an agreed-upon signal had been given. All have become pale and look at one another with troubled faces. In an instant the festive mood has been dispelled; the dreams of the conquering power of Judas Maccabeus, at whose side they had all enthusiastically stood in spirit, are submerged; gone is the splendid kingdom that had been before their eyes; once more they are poor, trembling, helpless Jews.

A frightened silence. The prayer book has slipped from the hands of the Reader; their bloodless lips refuse to shape words. A dreadful oppressiveness pervades the room and holds all throats gripped with an iron fist.

They know full well why.

Terrible tidings had come to them—fresh, unprecedented news, the bloody import of which they had to feel on their own people. The Flagellants had appeared in Germany, those savage religious fanatics who in Corybantic frenzy and ecstasy lacerated their own bodies with scourges, raging, intoxicated, maddened hordes who had tortured and slaughtered thousands of Jews from whom they sought to wrest forcibly their most sacred palladium, the ancient faith of their fathers. And that was the Jews' most burdensome fear. Being driven, beaten, robbed, serving as slaves—all that they had accepted with a blind, fatalistic patience; each one of them had lived through late-night raids with burning and pillaging, and time and again a shudder ran through their bones whenever they thought of such times.

Only a few days ago they had heard a rumor that their country, too, which had hitherto known the Flagellants only by name, was being invaded by a horde that was said to be no longer distant. Indeed, might they not be here already?

A terrible fright has gripped everyone's heart. Already they can see once more the bloodthirsty hordes with their wine-intoxicated faces storm into their houses with savage leaps, carrying flaming torches in their hands; their ears already ring with their wives' muffled cries for help against the wild lust of the murderers; they can already feel the flashing weapons. Everything is as in a dream, distinct and alive.

The stranger listens, and when he is not granted admittance, he repeats his knock, which again reverberates hollow and roaring through the muted, terrified building.

Meanwhile the master of the house, the leader of the service, whose flowing white beard and advanced age give him the appearance of a patriarch, has been the first to regain some composure. In a low voice he murmurs: "God's will be done." And then he bends to his granddaughter, a beautiful girl, who in her fright is reminiscent of a doe that turns towards her pursuer with large, imploring eyes, and says: "Take a look, Leah, and see who it is!"

The girl, upon whose face all eyes are fastened, goes to the window with timid steps and pushes the curtain aside with trembling, bloodless fingers. And she utters a cry which comes from the bottom of her soul: "God be praised, it is just one man."

"God be praised!" It resounds from all sides, like a sigh of relief. And now the rigid figures upon whom that frightful burden has rested begin to move; small groups form, some standing in silent prayer, others discussing in fear and uncertainty the arrival of the stranger who is now being admitted at the gate.

The entire room is filled with the sultry, oppressive odor of burning logs and the presence of so many human beings assembled around the richly-laden holiday table; on it stands the token and symbol of the sacred evening, the seven-branched candelabrum, whose individual candles burn dimly through the smoldering haze. The women are attired in sumptuous, jewel-studded dresses, the men wear flowing garments with white prayer shawls. And the narrow room is suffused with a profound solemnity such as only genuine piety can bestow.

Now the quick steps of the stranger are on the stairs, and he enters. At the same time a terrible, sharp gust of wind, admitted by the opened gate, penetrates the warm room. An icy cold streams in with the snowy air and chills everyone. The draught extinguishes the flickering candles on the menorah; only one flickers back and forth, dying. Suddenly the room is enshrouded in a heavy, uncomfortable twilight; it seems as though a cold night is about to descend precipitously from the walls. At one stroke the cozy, peaceful atmosphere has been dissipated, everyone senses the evil portent in the extinguishing of the sacred candles, and superstition makes them shudder anew. But no one dares speak a word.

At the door stands a tall, black-bearded man, scarcely more than thirty years old. He quickly sheds the wraps and blankets with which he has muffled himself against the cold. And at that moment, when his features become visible by the dim light of the last little flickering candle, Leah rushes up to him and embraces him.

It is Joshua, her betrothed, from the neighboring town.

The others, too, animatedly crowd about him and greet him joyfully, only to fall silent soon, for he holds off his fiancée with a serious, sad mien; heavy, sorrowful knowledge has etched wide furrows on his forehead. All glances are anxiously directed at the man who cannot marshal his words against the streaming flood of his emotions. He takes the hands of those standing closest to him, and softly his heavy secret wrests itself from his lips: "The Flagellants are here!" The glances that had questioningly rested on him have become rigid, and he feels how the pulses of the hands he is holding suddenly pause. With trembling hands the leader of the service grasps the heavy table for support, so that the crystal of the glasses begins to vibrate softly, emitting quavering tones. Again fright holds dismayed hearts in its grip and squeezes the last drop of blood out of the frightened, ravaged faces that are staring at the messenger.

The last candle flickers once more and goes out...

Only the hanging lamp dimly illuminates the troubled, crushed beings whom these words have hit like a stroke of lighting.

One voice softly murmurs the fate-accustomed phrase of resignation: "God has willed it!"

But the others still cannot control themselves. The stranger continues talking, disjointedly, violently, as though he himself does not want to hear his words: "They are coming—many of them—hundreds! And much rabble with them. Their hands are sticky with blood—they have murdered thousands—all of our people. They have already been in my town..."

A fearful scream in a woman's voice, the shrillness of which gushing tears cannot subdue, interrupts him. A woman, still young, only recently married, rushes up to him. "They are there? And my parents, my brothers and sisters? Have they been harmed?"

He bends down to her, and there is a sob in his voice as he tells her, gently, so that it sounds like a consolation: "They know earthly sorrow no more."

And again it has become still, quite still. The terrible spectre of death is among them and makes them tremble. There is no one there who does not have some loved one among the dead in that town.

And then the leader of the service, with tears streaming down his silver beard, begins to chant, in a broken voice that refuses to do his bidding, the age-old, solemn prayer for the dead. And all join in. They do not themselves realize that they are singing, they pay no attention to the words and melody which they repeat mechanically; each one thinks only of his loved ones. And ever mightier grows their chant, ever deeper are the breaths they draw; it becomes more and more difficult for them to restrain their overpowering emotions; their words become ever more confused, and finally they all sob in their savage, uncontrollable grief. Infinite sorrow has bound them together, a sorrow that is beyond words.

Profound silence. Only now and then a deep sobbing that will not be stifled. And then again the hard, deafening voice of the narrator: "They are all resting with God. None of them escaped the hordes. I alone fled through an act of God..."

"His name be praised," murmurs the congregation with an instinctive religious feeling. Like a worn-out formula the words come from the mouths of those broken, trembling human beings.

"I returned late to the town from a trip; the ghetto was already swarming with plunderers. I was not recognized. I could have fled—but something instinctively drove me there, to my place, to my people, into the midst of those who were being felled by the Flagellants' blows. Suddenly one of them rides up to me, lashes out at me—he misses and sways in his saddle. And suddenly the will to live takes hold of me—this passion gives me strength and courage. I pull him off his horse and use it to storm into the distance, into the dark night, to you; one day and one night I spent in the saddle."

He pauses for a moment. Then he says in a firmer voice: "Enough now of all this! What is to be done next?"

From all sides comes the answer: "Flight!" "We must flee!" "Let us escape to Poland!"

This is the only expedient they all know, the time-worn, shameful, and yet inevitable way in which the weaker fight the stronger. No one thinks of offering resistance. A Jew should fight or defend himself? In their eyes that would be something ludicrous and inconceivable; they are no longer living in the time of the Maccabees; the times of bondage, as in Egypt, have come again, times that have imprinted upon the Jewish people the eternal stamp of weakness and servility which the floods of centuries cannot efface.

Flight, then!

Someone had timidly wanted to suggest that they might claim the protection of the burghers, but a scornful smile had been the answer. Time and again fate had thrown the enslaved upon their own resources or led them to their God. They no longer knew trust in a third party.

Now they discussed the details. These men who had always been so intent upon scraping money together now agreed that no sacrifice must be spared to hasten their flight. All possessions must be turned into ready money, even on the most unfavorable terms; carriages had to be procured as well as horses and what was most needful for protection from the cold. At one blow the fear of death had blurred their ghetto characteristics, just as it had welded individuals into one single will. In all the tired faces thoughts were working toward one goal.

And when morning kindled its blazing torches, everything had already been discussed and decided upon. With the mobility of a people that has roamed the earth they bowed to the harsh compulsion of the situation, and their final decisions and dispositions again ended with a prayer.

Each went away in order to carry out his assignment. And the soft whispering of the snowflakes which had piled up high drifts in the shimmering streets drowned out many a sigh...

Behind the last carriage of the fugitives the big town gate boomed shut.

In the sky the moon shone only as a weak glow, but it put a silver sheen on the myriad snowflakes which formed merry patterns, hid in people's clothes, danced around the snorting nostrils of the horses, and crackled about the wheels which ploughed through the thick drifts only with difficulty.

From the carriages came soft, whispering voices; those of women who in a gentle, melancholy sing-song exchanged reminiscences of their native town which still lay so close to their eyes in its secure, proud massiveness; the bright children's voices that inquired about a thousand things, but became ever more quiet and unnatural and finally gave way to an even breathing, melodiously contrasting with the sonorous voices of the men who were worriedly discussing the future and softly mumbling prayers. All nestled close in the consciousness of their belonging together and out of an instinctive fear of the cold which blew in like an icy breath through all the gaps and openings and froze the fingers of the coach drivers.

The first carriage came to a halt. Immediately the whole procession stopped. From all those traveling tents pale faces peered out to ascertain the reason. The eldest of the group had climbed from the first carriage, and now all followed his example, for they had recognized the cause of the delay.

They were not far from the town as yet; through the white veil one could still see indistinctly the tower rising from the wide plain like a threatening hand, with its top radiating a shimmer like that of a precious stone on a hand.

Here everything was smooth and white, like the frozen surface of a lake. Only in spots were there visible, within marked limits, small, uniform mounds under which they knew their loved ones lay, who, cast out and lonely, like their entire people, had here found a silent, perpetual bed far from their homes.

Deep silence, broken only by soft sobbing.

And hot tears stream down over the rigid, careworn faces and turn to shiny pellets of ice in the snow.

Gone and forgotten is any fear of death as they contemplate this deep, mute peace. And of a sudden there comes over all of them an infinite, tear-laden, savage yearning for the perpetual peace in the "Good Place," together with their loved ones. So much of their childhood sleeps beneath this white blanket, so many blissful memories, such an infinity of happiness as they will never experience again. Everyone feels this and is gripped by longing for the "Good Place."

But time presses them to move on.

They crawl back into the carriages, closely and firmly huddled together, for while they had not felt the biting cold in the open, the icy chills now again creep up their quivering, trembling bodies and make their teeth chatter. And in the darkness of the carriages their eyes meet with the expression of an unspeakable fear and an infinite sorrow...

Their thoughts continually turn back along the paths which the wide carriage wheels have carved in the snow, back to the object of their yearning, the "Good Place."

Midnight has passed. The carriages are now far from the town, in the middle of the huge plain flooded by bright moonlight and enshrouded by white, flowing veils through the shimmering reflections of the snow. With great exertion the horses plough vigorously through the thick layers of snow which cling tenaciously to the wheels; slowly, almost imperceptibly the vehicles rumble on; it looks as though they might stall at any moment.

The cold has become severe and cuts as if with icy knives into their limbs which have already lost much of their mobility. And gradually a strong wind has sprung up, too, which chants savage songs and rattles the carriages. As though with greedy hands reaching out for a victim it tears at the tent covers which are shaken without let-up and can be secured only with difficulty by their numbed hands.

Louder and louder roars the storm and drowns out the praying, softly lisping voices of the men whose ice-congealed lips can scarcely shape the words. The shrill whistling smothers the uncontrollable, hopeless sobbing of the women and the self-willed weeping of the children roused from their fatigue by the cold.

Groaning, the wheels roll through the snow.

In the last carriage, Leah nestles up to her betrothed who in a sad, droning voice tells her about the great tragedy. And he tightly wraps his stiff arm around her girlish, slender body, as if he wanted to shield her against the attacks of the cold and any pain. She looks at him with grateful eyes; and the cacophony of laments and the storm drown out a few words, tender with longing, which make both forget death and danger...

Suddenly there is a hard jerk which makes everything totter.

And then the carriage stops.

From the vehicles in front one can hear through the raging flood of the storm loud words, the cracking of whips and the murmuring of excited voices that will not be silenced. They leave the carriages, rush through the biting cold up front where one horse of the team has fallen and pulled the other one down with it. The men are surrounding the horses, trying to help, but unable to, for the wind blows them about like flimsy puppets, the snowflakes dazzle their eyes, and their hands are stiff and feeble, the fingers like blocks of wood. And far and wide there is no help, only the plain, which in the proud consciousness of its expanse loses itself without a horizon line in the dim snowy light, and the storm, which heedlessly swallows up their cries for help.

Now there awakens in them again the sad, full realization of their predicament. In a new and fearful guise death again reaches for them as they helplessly stand there, defenseless against the unconquerable, unabating forces of nature, against the ineluctable weapon of frost.

Again and again the storm trumpets into their ears: Here you must die—die!

And the fear of death within them grows into hopeless resignation.

No one expresses it aloud, the thought came to all simultaneously. Clumsily, as their stiff limbs permit it, they clamber into the carriages, close together, in order to die.

They no longer hope for succor.

They nestle together, each to his loved ones, to be united in death. Outside, the storm, their constant companion, sings a song of death, and the snowflakes fashion a great shimmering coffin around the carriages.

And slowly death comes. Through all crevices and pores the icy, stinging cold seeps in, like a poison which, sure of its effect, deadens sense after sense...

Slowly the minutes trickle by, as though they wanted to give death time to accomplish its great work of deliverance...

Heavy, long hours move by, each one transporting disheartened souls to eternity.

The storm sings gleefully and laughs in savage mockery at this everyday drama. And unfeelingly the moon strews its silver over life and death.

In the last carriage there is deep silence. Some are already dead, others in that hallucinatory trance with which freezing ameliorates death. But all are silent and lifeless, only thoughts still flit about in a confused tangle, like hot flashes of lightning.

Joshua holds his beloved in an embrace with freezing fingers. She is already dead, but he does not know it.

He is dreaming...

He is sitting with her in a fragrant, warm room; the golden candelabrum burns with its seven candles, and they are all sitting together as of old. The reflection of the joyful feast is on their smiling faces, and friendly words and prayers are being said. And long-dead persons come in through the big door, even his deceased parents, but he is no longer surprised. And they kiss tenderly and speak intimate words. And more and more approach, Jews in old-fashioned, faded costumes and garments, and the heroes come, Judas Maccabeus and all the others; they sit down with them and converse and are of good cheer. And more and ever more come. The room is full of figures, his eyes get tired from the change of characters who rush faster and faster and intermingle in a jumble, his ears ring with the confusion of noises. His pulse hammers and throbs hotly, ever more hotly—

And suddenly all is still and past...

The sun has risen now and the snowflakes that are still hastening down shimmer like diamonds. And there is a shimmering on the wide mound which, covered all over with snow, has risen out of the plain overnight.

It is a radiant, powerful sun, almost a spring sun, which has suddenly begin to shine. And actually spring is no longer far off. Soon it will make everything bud and burst into leaf again and will remove the white shroud from the grave of the poor, strayed, frozen Jews who in their lives have never known a spring.

Stefan Zweig:

THE LEGEND OF THE THIRD DOVE

In the Book of Genesis we read the story of the two doves which the patriarch Noah sent forth from the ark when the floodgates of heaven had closed and the waters of the deep had subsided. But as for the flight and fate of the third dove—who has related that? The ark of rescue which sheltered all life spared from the deluge came to rest atop Mount Ararat. When Father Noah looked out from the ark and saw only waves and billows, an endless expanse of waters, he sent forth a dove to learn if somewhere under the cloudless firmament land was to be found.

The first dove—so the Bible tells us—soared upwards, spreading her wings. She flew east and she flew west, but the waters still covered the face of the earth. Nowhere did she find rest for the sole of her foot, and gradually her wings grew tired. So she returned to the only solid thing on earth, the ark, fluttering about the vessel at rest on the mountain top until Noah put forth his hand and took her in.

Noah waited yet another seven days, during which time no rain fell and the waters receded. He then took a second dove and sent her forth for tidings. This dove flew out in the morning, and when she returned at eventide, behold, she carried in her mouth a freshly-plucked olive leaf, a first token of the liberated earth. So Noah knew that the tops of the trees were already above water and that the trial was over.

After another seven days Noah sent forth a third dove who flew out into the world. In the morning she flew away, but she did not come back in the evening. Noah waited many days, but the dove did not return. Now Father Noah could be certain that the earth was clear and that the waters had subsided. But the dove, the third dove, was never heard of again, neither by Noah nor by mankind; never, to our days, has her legend been told.

But what was the fate of the third dove? In the morning she had flown out of the musty quarters of the ark where the animals, closely pressed together, crowding hoofs and claws, growled with impatience in a confusion of roaring, whistling, hissing, and barking. She had flown out of confinement into the open sky, out of darkness into light. Raising her wings into the bright, clear, rain-washed air, she suddenly thrilled to her new-found freedom, knowing the bliss of the infinite. The waters of the deep shimmered; the forests shone green as dewy moss; the white early-morning vapors rose from the meadows; and the fragrant fermentation of the plants sweetened the fields. The metallic skies glistened brilliantly; the mountain tops diffused the light of the rising sun in an endless red glow which made the sun shine like red blood and the blooming earth steam as from boiling blood. To watch this awakening was something divine, and the dove blissfully and with level wings hovered over the radiant world. She flew over lands and seas, dreaming all the while, until she herself became a winged dream. She was now the first to see, as God Himself had seen, the liberated earth, and her looking knew no end. She had long since forgotten Noah, the white-bearded master of the ark, and his commission, long since forgotten about her return. For the world was now her home, all the heavens her very own dwelling place.

And so the third dove, unfaithful messenger of the patriarch, flew over the uninhabited earth, borne father and ever farther by the tempest of her joy, by the wind of her blissful unrest; onward she flew until her wings grew heavy and her plumage leaden. The earth drew her downward with a mighty force; her weary wings sank lower and lower, grazing the moist tree tops. On the evening of the second day she finally descended into the depths of a forest, nameless, as were all things in that beginning of time. In the thicket of the branches she found shelter and rested from her flight. Brushwood covered her, the wind lulled her to sleep; it was cool in the foliage by day, warm in the wooded abode by night. Soon she forgot the windy skies and the lure of the faraway; the verdant vault enclosed her and time, unmeasured, passed over her.

The stray dove had chosen for her domicile a forest of our nearby world, where no people lived as yet, and in her solitude she gradually turned into a dream herself, nesting in the night-green dark. The years passed her by, and even Death forgot her; for all those animals who knew the world before the deluge are immortal and no hunter can harm them; invisible, they live in the unexplored crevices of the earth, just as this dove lived in the deep of the forest. At times, to be sure, she sensed the presence of men. A shot would ring out and echo a hundredfold from the green walls; woodchoppers would strike against the tree trunks, their blows resounding through the forest; the soft laughter of lovers, arm in arm, seeking secluded spots, rippled softly through the shrubbery; and from afar, barely audible, could be heard the singing of children looking for berries. The dream-laden dove, entangled in foliage and reveries, sometimes heard those voices of the world; but she listened to them without fear and remained hidden.

One day, however, the whole forest began to roar and thunder as though the earth were erupting. Masses of black metal whirled through the air, and where they fell the earth blew up in horror and the trees broke like straws. Men in colored garments hurled death at one another, and the terrible machines spat out fire. Lightning rose from the earth to the clouds, and thunder followed; it seemed as if the earth wished to burst into the sky or the sky crash down upon the earth. The dove started from her dream. Death and destruction were about her; fire now engulfed the earth as had the waters once before. Quickly she spread her wings and soared into the air to seek asylum, a place of peace beyond the crashing forests.

She darted upward and flew over our earth in search of peace, but wherever she flew there was this man-made lightning and thunder; war was everywhere. As of old, an ocean of fire and blood was flooding the earth; the deluge had come again. Hurriedly she winged her way through the world, to espy a place of rest and then to soar up to Father Noah to bring him the Olive-leaf of Promise. But this was nowhere to be found in those days; the flood of perdition rose higher and higher, the conflagration spread farther and farther. The dove has still not found rest, just as mankind has not found peace; while she still searches, she may not return home, nor may she rest.

No one has seen her in our days, this stray mythical dove, this peace-seeker. Nonetheless, she is fluttering over our heads, frightened and weary of wing. Sometimes, in the night, starting from sleep, one hears a rustling in the air, a stirring in the darkness, a troubled flight and a helpless escape. Upon her wings ride all our forebodings, in her fright all our hopes fluctuate. This stray dove, this unfaithful messenger of old, trembling between heaven and earth, now proclaims our own fate to the patriarch of mankind. And once again, as thousands of years ago, a world awaits one who will hold out his hands to her, acknowledging that there has now been trial enough.

Stefan Zweig:

THE TOWER OF BABEL

Mankind's profoundest legends are concerned with its beginning. The symbols of origin have wonderful poetic power, and as if of their own accord, they make reference to every subsequent great moment in history in which nations renew themselves and significant epochs have their beginnings. In the books of the Bible, on the very first pages, right after the chaos of Creation, there is told a wonderful myth of mankind. In those days, when men had scarcely sprung from the unknown, when the twilight shadows of the unconscious were still about them, they banded together for a joint project. They found themselves in a strange, uncharted world that seemed dark and dangerous to them, but high above them they saw the firmament, pure and clear, the eternal mirror of the infinite for which they had an innate longing. And so they came together and said, "Come, let us build ourselves a city and a tower whose top shall reach the heavens, so that we may leave our names to all eternity." And they gathered, kneaded clay, baked bricks with it, and began to build a tower that was to extend into God's realm, to his stars and to the shiny shell of the moon.

From His heavens God saw the petty toil, and He may have smiled when He saw the men who, themselves small, looked from a distance like tiny insects as they put even smaller things together—kneaded clay and hewn stones. It may have seemed like a game to Him, a simple and harmless game, this undertaking that the men down below had started in their confused longing for eternity. But soon God saw the foundation of the tower grow, because the men were peaceable and single-minded, because they did not tarry over their labors and devotedly helped one another. And He said to Himself, "They are not going to desist from building the tower until they have completed it." For the first time He appreciated the greatness of the spirit that He Himself had instilled in human beings. He became aware that it was no longer His spirit, which had rested forever after seven days of work, but another, dangerous, wonderful spirit of indefatigability that does not stop short of fulfillment. And for the first time God grew alarmed at men, for they were strong when they were like unto Him, a unity. He began to consider how He could impede the work and came to the conclusion that He would be stronger than they only if they were no longer single-minded. And thus He sowed dissension among them, saying to Himself, "Let us confound them so that they may not understand one another's speech." That was the first time God was cruel to mankind.

And God's ominous decision became deed. He stretched out His hand against the industrious men who were working below in busy harmony, and He smote their intellect. The darkest hour of mankind had come. Suddenly, overnight, in the midst of their work they no longer understood one another. They shouted to one another, but one man did not understand the next man's speech, and because they did not understand their neighbors, they grew angry at one another. They threw away their bricks, their pickaxes, and their trowels; they quarreled and they squabbled, and finally they all ran away from their joint work, each to his homeland, to his house. They dispersed over all the fields and the forests of the earth, and each built only his narrow homestead, which did not rise up to the clouds and to God but merely protected his physical self and his nocturnal slumber. The Tower of Babel, however, that tremendous edifice, remained abandoned. The rain and the wind beat against its battlements, which had already approached the heavens; gradually they gave way, crumbled, and broke off. Soon the tower was but a legend, recorded only in song, and mankind forgot the greatest project of its youth.

Hundreds of thousands of years passed, and men continued to live in the seclusion of their tongues. They put boundaries between their fields and their lands, boundaries between their faiths and their customs. They lived next to one another as strangers, and if they crossed these boundaries, it was only to rob one another. For hundreds and thousands of years there was no unity among them, only secluded pride and self-seeking. And yet—from their common childhood there must have been in them a dim memory of the great project, like a dream, for as they gradually advanced to the maturity of years, they began to inquire about one another again and unconsciously seek the lost connection. A few bold men made the beginning. They visited other lands and brought home knowledge of them. Gradually the peoples became friends; one nation learned from another; they exchanged their knowledge, their values, their metals, and gradually they discovered that different languages need not mean estrangement and that a boundary need not be a gulf between nations. Their sages recognized that no nation's scholarship could comprehend infinity by itself, and soon the scholars, too, saw that an exchange of information would advance universal knowledge more quickly. The poets translated the words of their brethren into their own languages, and music, the only thing that was free of the narrow bonds of language, suffused the emotions of all. Men loved life more since they knew that unity was possible beyond language. In fact, they thanked God for what He had imposed upon them as punishment; they thanked Him for having bestowed this diversity upon them, because with it He had given them a chance to enjoy the world in many ways and, thanks to this variety, to love their own individuality with heightened intensity.

And so it gradually began to rise again on European soil, the Tower of Babel, this monument of brotherly community, of human solidarity. It was no longer dead matter—bricks and clay, mortar and earth—that people chose in order to reach the heavens, to turn God and the world into brothers. The new tower was built of the finest, the most indestructible material available to earthly creatures: of intellect and experience, of the sublimest spiritual substances. Broad and deep was its foundation; the wisdom of the East had deepened it, Christian doctrine gave it its equilibrium, and its iron-squared stones derived from classical antiquity.

Everything that humankind had ever done, all that the human spirit had ever accomplished was incorporated into this tower, and it rose heavenward. Each people contributed its creations to this monument of Europe; young nations eagerly came forward to learn from the old and added their virgin strength to the experience of the wise. They learned the tricks of the trade from one another, and the fact that their working methods differed only heightened their common zeal; for if someone did more work, that was an incentive for his neighbor, and the disputes that sometimes caused confusion within a nation could not bring the joint labor to a standstill.

And so the tower, the new Tower of Babel, grew, and never did its top rise higher than in our time. Never had the nations penetrated into one another's spirit so deeply, never had their sciences been so closely knit together, never had commerce been interwoven into such a wonderful fabric, never had the people of Europe loved their homelands and the whole world so much. In this rapture of unity they were bound to feel close to heaven, for precisely in those years the poets of all languages began to write paeans to the beauty of existence and creativity, and, like the builders of the mythical tower of yore, men felt Godlike because they were so close to fulfillment. The monument kept rising; all that was sacred to humanity was assembled in it, and music surrounded it like a great wind.

But the God above them, who is as immortal as mankind itself, was frightened when He saw the tower, which He had once smashed, rise again, and once more His concern grew. And again He realized that He could be stronger than mankind only if He again sowed dissension among men and prevented them from understanding one another. Once again He was cruel, again He produced confusion among them—and now, after thousands and thousands of years, this horrible scene is being reenacted in our lifetime. Overnight men no longer understood one another, men who had worked peacefully side by side, and because there was no mutual understanding, they grew angry at one another. Again they flung away their tools or turned them into weapons to fight one another. The knowledge of the scholars, the discoveries of the scientists, the words of the poets, the religion of the clergy—all the things that had formerly contributed to life-giving activity—were now turned into death-dealing weapons.

This is our terrible situation today. The new Tower of Babel, that great monument to Europe's spiritual unity, is decayed and the workmen have dispersed. Its battlements are still standing, its invisible squared stones still rise over a confused world, but without the shared toil, the conserving, continuing labor it will fall into oblivion, like that other tower of mythical times. Today there are many among all nations who desire this, who would like to detach from the wonderful edifice the part that their people have contributed to the common cause, unconcerned over whether the tower might fall to pieces, who want to try to reach the heavens and infinity by themselves with the limited strength of their fellow countrymen. But still there are others, those who believe that no people, no nation could ever succeed in attaining what the united strength of Europe was hardly able to achieve in centuries of heroic common effort. These are people who sincerely believe that this monument must be completed here, in our Europe where it was begun, rather than on foreign continents like America or Asia. The time is not yet ripe for joint activity; the confusion that God has instilled in souls is still too great, and it may be years before the brethren of yore work again in peaceful competition with eternity. But we must go back to the edifice, each to the place he left in the moment of confusion. Perhaps we shall not see one another at the work for years; perhaps we shall rarely hear from one another. But if we toil away now, each at his post, with the old ardor, the tower will rise once more, and on its pinnacle the nations will meet again.

Stefan Zweig:

THANKS TO BOOKS

They are there, waiting and silent. They neither urge, nor call, nor press their claims. Mutely they are ranged along the wall. They seem to be asleep, and yet from each one a name looks at you like an open eye. If you direct your glances their way or move your hands over them, they do not call out to you in supplication, nor do they obtrude themselves upon you. They make no demands. They wait until you are receptive to them; only then do they open up. First there has to be quiet about us, peace within us; then we are ready for them. Of an evening, on returning home from tiresome errands; some day at noon, when one is weary of his fellow men; in the morning, when one is cloudily half-awake after dream-laden sleep—only then is one ready for books. You would like to have a conversation and yet be alone. You would like to dream, but in music. With the agreeable anticipation of sweet sampling you step to the bookcase; a hundred eyes, a hundred names meet your searching glance silently and patiently, the way the slave women of a seraglio greet their master, humbly awaiting the call and yet blissful to be chosen, to be enjoyed. And then—as the finger gropes about on the piano to find the key for the inner melody, gently it nestles against the hand, this dumb white thing, this closed violin; in it all the voices of God are locked up. You open up a book, you read a line, a verse, but it does not ring clear at the moment. Disappointed, almost rudely, you put it back. Finally the right one is at hand, the book that is right for this hour—and suddenly you are gripped, your breath mingles with another's breath, as though the warm, naked body of a woman were lying next to yours. And as you carry it away to your lamp, The Book, the happily chosen one, glows with an inner light. Magic has been done; from delicate dream-clouds there arises phantasmagoria. Broad vistas open up, and your senses fade away into space.

Somewhere a clock ticks. But it does not penetrate into this time which has escaped from itself. Here the hours are measured by another unit. There are books which traveled through many centuries before their words came to our lips; there are new books, born only yesterday, just yesterday begotten out of the confusion and distress of a beardless boy. But they speak with magic tongues, and one like the other soothes and quickens our breathing. And as they excite, they also comfort; as they seduce, they also soothe the open mind. Gradually you sink down into them; you experience repose and contemplation, a relaxed floating in their melody in a world beyond this world.

You pure leisure hours, transporting us away from the tumult of the day; you books, truest and most silent companions, how can we thank you for your ever-present readiness, for this eternally uplifting, infinitely elevating influence of your presence! What have you not been in the darkest days of the soul's solitude! In military hospitals and army camps, in prisons and on beds of pain, in all places, you, the eternally wakeful, have given men dreams and a hand's breadth of tranquility amidst unrest and torment. God's gentle magnets, you have always been able to draw the soul out into its very own sphere when it was buried in everyday routine. In all periods of gloom you have always widened the expanse of our inner horizon.

Tiny fragments of eternity, mutely ranged along an unadorned wall, you stand there unpretentiously in our home. Yet when a hand frees you, when a heart touches you, you imperceptibly break through the workaday surroundings, and as in a fiery chariot your words lead us upward from narrowness into eternity.

Z.F. Finot:

PURIM IN THE POLISH GHETTO

Purim is Purim—but the Jews of Lvov hadn't had such a good laugh in a long time as they did on that memorable 14th of Adar. It is true, it was another hard East Galician winter, with a biting, stinging frost, but what Jew pays attention to frost and snowstorms on this merriest day of the whole year? There is only one Purim, and on this occasion even the *Shulhan Arukh* permits one to transgress all commandments and to let off steam with drinking, dancing, masquerades, and all sorts of practical jokes.

In the narrow, dirt-filled, snow-clogged lanes of the Jewish quarter in Lvov things have been cooking and bubbling for days. Every household is getting ready for the traditional festive meal, and even the poorest are preparing colorful plates with presents, the so-called *shalakhmones,* for children, relatives and friends, and especially for the Rabbi. Weeks before the day of Purim people drag all sorts of costumes out of the most remote corners or lending establishments, and at the same time they make masks out of cardboard, ribbons, and other varicolored material.

The actual festival of Purim does not begin until after the fast day in memory of Queen Esther. Young and old flock in droves to the age-old *Vorstadtschul* (suburban synagogue), which is located in the heart of the Lvov ghetto, in order to attend the reading of the *megillah.* At the words *vaihi bimey Ahashverosh* (and it happened in the days of Ahasuerus) there fairly streams forth the hotly glowing breath of a typically Jewish fervor from the closely packed crowd, a fervor which on one day in the year always finds untrammeled expression even in the sacred precincts of the synagogue. Hardly does the depraved name of *Haman harosho* (the wicked Haman) resound from the *almemor* (tribune) before the old walls shake with deafening tooting, screaming, squealing, and brandishing of the traditional Purim rattle, the *gragger.*

But soon after the *megillah* there is a breather. Not until the next day is the Jewish market around the synagogue flooded with housewives doing their last-minute shopping for the festive evening meal. Whole mountains of *hamantashn, kreplakh,* and silver-covered nuts are offered for sale by the market women. *Koifts, vaiber, koifts nisselekh yn oibst!* (Buy, women, buy nuts and fruit) they scream with shrill, hoarse voices while warming their numb hands by the redhot braziers.

Presently evening descends, and only now is the gray, heavy everyday atmosphere of the whole year rolled back by an irresistible wave of merriment and lust for life. From the windows of the Jewish quarter flares the light of flickering candles which light up the pitch-dark lanes and squares like dim little stars. Families and invited guests keep streaming in, wandering through the dark streets from house to house, masked and with burning lanterns. Mixed in with the guests who push their way in are whole swarms of masked children who hop over tables and benches with their jingling collection boxes and their rattling *graggers,* asking for donations in a shrill sing-song: "*Haint is Purim, morgen is oys / gebt uns a kreuzer yn warft uns aroys*" (Today is Purim, tomorrow it's over; give us a penny and send us packing).

So the Purim night holds sway in the cramped dwellings of the ghetto until midnight, working up to a climax of exuberant jollity.

After the Purim feast, as though at a command, a stream of humanity pours out into the snow-covered lanes. From every nook and cranny whole bands of spookily disguised forms emerge out of the shadows of the dimly flickering gas lights. The professional Purim players, who used to come to Lvov from the neighboring Polish border town of Brody and then toured the provincial town with all sorts of Purim plays, quick as a flash in the icy cold winter night organize the Purim guests as they stream out into an orderly procession. Like a stirred-up ant-heap this procession moves, amid the sounds of the band leading it, in the direction of the old synagogue on Market Square. With Chinese lanterns, burning torches, and illuminated signs, masked men, women and children, whose age and gender is hardly recognizable through the peculiar disguises, sing and dance along. Above the marching crowd, from house-high gallows dangle the stuffed figures of Haman and his minions, marching along like ghosts in the shadow of the glowing torches. Trumpets and drums blare madly, the crowd howls as if possessed, dances and hops along under the leadership of the "Brodyites," and in between engages in all kinds of horseplay with stinging thistles, throwing snowballs, nuts, beans, and confetti.

Only the two giant policemen whom the imperial authorities of Lvov have assigned to watch over the Jewish festival of Purim waddle along, with deeply serious official mien, by the side of the bandmaster with his quick, trim step. Their pointed black shakos with flashing white peaks and their oversize curved cuirassier sabres which rattle on the ground at every step, in time with the bandleader's baton, fit harmoniously into the marching panorama of masks, Hasidic *kapotes, shtreimlakh,* checked trousers, colorful wigs, dazzling garments, and the black Haman gallows swinging over everything. Finally the procession crowds, shoving and screaming, over the cellar-like threshold of the medieval synagogue, which is made available once a year for the celebration of Purim. Soon an exultant audience fills the enormous subterranean hall with its anterooms and women's galleries to witness the actual performance of the Brody Purim Players. The band blares out popular tunes, and on the raised platform in the center of the *shul* the Purim players grimace, sing Jewish folk songs, reproduce the play about Haman, Esther and Ahasuerus, and finally, amidst a fanfare from the band and tempestuous applause, kick Haman *harosho* to hell.

During all this, volunteers make their way through the packed rows of spectators and distribute schnapps and *hamantashn* which the elders of the synagogue have donated for this evening. People sing as if transported with ecstasy; they dance, rage, bawl, push, and jump over the balustrade of the *almemor,* with masks and clothes flying in shreds. Only the two imperial policemen lean, sad and shivering, against the outside wall of the synagogue. Their official non-Jewish character forbids them to cross the threshold of a synagogue. But finally they let themselves be persuaded by a few roguish Jewish boys, who dare to approach them, to descend out of the raging snowstorm into the warm cellar vault of the brightly lit synagogue. They are all the more eager to do so because outside they have got a whiff of the familiar smell of the plentifully flowing liquor. Thus the two, with their uniforms and rattling sabres, get right into the seething center of the Purim celebration.

In a trice, as if by a whirlwind, the two latecomers, who are taken for especially ingenious masqueraders, are swept into the midst of the dancing couples, and gradually a goodly amount of schnapps and slivovitz is poured into the wide-open mouths of the two giants. It isn't long before the two guardians of the law are tottering about in a circle, half drunk. Their heavy bearskin caps roll about between the feet of the dancers, and since even on Purim no one is allowed in the synagogue without a head covering someone quickly claps two old, torn *shtreimlakh*, picked up somewhere, on their skulls.

Haze, heat, alcohol, and the earsplitting noise gradually befuddle their senses. Soon they mechanically unbutton their heavy fur coats, which prompts the waggish boys who lured them inside to throw long, flowing women's dresses over them. Only their sabres stick out from under their dresses, and that is why someone also ties a white bedsheet around their bellies, as a sort of *arbe kanfes* (four-edged prayer shawl). When it is time for the competition for the best Purim mask, there is a unanimous vote, and amidst the blaring victory trumpets of the band the two unsuspecting policemen are dragged up on the platform, where their side-splitting figures that reach up to the ceiling constitute the climax of this year's Purim celebration.

The band played on until dawn, and the couples went on dancing in the stifling hot air. Gradually the hall emptied. Some of the exhausted dancers squatted down along the synagogue walls, beside their discarded masks, to get some sleep. Only the two drunken guardians of law and order still went reeling through the synagogue corridors, lost to the world, got into the women's gallery, and amid squealing and cursing stumbled over women's feet and heads, until once again a gang of fun-loving youngsters came up and, pooling their strength, took them out into the open air. Since, however, they could hardly make out from the babbling of the policemen where they wanted to be taken, they pluckily took the two drunks under their arms and dragged them, panting and wheezing, to the nearest police station. At the threshold they pushed the two wobbly Purim heroes, still wearing their full "war paint," into the dark room. Quick as a flash the young heroes cleared out and disappeared in the snowstorm of dawn. From their hiding place they presently caught sight of the policemen in their Purim get-up being dragged by their own colleagues in the direction of the municipal jail. Since the two, in their drunken stupor, had only uttered incomprehensible sounds, they had been taken for two impudent Jewish masqueraders who had ventured into a police station in their besotted state. The real perpetrators of this Purim prank took to their heels while the taking was good, and the inhabitants of the Lvov Jewish quarter laughed for a long time about the successful prank on that memorable 14th day of Adar...

But the imperial authorities took a very dim view of it. An official report was despatched to the imperial city of Vienna, and soon a severe reprimand went to the Lvov Jewish community for its disrespect toward the state's police authorities. From that day on the authorities granted no more police protection for the celebration of Purim.

Z. F. Finot:

CHESS AT CHANUKAH

It is Chanukah and people play chess—a game that can be continued even when the Chanukah candles have been lit. There are three festivals, in fact, on which Jewish merriment may hold sway even at the sacred places dedicated to the Torah: namely, Simchas Torah, Chanukah, and Purim. So people sat in the *klaus,* which was located on the very edge of the ghetto, and tirelessly played chess. This royal game was the most popular of all—no other so stirred feelings to tempestuous passions. Judah Halevi once called a chessboard a reflection of higher reality. The game provided a satisfactory battleground for brains sharpened over generations by hair-splitting *pilpul,* and it furnished diversion from the gloom of the everyday world.

A few benches and tables, in a corner a desk with old folio volumes, and on the east wall a closet for the sacred Torah scrolls—this was the *klaus,* the seat of the Rabbi and his disciples. From early morning the rhythms of Jewish small-town life echoed here: an eternal coming and going from the street, where life rolled along in lazy waves of bargaining and haggling. The *klaus* was the spiritual center, where all the pent-up hopes of a national life squeezed into a narrow space found a meaning and an expression.

Only on holidays did the nightmarish pressure of cares and anxiety give way for a while. During the Chanukah days, there was added the distant echo of a heroic combat filling souls with pride and joy. "*Nes gadol haya sham*—a great miracle took place there." Perhaps it was a reflection of the Jewish fighting spirit of yore which especially attracted the epigones to hold chess tournaments at Chanukahtime. The best players entered the tournaments, and the winners, by way of reward, were even called up for an *aliyah* during the religious services.

Right after the first morning prayer, the race for opponents began. From the cluster of congregants a few figures soon detached themselves: with crafty smiles on their faces, they looked around for players who would be a match for them. Everyone knew who the impassioned players were; in a trice they had gathered in a corner of the *klaus,* around a little table upon which the master of this room, the *shammes,* had placed a chessboard.

Only two can take part in the game, but each match starts off with the yelling and squabbling of the spectators crowding round. One of the players, an elderly Hasid with a face shaded by thick hair, phlegmatically props his head on one hand while he lights his pipe with the other. His opponent, a man with a pointed nose and bulging eyes, meanwhile closely watches the Hasid's first moves. While they play, their two backs rock in rhythm as during prayer, and soon there comes the murmur of a monotonous intoning: "*Gey ich aher—geyt er ahin*—If I go here, he'll go there." Suddenly the Hasid picks up a chessman and jerkily pushes it forward. The crowd, pressing constantly closer to the table, yells: "*Mottie, vi ahin kricht ir?*—Mottie, where do you think you're going?" Screaming out warnings or cheering the players on, the crowd has its own influence on the game. "*Vi loift ir, Tipesch?*—Where are you running to, Tipesch?" someone suddenly says in a warning voice. "*Antloift, der rosh iz in a sakuneh*—Get out, the king is in danger!" comes back from the other side.

The center of gravity of the game visibly shifts to the surrounding kibitzers, who scream in rhythm with the game's ups and downs, while the silhouettes of their swaying heads throw flickering shadows on the whitewashed walls behind them. Suddenly there resounds a short, clipped shout: "Check!", like the hissing of a snake. A scream—at once of horror and of victory. But the danger has been averted for the moment. The Hasid nervously tugs at his beard; his cheeks turn brick-red, his hands grope uncertainly about the chessmen. One can see by his tense expression that the end of the game is near. As if it were a matter of life and death, he pushes the pieces forward, visibly resigned. *"Pooh, a metzieh*—some bargain," mocks the Hasid, who has already recognized the superiority of his opponent: The old Hasid has obviously underestimated the young upstart. He puts his pipe in his belt and with his elbows pushes away the kibitzers who have been crowding too close to the table.

Meanwhile, the veins swell out on his opponent's forehead, looking like charcoal smudges in the murky gloom of the wintry light that comes through the windows.

"Antloift, antloift!" the crowd's shrill warning comes again. The eyes of the old Hasid are aglow, for this time the cry is meant for him. He stares at the bloated hands of his opponent as if to paralyze them. Suddenly he opens both eyes wide: "The king is lost!" At the same moment the whole room resounds with cries of "Checkmate, checkmate, checkmate!"

The old Hasid is shaken as by an electric current. Ponderously he raises his massive body from the chair, but presently he straightens up with pride, whips his pipe from his belt, and mockingly cries out to his opponent. "Pooh, it's Chanukah, the time when miracles happen. A return game tomorrow, *Reb Yid!*" He hurries out of the room. Another pair of players rush to occupy the chess corner. The obliging *shammes* meanwhile passes out *dreydls,* pastry, and drinks to the new arrivals for the sanctification of the Chanukah festival.

Dusk approaches: new players and new spectators keep coming in. Outside is heard the shouting and singing of children at play. They come up to the low hut of the *klaus* and bang against the window with their *dreydls.* Inside, the game is still on. *"Gey ich aher—geyt er ahin..."* The sing-song of the chess players sounds like the chorus of the unassuaged longing of many generations, on these twilit days of Chanukah.

Alfred Polgar:

THEORY OF THE CAFÉ CENTRAL

The Café Central in Vienna, you see, is not like other cafés; it is a way of viewing the world, one whose innermost substance it is *not* to view the world. What do you see when you do view it, anyway? But more about this later. Experience has shown one thing: no one is in the Café Central who does not contain a piece of the Central—that is, whose personal spectrum does not contain the Central color: a mixture of ash-gray and don't-give-a-damask rose.[1] Whether the place has adapted to the people or the people have adapted to the place is a matter of dispute. I suspect there has been reciprocal action. "You are not in the place; the place is in you," says Angelus Silesius in *The Cherubinic Wanderer.*

If you put all the anecdotes that circulate about this café into a retort, crushed them, and vaporized them, a cloudy iridescent gas smelling faintly of ammonia would develop; this is the Café Central's so-called air. It determines the intellectual climate of the place, a very

---

[1] The translation attempts to reproduce an Austrian idiom involving a nonexistent color (in Polgar, "Ultra-Stagelgrün").

special climate in which only that which is not viable thrives, with complete preservation of its unviability. Here impotence develops the potency peculiar to it, the fruits of unfruitfulness ripen, and every non-property bears interest. Of course, only a real Centralist will fully comprehend this—a person who, upon finding his café closed, feels cast out into the jungle of life, a prey to the wild accidents, anomalies, and cruelties of alien places.

The Café Central is located below the Viennese latitude at the meridian of loneliness. Its denizens are largely people who want to be alone but need company for it. Their inner world needs a layer of outer world as insulating material; their wavering solo voices cannot do without the support of a chorus. They are indistinct personalities, rather lost without the security supplied by the feeling of being particles of a whole (the tone and hue of which they have a hand in determining). A Centralist is a person who does *not* get such a feeling from his family, his occupation, or his political party, and so the café lends a helping hand as a surrogate totality, inviting him to disappear and dissolve there. Thus it is understandable that it is particularly women, who of course can never be by themselves but need at least one other person to be alone with, who have a weakness for the Café Central. It is a place for people who know that they are fated to forsake and be forsaken but don't have strong enough nerves to live in accordance with this destiny. It is a real asylum for people who must kill time in order not to be killed by it. It is the homey hearth of those who loathe a homey hearth, the refuge of married couples and lovers from the horrors of undisturbed togetherness, a first-aid station for schizophrenics who, in their lifelong search for themselves and flight from themselves, use this place to hide their fugitive ego behind newspapers, boring conversations, and card-playing, forcing their pursuing ego into the role of the kibitzer who is supposed to keep his mouth shut.

Thus the Café Central constitutes a kind of organization of the disorganized.

In this blessed place any half-way indeterminate person is credited with a personality (provided he stays within the confines of the café, he can use the credit to defray all his moral expenses), and everyone who evinces contempt for other people's money is crowned with the anti-bourgeois crown.

A Centralist lives a parasitic life on the anecdote that circulates about him. The anecdote is the main thing. Everything else—the facts of his existence—is in small print, additions and fabrications that might as well be omitted.

The guests of the Café Central know, love, and despise one another. In the Café Central even those who have no relationship with one another regard this nonrelationship as a relationship. Even mutual repugnance has binding force; it recognizes and practices a kind of freemasonic solidarity. The Café Central is a whistle stop in the heart of the metropolis, steamy with gossip, curiosity, and scandalmongering. I believe that fish in an aquarium live like the regular customers of this café, always bustling about to no particular purpose, using the oblique refraction of their medium for all kinds of tomfoolery, always full of expectancy but also deeply worried that something new might fall into their glass tank, with a serious mien playing "Sea" on their artificial miniature sea-bottom.

Of course, the Central fish, who share the same few cubic meters of breathing space for so many hours of their lives, no longer have any inhibitions or secrets. A Centralist leads the private lives of the others, and his own life is an open book. Aided and abetted by the local tendency toward self-mockery and the nonchalant exposure of one's own weaknesses, this creates an atmosphere of vaporous *Gemütlichkeit* in which any prudishness withers and dies. There are Central customers who walk around in the psychic buff without having to fear that their childlike, innocent nakedness will be misinterpreted as shamelessness. A few years ago the proprietor of the café attempted to acknowledge this paradisiacal touch in the character of his regular customers by putting up a palm tree.

The only persons who can partake of the intrinsic charm of this wondrous café are those who want nothing from it but the chance to be there. Purposelessness hallows their sojourn. A guest may not even like the place or its noisy denizens, but his nervous system imperiously demands its daily dose of Centraline. Habit hardly suffices to explain this, nor can it be explained by saying that, like a murderer, *homo Centralis* is propelled to the place where he committed his deed, where he has killed so much time and eradicated entire years. What is it, then? The AURA! I can only call it the aura. There are writers who are able to do their writing chores nowhere but at the Café Central; only there, at the tables of idleness, is their working table set; only there, with the winds of sloth blowing about them, is their indolence fertilized. There are creative people who have no ideas only at the Café Central, and far less anywhere else. There are poets and other intellectuals who have profitable thoughts only there; constipated people who find the door to relief open only there; people who lost their erotic appetite long ago and find themselves hungry only there; mutes who find their voice, or someone else's voice, only at the Café Central; misers whose money gland secretes only there.

In the peaceless people who frequent it this mysterious café pacifies something that I would like to call cosmic discontent. In this place of loose relationships a person's relationship to fate is loosened as well. A creature slips out of his or her compulsory relationship to the universe and forms a non-binding, sensual, casual relationship to nothingness. The threats of eternity do not penetrate the walls of the Café Central, and within these walls you enjoy the devil-may-care sweetness of the moment. As to the love life of the Café Central, the equalization of social differences, and the literary and political currents by which its jagged coasts are laved; as for those buried in the Café Central who yearn to be excavated, hoping that they never will be; as for the masque of wit and dimwittedness that turns every night in these rooms into a Mardi Gras—a great deal could be said about these and other things. But anyone interested in the Café Central knows all this anyway, and as for those not interested in it, we are not interested in their interests.

It is a café, take it for all in all! You shall not look upon its like again. What Knut Hamsun said about the city of Christiania on the first page of his immortal novel *Hunger* applies to this café as well: It will not let anyone leave without first leaving its mark upon him.

Martin Buber:

BOOKS AND PEOPLE

If someone had asked me in my early youth whether I would prefer to associate only with people or only with books, I would surely have declared myself in favor of the latter. Later this changed more and more. Not that the experiences I had with people were so much better than those I had with books; on the contrary, even today I encounter entirely pleasant books far more frequently than entirely pleasant people. But the many bad experiences I have had with people have nourished my life's marrow in a way that the most exquisite book could not, and my good experiences with them have turned the earth into a garden for me.

On the other hand, no book can do more for me than transport me to a paradise of exalted spirits, where my heart of hearts never forgets that I am not permitted to stay for long and that I cannot even desire such permission. For, and I must say it right out to be understood, my heart of hearts loves the world more than it loves the intellect.

True, I am not as fit for living with the world as I would like to be; again and again I fail in my dealings with it; again and again I fall short of what it expects of me, and part of the reason is that I am so bound to the intellect. In a way, I am as much bound to it as I am bound to myself; but I do not really love it, just as I do not really love myself. Actually, I do not love this one that has seized me with its celestial claw and holds me fast, but the thing over there that keeps coming up and holding out a few fingers to me, the "world."

Both of them have gifts to distribute. The intellect gives me its manna, books; the world has dark bread for me on whose crust I loosen my teeth and with which I am never sated: *people.* Oh, these muddle-heads and ne'er-do-wells, how I love them! I respect books—those that I really read—far too much to be able to love them that way. But in the most respected living person I always get a bit more to love than to respect, always a bit of this world, which is simply there in a way that the intellect can never be there.

True, it is above me and "exists," but it is not there. It hovers over me powerfully and talks down at me with its exalted words, the books; how magnificent, how uncanny! The world of men, however, needs only to smile its mute smile and I cannot live without it.

It is mute, for all the talk of people does not add up to a word such as I derive from books time and time again. And I put up with all that talk in order to be able to hear the silence that comes through the muteness of created things. But it is that of *human* creatures! Which means, that of a mixture. Books are pure, people are mixed; books are spirit and word, pure spirit and purified words; people are put together out of talk and muteness, and the muteness is not that of animals but that of men, and lo, out of the human muteness behind the talk the spirit whispers to you, the spirit as *soul.* This, this is the beloved.

There is an infallible test. Try to imagine a primeval situation in which you are alone, all alone on earth, and you could get one of the two, books or people. Yes, I can hear some praising their solitude; but they are able to do that only because there *are* people in the world, even though far away in space. I knew nothing of books when I sprang from my mother's womb, and I want to die without books, with a human hand clasping mine. Now, to be sure, I sometimes close the door of my room and surrender to a book, but only because I can open the door again and see a human being looking up at me.

ACKNOWLEDGMENTS

Grateful acknowledgment is made to the editors or publishers of journals or collections in which most of the essays and translations in this volume first appeared.

Cross Currents: A Yearbook of Central European Culture first printed the following: "The Vitriolic Viennese" (No. 3, 1984), "Three Austrian Aphorists" (4, 1985), "Gustinus Ambrosi" (8, 1989), "July Sunday in the Prater," "The Cholent War," "Theory of the Café Central" (all 9, 1990), and "Memorial Address on Wolfgang Amadeus Mozart" (11, 1992).

"The Jewish Contribution to Fin-de-Siècle Vienna" is reprinted from *The Jewish Response to German Culture,* ed. by J. Reinharz and W. Schatzberg, University Press of New England, 1985. "The Burning Secret of Stephen Branch" first appeared in *The World of Yesterday's Humanist Today,* ed. by M. Sonnenfeld, State University of New York Press, 1983. "The Herzl Diaries: A Self-Portrait of the Man and the Leader" is taken from *Herzl Year Book,* ed. by R. Patai, Herzl Press, vol. 3, 1960. "Translating Theodor Herzl" first appeared in *Silver Tongues,* Proceedings of the Annual Convention of the American Translators Association, ed. by P.E. Newman, 1984. "Trakl, Kraus and the Brenner Circle" is from *Internationales Georg Trakl-Symposium,* ed. by J.P. Strelka, Peter Lang, 1984. "Notes on a School Text and Related Matters" is reprinted from *Unser Fahrplan geht von Stern zu Stern,* ed. by J.P. Strelka et al., Peter Lang, 1992, "Franz Theodor Csokor's 'Allerseelenstück'" first appeared in *Immer ist Anfang,* ed. by J.P. Strelka, Peter Lang, 1991, and "The Austro-American Jewish Poet Ernst Waldinger" is reprinted from *Identity and Ethos* (Festschrift for Sol Liptzin), ed. by M.H. Gelber, Peter Lang, 1986.

"The Bell on the Left" is reprinted from *Midstream,* May 1987 and "Trudel's Tear" from *The Jewish Advocate,* Aug. 24, 1972. "In the Snow" first appeared (as "Escape") in *Jewish Quarterly,* Summer 1954, "The Legend of the Third Dove" in *The Jewish Advocate,* Sept. 23, 1954, "The Tower of Babel" in *Jewish Affairs,* Mar. 1961, and "Thanks to Books" in *Saturday Review,* Feb. 8, 1958. "Purim in the Polish Ghetto" is reprinted from *Jewish Affairs,* Feb. 1961, and "Chess at Chanukah" from *Commentary,* Dec. 1959. "Books and People" first appeared in *The Jewish Advocate,* Jan. 5, 1961.